Two Homelands

Two Homelands

A Historian Considers His Life and Work

O<small>DD</small> S. L<small>OVOLL</small>

N<small>ORWEGIAN</small>-A<small>MERICAN</small>
H<small>ISTORICAL</small> A<small>SSOCIATION</small>

MINNESOTA
HISTORICAL
SOCIETY PRESS

The publication of this book is supported by an anonymous endowment for Norwegian American History in Minnesota.

Unless otherwise indicated, all photos are taken by or in the possession of the author.

www.mnhspress.org
www.naha.stolaf.edu
The Minnesota Historical Society Press is a member of the Association of University Presses.

Manufactured in the United States of America

10 9 8 7 6 5 4 3 2 1

International Standard Book Number
ISBN: 978-1-68134-115-6 (paper)
ISBN: 978-1-68134-120-0 (e-book)

Library of Congress Cataloging-in-Publication Data available upon request.

This and other Minnesota Historical Society Press books are available from popular e-book vendors.

for ELSE

Contents

Two Homelands

SUNNMØRE

Vigra
Ålesund
Godøy
Langevåg

Sandsøy
Åram
Sørbrandal
Larsnes
Ørsta
Volda
Koparnes
Bjørlykke
Eidså
Fiskå
9

Tromsø

Andøya

Trondheim

Molde

INSET MAP

Ålesund
Åndalsnes
2
10
Bryggja
13
11
Hjelle
1
Loen
7
Stryn
3
14
12
Voss
8
Garnes
Osterøy
Oslo
Bergen
Drammen
Moss
4
5
Halden
Tysvær
Sandefjord
Karmøy
Stavanger
6
Listafjord
Kristiansand
Lista
Farsund

1 Hedmark
2 Møre og Romsdal
3 Sunnfjord
4 Telemark
5 Vestfold
6 Vest-Agder
7 Gudbrandsdalen
8 Hallingdal
9 Nordfjord
10 Østerdalen
11 Strynsvatnet
12 Sogn
13 Sunnmøre
14 Valdres

Introduction

MY MEMOIRS REFLECT strong ties throughout my life to my native land—Norway—and to my new homeland—America. During my childhood, my family's geographical universe was limited to the small farmstead Bjørlykke on the Rovdefjord, then in the municipality of Sande, in the southern district of Sunnmøre. Sunnmøre is the southernmost district in the coastal province (*fylke*) of Møre og Romsdal, part of a region identified for centuries as Northwest Norway (*Nordvestlandet*). Ålesund constitutes the main urban center.

Personal relationships—most especially with my immediate family—represent a major theme of my life and are lovingly included in this book: my father, Alf Løvoll (Lowell) (1901–1986); my mother, Astrid Aase Løvoll (1907–1994); my siblings, Magnar Bertel (1931–1950) and Svanhild (1937–); my wife, Else Olfrid Navekvien Lovoll (1935–2011); our children, Audrey Merete (1960–) and Ronald (1963–); and their spouses and our five grandchildren have all been an essential and priceless part of my life.

A second theme relates to my strong interest in and contributions to scholarly historical topics associated with Norwegian migration to America and with Norwegian American history. My journey as a citizen of both Norway and the United States awakened and sustained a lifelong interest in the immigrant experience—and it all began as an odyssey of self-discovery.

With the opening chapter, the narrative of my life—my personal reflections and memories—is placed in a larger historical context. Sunnmøre had a late and relatively small overseas migration, yet only my grandfather, one of five brothers, did not emigrate. My father had spent six years in the Pacific Northwest when I was born. America was thus a close reality. Alf found employment on a Norwegian whaling factory ship and was in Africa when the Germans occupied Norway in the spring of 1940. As a US citizen, he returned to America and was "a missing father" for seven long years. The difficult half decade of German occupation is placed in a broad context, with connections to the Holocaust and the painful and lasting memory of Norwegians of Jewish heritage being deported and executed in gas chambers.

The second chapter shows how an established and aging Norwegian American community responded to the German occupation of Norway. A large Norwegian community in exile existed, consisting of the Norwegian royal heirs, politicians, prominent people, and seamen. Relief efforts for Norway, the free Norwegian merchant fleet organized as Nortraship, the Little Norway training camp in Canada, and the Norwegian-speaking 99th Infantry Battalion activated at Camp Ripley in Minnesota are all a part of the story.

The third chapter features a new life in America, which began the summer of 1946 when my mother, brother, sister, and I joined Alf in Seattle, Washington. As part of the growing postwar Norwegian American community, we immigrant children faced challenges in adjusting to the demands of accepting and acclimating to a new society—a topic much neglected in scholarship. My personal relationship to religion and how it was altered by new circumstances is a part of the narrative.

In chapter four, I deal with my family's repatriation, brought about by the drowning death of my brother, Magnar, off our father's fishing vessel, *Attu,* and our father's long-held wishes to return to Norway in retirement. By then we had become "Americans," and the new adjustment was both demanding and stressful. The chapter treats repatriation, also a neglected topic, and its place in the history of migration. And then I married Else, the love of my life, and we started a family: Audrey, born in 1960, and Ronald, in 1963.

In chapter five, America comes calling. Eventually the entire family, including my father, felt the return to Norway had been a mistake. In 1967, Else and I and our two children moved to Grand Forks, North Dakota, where I would teach at the University of North Dakota. I pursued my graduate studies, and in 1973 earned a doctoral degree in US history with specialization in immigration at the University of Minnesota. From 1971 until retirement in 2001, I served on the faculty of St. Olaf College. My ties to Norway were apparent in my appointment as adjunct professor of history for nine years, 1996–2005, at the University of Oslo.

In the sixth and final chapter, I focus on some of my published works and my passionate interest in comprehending and communicating the complexity and disparate aspects of Norwegian American history. Through it all, my family takes center stage. My life has indeed been enriched by my two homelands and the many people who have been an integral part of it.

A Missing Father

Seven Long Years

REFLECTING ON MEMORIES from my childhood, I see myself as an eight-year-old boy walking on the isolated gravel roadway pushing a stick in front of him, making lines in the wet surface. Viewing myself initially in the third person creates a positive distance to a better understanding of my youthful qualities—and seems an appropriate introduction to my life's story. At times the boy in my memory stops to look at the rushing brooks, flooded by the melting snow, in the steep hillside above the road. On the other side is the desolate beach along the fjord. He nourishes his daydreaming by stopping to draw animals and people and to formulate words with his stick. It is spring, and the eight-year-old, I clearly recall, is on his way home from the one-room country school, a distance of nearly five kilometers, wandering in uninhabited territory marked by avalanches of rock and snow from the towering mountains, brown except for rectangular patches of planted evergreens.

In the distance he views three lonely farmsteads, all bearing the name Bjørlykke; the farthest one is the boy's destination. His mother, Astrid, and two siblings, an older brother, Magnar, and a sister not yet of school age, Svanhild, will be awaiting his return. As he shakes himself out of his reveries, he is startled by someone calling to him; it is a young man in German uniform on a bicycle. This man represents the hated occupying enemy, though, as I recall the incident, the

The farmstead Bjørlykke on the Rovdefjord showing the house
Alf Løvoll built in the 1930s. In the 1940s, the nearby community of
Sørbrandal had a landing dock, a general store with postal service,
and the local country schoolhouse.
Photo by Svanhild Wergeland

boy feels no fear or hatred, and when the German soldier motions to
him to climb onto the bicycle behind him, the boy gratefully accepts.

"Odd, you are home early," his mother calls out as he walks up to
the second story of the large farmhouse. On the main floor live his
uncle Petter Løvoll and family, who rent the farm owned by Odd's
father, Alf Løvoll.

Earlier recollections, happy as well as sad, come easily to mind. The
eight-year-old Odd is an impressionable and frequently lonely child,
falling prey to introspection and his own lively imagination. It is April
1942, and the whereabouts of a father he barely remembers is a constant source of pain and speculation.

There are, however, certain vivid memories of his father. Alf's returns from the Norwegian whaling expeditions to Antarctica were

happy moments. Unique toys purchased in exotic faraway places became the envy of other children. Odd as a toddler of three or four was especially fond of a wooden man that could be wound up to rotate one way, stop, then go in the opposite direction. Odd imitated the foreign doll until his head began swimming and he had to rest.

Never forgotten was the consequence of gorging on candy his father brought home—a visit to the community physician to have an aching tooth pulled. The trip to the village of Fiskå, some fourteen kilometers away, was made in the area's only taxi, owned by Alf's cousin. Odd sat on his father's lap as the doctor pulled the tooth without the benefit of any anesthetic. It happened so quickly that Odd neglected to cry until he sat in the taxi, comforted first by his father, who held him close, chuckling warmly to let him know that everything would be fine, and also by the doctor's praise of being *"en hardbalen kar"* (a hardy fellow).

During these wondrous days of carefree childhood, there were also the annual late-summer treks to a mountain cabin located on a small lake filled with tasty trout. In 1939, young Svanhild rode in a new baby carriage with Odd sitting at the foot, and the oldest, Magnar, walked with Astrid and Alf, both in their thirties. Up the steep incline the two youngest were carried, and the family rested midway by a crooked birch tree with a particular shape, known locally as *kamelen*—the camel.

In the cabin, all slept in bunks, Magnar and Odd's below Alf's, whose resting place was held up by two straps fastened to the ceiling. One night, as all were deeply asleep, the straps suddenly broke and a surprised father landed on top of two astonished boys, who let out a simultaneous surprised scream, which startled baby Svanhild, who began wailing for no good reason. She shared a third bunk with Astrid, who was left to calm everyone as Alf liberated himself from the bunk, his memorable warm laughter comforting the boys. The excitement deprived everyone of sleep, making for a short night.

Then there was the emotional good-bye in early fall of that year as Alf left his family to make the long journey from Bjørlykke to the city of Sandefjord on the Oslofjord some one hundred kilometers or more south of Oslo. In distant Sandefjord, he joined the crew on the whale factory ship *Kosmos I* and on October 5 headed south for the southern hemisphere's summer whaling season. Alf was to return the next spring—but the German invasion on April 9, 1940, prevented his homecoming. He instead joined his uncles and their families in America, where as a young man he had spent some six years of his life. Seven long years passed before he saw his family again.

As America played a decisive role in the Løvoll family's lives, it seems appropriate at this point to introduce how emigration to America from Sunnmøre affected the Løvolls, and how the Sunnmøre experience differed from that of the rest of the country. A further chronicle of the Løvoll family and the war years will follow.

THE AMERICAN CONNECTION

Sunnmøre constitutes the southern district in the province of Møre og Romsdal on Norway's northwestern coast. A classical description in the 1898 travel manual *Sunnmøre* by Kristofer Randers honors the place of my birth: "The distinctive characteristic of Sunnmøre's scenery is its exceptional combination of fjords and mountains, valleys, glaciers, rivers and waterfalls—and out on the coast islands, islets and reefs that shield against the open ocean. It is like a painting from the hand of an ingenious artist without a single dead spot. The contours steadily shift, the vistas change at every turn of the road or along the fjord—the landscape seems to be in eternal motion."

While America came calling to the area, the desire to seek a better life distant from the homeland lagged far behind that of other Norwegian districts. A popular saying, "the spring cod is our America," identified an important resource at precisely the beginning of the emigration season. The flourishing coastal cities and the prosperous fisheries created a shortage of labor, and as a result wages rose. Workers were attracted to the area from other parts of Norway.

Nineteenth-century Norwegian emigration had its dramatic and historically significant beginning with the sailing of the sloop *Restauration*

Magnar and Odd clearing land in Bjørlykke
Photo by Borghild Løvoll Andreassen

from Stavanger on the southwestern coast of Norway on July 4, 1825. The fifty-two persons on board, crew and passengers, all intended to settle in the New Land. A baby girl was born during the crossing. The *Restauration* reached the port of New York on October 9 after an adventurous voyage of fourteen weeks across the Atlantic. Truly a long journey.

After annual emigration began in 1836, the urge to go to America spread like a dangerous disease—indeed, an "America fever"—from the southwestern coastal regions, where it had begun, to coastal districts farther north and to the interior valleys. Places like Voss, Sogn, Hallingdal, Telemark, Valdres, and Hedmark were especially affected, but by the mid-1850s nearly all of Norway participated in the migration across the ocean. A striking feature of the overseas exodus was how it affected districts in different ways. The uneven spread of information about opportunities through "America letters" and the example and encouragement of visiting Norwegian Americans, as well as local circumstances at home—as seen in the northwestern coastal communities of Sunnfjord, Nordfjord, and Sunnmøre—might to some extent explain the varied response to the emigration alternative.

Grandfather Martin's brothers, four in all, became exceptions to the comparatively modest emigration from the district of Sunnmøre and, indeed, from the entire province of Møre og Romsdal. In the decade 1866 to 1875 it had the lowest emigration rate of all provinces—1.9 per thousand of its median population. Only in the 1880s did emigration really take hold. By the early 1900s the number of emigrants proportionately equaled closely the figure for the whole country, 8.2 per thousand of population.

In a study of three municipalities in southern Sunnmøre not far from the Bjørlykke cluster of farmsteads—Ørsta the largest—historian Ragnar Standal explains the delayed emigration, and why the trickle of emigrants swelled to a wave in the 1880s. Standal concluded that the early 1880s and 1890s were an economically depressed period for the district. In a broad sense, then, those who left were economic migrants seeking an improved financial position and a higher standard of living elsewhere. It is also important to keep in mind that until about 1880 the excess population found that nearby places, such as the rapidly growing city of Ålesund and the island districts, offered new opportunities to make a living, postponing emigration from Sunnmøre as a whole. As indicated above, the regular income from fishing made emigration less attractive as well. Standal also considers the more equally distributed soil resources in his district compared to other places in western Norway like Sogn and contends that the consequent lower social distinction eased the district's general spirit of discontent and the urge to emigrate.

Information about conditions in America, though not plentiful, was sufficiently adequate by the 1880s to make people sensitive to shifting economic conditions and events there. The news influenced their decision to either postpone migrating until better times arrived or leave immediately to seek a better life. Standal points to the fact that Sunnmøre skipped the first phase of the emigration, which nationally was strongly marked by family migration. From the late 1870s, the emigrant groups throughout Norway increasingly consisted of unmarried young people, with men outnumbering women, and the average age was lower—more a youth migration.

One by one, Grandfather Martin's brothers sought a better life away from the homeland. Later interviews showed that they had spent an entire summer going from one farm to the next seeking employment—without any success. Bent Brudevold and family, relatives from the farm located at the end of the fjord some ten or more kilometers from Koparnes, had emigrated and made their home in Page, North Dakota. This personal connection inspired intense debate about going to America. For the Løvoll clan, Brudevold thus came to play the role of an "innovator"—a person who plants the idea of emigration. By the end of the nineteenth century, the Pacific Northwest and Alaska had become major destinations, especially for immigrants from western and northern Norway. Granduncle Ole left for Seattle, Washington, at age twenty, in 1898; Ivar, at nineteen, in 1901; Elias, at eighteen, in 1905, settling in Everett, Washington; and Johan, at nineteen, in 1909. Johan had tried his hand at running a country store before emigrating. He first settled in Seattle to be near his brothers; in 1913, he moved to Juneau, Alaska, where he made a living fishing. He later became the prosperous owner of fishing vessels.

Following a common path for women, Grandpa Martin's only sister, Petra, did not emigrate but instead found employment in a nearby city. In 1910, when twenty-five years old, she married Laurits Grytten. They made their home in Ålesund. I recall how impressed I, like many adults, was when newly minted city folk, with their adopted urban speech and outlook, visited simple rustic places such as Koparnes and Bjørlykke, with their country lingo and unadorned ways.

In 1908, Ivar repatriated. He married Oline Rasmusdatter Solbakken, a *gardjente*—heiress to a farm—who had inherited her father's land in the community of Eidså, some ten kilometers from Grandfather Martin's farmstead. Ivar was an adventurous man, and alongside farming he became an agent for Singer Sewing Machine Company; up and down the coast of Norway Ivar Løvoll became known as Mr. Singer. I recall his strong social presence.[1]

YEARS OF WAR

Childhood memories may at times seem more like a dream than reality, their content both happy and troubling. In thinking back on the five years of the German occupation, 1940–45, however, I have a strong clarity in regard to circumstances and events. They left a lasting impression.

In April 1940, Germans bombed Ålesund, the major urban area in the district of Sunnmøre—the Bjørlykke farms situated in its southern reaches. Bombs were also dropped on rural communities. The city of Molde to the north was viciously bombed by German pilots in pursuit of Norwegian King Haakon and Crown Prince Olav as they fled with members of the royal Norwegian government. The three Bjørlykke farms had a joint subscription to *Sunnmørsposten*, the main daily journal in Sunnmøre, with copies shared among the households. Its front-page news had been the spread of the European warfare, and its editorial on April 9, 1940, carried the heading "Norway's Hour of Destiny." The editorial's concluding paragraph reads: "It is a heavy weight that at this time imbues the Norwegian people, a gravity that places the most stringent demands on the steadfastness and patriotic standpoint of all women and men, young and old. It is a demand on all of us to preserve equanimity and thoughtfulness. It seeks *one* people that united and in accord can face whatever the heavy burden in time will offer us."

Hitler had ordered the German occupation of Denmark and Norway to take place on April 9, 1940. The German campaign caught the Norwegians both mentally and physically unprepared, as historian Olav Riste describes: "the armed resistance to the German assault was improvised and inadequate, and did little more than delay the invasion timetable." Yet, Norway's government refused to accept Germany's ultimatum to surrender, and resistance against the invaders became a reality. *Sunnmørsposten* reported in large print on Norwegian troops being mobilized and the campaign against the Germans advancing; on April 15, it reported that British naval forces shot down three of the eight German bombers attacking Ålesund and surrounding areas. On April 22, *Sunnmørsposten* carried in large print the encouraging news that "The Norwegians are Persevering and Making Successful Resistance throughout the Entire Country." On April 27, the front-page headline read: "The Situation for the Allied Forces in Norway is Steadily Improving."

The picture changed quickly. South Norway was relinquished May 1, and the state authorities were evacuated to Tromsø. In early May, the headline reports were that "Defeat in South-Norway Conceded"; German news from Oslo, as printed in *Sunnmørsposten*, was that the German flag was flying over Åndalsnes, a municipality in Møre og Romsdal province. On May 3, it observed that "The situation now is that also our city and likely our districts are coming under German high control." By June 7, despite assistance from Allied forces—British, French, and Polish troops—the Norwegian resistance was crushed by German military superiority. The Norwegian government decided to abandon the struggle in the homeland, with capitulation of the remaining Norwegian forces, and move to exile in Britain. On June 10, *Sunnmørsposten* informed its readers that "Norway Lays Down its Arms," with the news that England and France had pulled back their forces and all their materiel and left the country. By then, King Haakon VII, Crown Prince Olav, and the Norwegian government were on the high seas en route to Great Britain.

How much of the reality of these disturbing developments was known to people in Bjørlykke and neighboring communities beyond what was reported in the press is difficult to determine. Vidkun Quisling and his Nazi party, *Nasjonal Samling (NS)*—National Unification—on the very day of the invasion, assumed control of *Norsk rikskringkasting*—Norwegian National Broadcasting—and declared a state coup with himself as both prime and foreign minister; the radio enabled the German occupying forces to spread their message to the Norwegian people. Speculations about future hardship and oppression abounded throughout the country.

When the Germans finally made their appearance in this remote coastal region on the country's northwestern coast, they came marching quite regularly or were transported in large military vehicles. They aroused more curiosity than fear. Since the community was located along a major coastal route, large German military installations were set up at Åram, farther out on the fjord. Construction began in May 1941, with the work being done by German soldiers, Norwegian workers, and Russian and Polish prisoners of war. A construction firm in Ålesund erected the barracks. The German occupiers sought to engage and collaborate with the local population. A coastal artillery with mounted cannons was in place, as were antiaircraft defenses in order to, among other military commissions, protect an important sea lane. A dock made delivery of provisions and military equipment convenient. The blinking light on the small island of Saudeholmen—the sheep isle—across the fjord from Bjørlykke, had long helped ships navigate the fjord. The Germans expropriated land close to the local Lutheran church at Åram; stringent controls were imposed as locals walked past the array of barracks, weaponry, and minefields to attend church on Sunday morning. And pillars of rock on either side of the narrow road could easily be deployed to block the advances of an invading liberating army.[2]

Prisoners of war, toiling outside the confines of the military installation, became visible evidence of the raging war beyond Norway. The German occupiers built telephone lines where they earlier had not existed, including on the small farm where the Løvoll family lived. At first, Polish and Russian prisoners dug holes and placed the telephone poles while armed German soldiers gave orders and kept guard. One of the soldiers walked up to the farmhouse and showed a photo of his children, saying in Norwegian, *"Krig dårlig"*—war bad. The human drama and suffering were shared by both sides in the cataclysmic wartime reality.

Local people stood by and watched. Most were likely unaware, as Guri Hjeltnes notes in her fine history of everyday life in wartime Norway, *Hverdagsliv i krig. Norge 1940–45* (Everyday Life in War: Norway 1940–45), "that more foreigners than Norwegians lost their lives on Norwegian soil" during the years of war. Hjeltnes states that between fourteen and fifteen thousand foreign prisoners of war perished in German prison camps, subjected to inhuman hard labor, while attempting to flee, or by execution. In its June 11, 1942, issue a well-informed *Nordisk Tidende* carried the headline, "Brutal Treatment of Russian Prisoners of War"; the paper then reported how prisoners had died from the suffering they endured, that food was rationed to one loaf of bread daily shared by three men, and that many prisoners had been shot in the prisoner of war camp under consideration. There were, according to *Store norske leksikon* (The Large Norwegian Encyclopedia), 100,000 Soviet prisoners of war in Norway—and 13,700 of the prisoners who succumbed were Russian.

THE STEINFELD FAMILY

As the German occupational forces and their Norwegian collaborators became entrenched, dreadful rumors of the torture of innocents, of arrests and deportation, and of resistance by Norwegian patriots spread throughout the district. The destruction of the small community of Jewish residents in Ålesund in 1942 will never be forgotten; it was reported in the press and discussed with much emotion. Only one Jewish family at that time lived in Ålesund: Lea and Israel Steinfeld and their two children, Reidun and Morten. In the fall of 1942, *Sunnmørsposten* covered both the military advances abroad and the fate of the Jewish population at home. A series of disturbing directives and incidents called for the expropriation of all Jewish assets; the requirement that "full Jews, half Jews, and quarter Jews" register with local authorities; the internment of Jewish men. Other reports included quotes from Martin Luther's anti-Semitic command, "Away with the Jews"; and Minister President Vidkun Quisling, as nominal head of the Norwegian government, publicly declaring that "It is the international Jewish might that staged the war." These and other legislative acts and public indictments created a negative environment and attitude that led to the arrest and deportation of Norwegians of Jewish heritage—first men, then women and children.

The Steinfeld family had moved to Ålesund following a devastating 1904 fire that destroyed much of the city. I include their story in some detail because of the nightmarish visions I as a child had of their final fate and my persistent preoccupation as an adult with the inhumanity of waging war and the atrocities committed against fellow human beings. The Holocaust, the deadliest genocide in history, bore witness to an unimaginable cruelty, and must never be forgotten.

Moses Steinfeld, Israel's father, visited Ålesund in March, a month or so after the fire, and declared his intention to start a business, but already in September he discontinued all such activity. In 1909 he opened a clothing store in Ålesund, having first operated one in Bergen, and lived in Ålesund until his death in 1923. Moses was born in present-day Latvia in 1853; his wife, Dora Gittelson Steinfeld, was born in 1859 in Szaki, located in Russian Poland. For them, as for many Jewish residents who suffered under the Russian pogroms, America was "the promised land," but lack of financial resources forced them to choose a different destination. As outlined by Joel Perlmann in *Ethnic Differences*, the immigration of eastern European Jews was the critical event in American Jewish history. Russian Jews began arriving in the United States in large numbers just after 1880. By 1900, the Jews were the second-largest immigrant group to enter the United States each year.

Moses and Dora immigrated to Sweden. Israel was born in 1889 as their fifth child. When he was three years old, the family moved to Trondheim, Norway, which had a growing Jewish population. In 1905, a Jewish congregation gained approval as a separate dissenter congregation. Moses was the first treasurer of the Mosaic Communion in the city.

Israel moved to Ålesund at the age of sixteen in 1905. He joined the local Turner Society (gymnastics club), making a great effort on its behalf and engaging in its activities—one of many examples of how the Steinfelds became an integral part of the city's life. In 1910, when twenty-one years old, he started his own business on Ålesund's main street Kongens gate, and in 1929 a second department store, also in Kongens gate. Therese Alvik in an engaging account quotes people who told her "that they shopped there because of the large selection, high quality and acceptable prices."

In 1918, Israel married Lea Levin. Her parents, Henriette and Leib (Leopold) Levin, had immigrated to Norway in the late 1800s, and Lea was born into a large family in 1896. She was actively engaged in public health societies, and she and Israel had a large circle of friends. In 1922, their daughter Reidun was born, and in 1925, son Morten. They became *skolebarn* (schoolchildren), like all other youngsters in Ålesund. Their schoolmates said, "They were exactly like us, they were not different in any way." And of course they were Norwegian-born children.

At the time of the German invasion, Reidun and Morten were teenagers, both enrolled in the Latin school, or gymnas; Morten was known to be skilled at expressing himself in written Norwegian. He co-edited the student paper, *Aqua Vitae*. Reidun earned her *examen artium*—university entrance exam—and proudly wore her student cap. And then their father was arrested.

On the German Gestapo's orders, Israel was seized by regular Norwegian police on October 26, 1942. Participants in such arrests were Norwegian Nazi *hird* members—Quisling's storm troopers— and Germanic SS Norway (GSSN), a military organization established in Norway in July 1942. It was thus not the German occupiers who directly arrested the Jews. There was a general Nazification of the Norwegian police forces throughout the country, but because Ålesund was a major port for people fleeing across the North Sea to England, the Gestapo strongly distrusted the regular police and replaced officers and the chief with members of the Nazi SN party. Regardless, Norwegians arrested fellow citizens who had committed no legal offense—a fact not to be forgotten. Only in January 2012, seventy years later, did Norway's prime minister Jens Stoltenberg

Reidun and Morten Steinfeld, about 1942
Courtesy Therese Alvik

recognize the part Norwegians had played in the persecution of Jewish residents. He expressed his regrets as quoted by Therese Alvik in *Familien Steinfeld. Da byen gråt* (The Steinfeld Family: When the City Wept): "Without excluding the Nazis of responsibility, the time has come for us to recognize that the police and other Norwegians participated in the arrest and deportation of Jews. I find today appropriate to express our deep regret that this could happen on Norwegian soil."

Lea, Morten, and Reidun were incarcerated on November 26. Friends had tried to postpone Morten's arrest by having him undergo an appendectomy in the local hospital. Claiming he was too weak to travel did not delay the inevitable. Israel arrived in the German death camp Auschwitz the day his family was detained and as an able-bodied person was among those picked to work; he died in the camp May 15, 1943. Lea, Reidun, and Morten too met their fate in Auschwitz; they were put to death in a gas chamber on March 3, 1943, for no other reason than being of Jewish heritage. This particular wartime atrocity, more than any of the many others, haunted the sensitive eight-year-old I then was and continues to haunt me to this very day.

Kristian Ottosen, himself a survivor of German concentration camps, describes in his book *I slik en natt* (In Such a Night) the deportation of 767 Norwegian Jews; in an addendum, he lists their names, when born, residence when arrested, occupation, when deported, transport, date of death, and finally place of death. Most arrived on the troop transport ship *Donau,* and with few exceptions all perished in the Auschwitz death camp. According to Ottosen, only twenty-six of the deported Jews survived. An astounding number, some 45 percent, of the more than seventeen hundred Jewish residents in Norway in 1940 thus became the innocent victims of the Holocaust. The *Donau* met its end the night of January 16, 1945, when two resistance men, Max Manus and Roy Nielsen, placed explosives on the side of the ship; they detonated just past the city of Drøbak on the Oslofjord. The ship was beached with the bow and forepart on land. Visiting the

Holocaust Center on Bygdøy near Oslo in October 2016, I felt a chill down my back when holding a lifebuoy with *Donau*'s name on it.

Jews not arrested managed to escape to neutral Sweden with the help of the Norwegian resistance movement. Jo Benkow, the first Norwegian of Jewish descent to be elected to the Storting (Grand Assembly; the Norwegian parliament), and who served as *stortingspresident* (speaker of the Storting), 1985–93, observed the following: "Although it did not prove possible to take the lives of all the Norwegian Jews, the economic liquidation of the Jewish community in Norway during World War II was total and absolute."

Ottosen provides personal accounts for those who did not escape, making manifest the individual tragedies associated with Germany's determination to exterminate all Jews. These thought-provoking stories display the evil that people are capable of committing against their fellow human beings.[3]

PERSONAL MEMORIES OF WAR

Wartime recollections from Sunnmøre and Bjørlykke are vivid. Low-flying German planes, the *Fliegende Festung*—flying fortress—created much bewilderment. Transport ships moving out of the fjord with their protective blimps or barrage balloons flying above aroused wonderment. And yet, there were Allied bombings and sinking ships on the fjord just below the two-story farmhouse, calls for help from injured men, and discharges from German antiaircraft guns farther out unto the fjord. There were explosions and shattering windows as the Løvolls huddled in the basement.

The local schoolhouse, located in Sørbrandal, was from time to time confiscated by the Germans, whose military installations at Åram were only a few kilometers farther out on the fjord. The teacher, Einar Vik, gathered the students in the area's largest living rooms—the realities of adjustment and survival.

Christmas was still observed as a public celebration with all the festivity that the teacher and parents could muster. When not occupied by the Germans, the small schoolhouse was the community's regular meeting place. A decorated tree stood in the center of the room; people walked around it while holding hands and singing Christmas carols; Einar Vik gave a little talk about the Yuletide season. The basement was the serving area. Children brought rationing cards to school so that cookies could be purchased from the baker. These bakery products always seemed to taste better than those made at home, even though the baker likely had the same limited and poor ingredients. This simple and locally noteworthy festival brightened a few hours during the dark days of the occupation.

One Christmas Eve became particularly memorable. There was no flour for making cookies, but then unexpectedly each family was allotted a small amount of wheat flour, usually available only to families with babies. Our mother immediately set out for the store some eight kilometers away in Eidså, and after her return made *smultringer*—doughnuts—two or three for each of us children. There are also painful memories of a mother desperate to provide food and clothing, often going hungry or cold herself, visiting local farmers and, when she could, outbidding the German troops on the black market. Grandpa Martin on patriotic principle never traded with the occupiers.

Some mornings there were eggs, and some dinners included meat. Even those not famished had to swallow bread made from the so-called crisis flour—unripe harvested grain roughly ground and with chalk added; there was no alternative. Local talk and imagination added other more objectionable ingredients; the flour's quality deteriorated through the years of occupation. People regularly added potatoes and even seaweed to the flour. But after the barley and oats had been harvested and the grain ground—often covertly on primitive water-powered millstones to avoid reporting the flour to the authorities—the Bjørlykke neighbors gathered on one of the farms and spent a day rolling out and baking *flatbrød* (flatbread). These were good and memorable times for the children.

The German occupiers confiscated meat and other farm products and fish, leading to shortages for the locals. Resourceful people developed new sources of food, including dishes made from rabbits, squirrels, sea gulls, and thrush—never to be served again when peace finally ruled. Guri Hjeltnes describes people's ingenuity, both in the countryside and in urban areas: "Many people made a debut raising animals." "Rabbits, ducks, and pigs became new family members." "*Villagrisen*, the villa pig, was likely the most talked about as well as unruly resident."

Along Norway's long coastline, people consumed fish as never before, as Hjeltnes explains: "The Norwegian household had to base itself on fish and herring to a degree not known earlier—if the country should make it through [the war] without famine." And fish and herring were indeed a major source of food at Bjørlykke, located on a well-stocked fjord. I remember large catches of herring hung to dry on the sides of the barn; after dark, *morild*—phosphorescence from the drying herring—lit up the structure. Herring was also salted and stored in barrels; one dish, *boknasild*, boiled half-dried herring, especially comes to mind.

On rare occasions generous people in occupied Denmark or neutral Sweden sent special gifts of food to the Løvoll family. *Nasjonalhjelpen* (The National Aid) distributed "godparent presents" to us because we were technically orphans, not having a father present. One Christmas, Svanhild even got a Swedish doll that could close its eyes, a miracle if there ever was one.

And from neutral Sweden came the only news of our father, arriving in the form of heavily censored Red Cross letters, or telegrams, several months old. A return message was permitted, though its fate after given to the Red Cross could never be ascertained. Hopefully it would in time reach our dearly missed father. His absence was always blamed on the Germans, and long after I was no longer a child I nurtured hostility against a nation that I felt purposefully had deprived me of the care and succor of a loving father.[4]

LIFE WITHOUT A FATHER

Even lacking our father's presence, we grew up. Magnar, my senior by three and a half years, assumed, to the extent possible at his young age, a fatherly role to the benefit of his younger siblings. He matured quickly. Magnar had a great sense for the burden our mother carried.

Mother Astrid was a deeply religious woman, and the tribulations and responsibility of these years of bringing up the children alone were accepted as her simple duty. But at times it all seemed to over-whelm her—and no wonder, considering the dire circumstances. Under these extreme pressures big brother Magnar was called upon to act as comforter to his mother and reassuring force to his siblings.

From time to time, our maternal grandfather, Odin Aase, who had retired as *tømmermann* (a ship carpenter) when prematurely wid-owed, rowed over from the village of Volda. We children watched his small boat, which he himself had fashioned, come ashore. Grand-father Odin was a man with many tales. He had sailed the seven seas and could tell of places, people, and events beyond his young listen-ers' wildest imagination. His northern brand of Norwegian added color to his accounts.

Everyone's eyes grew big when he spoke of Africans, black people being totally foreign to his grandchildren except as presented in missionary literature, and then only as "heathens" to be saved from eternal damnation by Norwegian Lutheran missionaries. Viewed at a national level, this groundless prejudice did not bode well for toler-ance, much less appreciation, of worldwide cultural, religious, and racial differences. No contending view was forthcoming.

Every evening, our mother led us in prayer for the unenlightened heathens. A fearful portion of the invocation was a plea to God to save our souls should we die during the night. I recall nightmares about that potentiality. Children were not spared the reality of death. At the passing of a neighbor who was simply styled *Gamlelars* (Old Lars), a picture shows children, including me, standing by the casket. Lars was to be buried in the graveyard surrounding the main parish church located on the island of Sandsøy; when all transportation was by sea, a central island was a logical location. A motorboat brought the mourners to the island, where the casket was lowered into a grave. On the way back to Bjørlykke, the adults on board discussed people who seemingly were dead (*skinndød*) and had been buried alive. I visualized with much dismay Gamlelars waking up in his casket deep under ground.

And, of course, good Christian behavior was inculcated; using bad language would make the angels cry. From time to time—troubled by a bad conscience due to uttering words from the great flora of Norwegian expletives—I could believe that crying angels fluttered above me.

The local schoolteacher, who served one year while Vik was on leave, started a society to support missionary activity in Madagascar, evidently an early destination for Norwegian missionaries. What difference these efforts would make in occupied Norway during a period of dire need is difficult to comprehend. Both the foreign (*ytremisjon*) and the home (*indremisjon*) mission societies continued to meet and promoted social activities. Astrid took me and Svanhild to mission meetings held in homes in the district (Magnar was old enough to be left home alone). My distinct impression was that unless Norway acted quickly, Norwegians would be nearly alone in heaven.

ASTRID AND ALF

Alf's father, Martin Larsen Løvoll, the oldest of five brothers and one sister, assumed operation of the small family farm Koparnes when he was only twenty-one years old, in 1896, on the drowning death of his father, Lars Olsen Løvoll. He also had responsibility for his widowed mother, Ane Karin Løvoll, four younger brothers, and a younger sister. The crowded situation must have represented a strong push factor for his siblings to move out, to emigrate. Together with his wife, Birte Bentsdatter Bjørlykke, Martin ran the farmstead and raised a family; Alf, born in 1901, was their third child and first son. Birte died shortly after giving birth to child number seven in 1910. Martin struggled to support his growing family on the barren small farm. He engaged in fishing, traded in horses, kept fur-bearing fox, and opened a bakery in the farmhouse's basement for the local fishing community. It was still a meager livelihood.

The grandchildren all loved their grandpa dearly. He was truly protective and concerned about their well-being. But he could also lose his temper when things did not go well; he always seemed to blame *Gamle Eirik* (Old Eirik)—a designation for the devil. Once I watched Grandpa Martin step down from the large mowing machine to get a drink of water, and the horse took off pulling the mower. And there was Grandpa, running as fast as he could to catch the horse as he shouted, *"No er Gamle Eirik laus igjen"* (Now Old Eirik is loose again).

Martin sought a wife and someone to help raise the flock of offspring. Grandpa Martin later reminisced about distantly related *tausekjerringar* (spinsters)—unmarried women past thirty—out on the coastal islands. One Sunday he set out on this special errand and returned with Karen Kristiansdatter Bergsnev, who became his wife and the mother of three children. She was a caring and patient woman with burdensome obligations and duties. She became simply *kjerringa til bestefar* (grandfather's wife), never grandmother to descendants of the first marriage. Some incidents linger in my childhood memory, among these a man putting his hand on my shoulder as he declared himself to be my uncle just as much as anyone else. Rumor had it that Grandpa Martin had fathered a child with a neighbor girl while a widower. Mother told me not to talk about it. It would perhaps be viewed as a family dishonor.

Alf became a part of a strategy; as a firstborn son he was to work in America and save money to help pay off the debt on the Koparnes farm. At the age of eighteen in early 1920, he accompanied his uncle Johan, whose name had been Americanized to John Lowell, and his wife, Anna Aase, when they returned to America. Anna, born in Ålesund in 1890, had emigrated in 1910, and like many Norwegian immigrant women worked in domestic service, first in Granite Falls, Minnesota, then in Seattle, Washington, where she met John visiting his brother Ole. Anna and John were married in the Medieval Borgund church in Ålesund on Anna's birthday, January 26, 1920, and shortly thereafter they left for Juneau.

John and his brothers had arrived using the patronymic Larsen as their surname. The story goes that, while employed at a sawmill in Everett populated by Norwegian immigrant workers, Ole discovered that, "if their name was not Ole Larsen it would be Lars Olsen"—which created great confusion. So when Ole took out his citizenship papers, someone suggested he should list his surname as Løvoll, the name of the farm his father, Lars Olsen Løvoll, had owned at Åheim before moving to Koparnes. Ole thought that name too Norwegian, so the helpful friend informed him that he had seen a similar name in an American newspaper: Lowell. And Lowell it became. Ole entered American citizenship as Ole Lowell. His brothers followed suit, as did Alf when he became an American citizen.[5]

Just before Christmas 1926, after engaging mostly in fisheries on the Pacific Coast, Alf returned to Norway. As a dutiful son, he fulfilled his commitment to his father and his large family eking out a living on the modest farmstead.

In 1929, he purchased a small farm, Bjørlykke, in the municipality of Sande a bit farther out on the fjord from Koparnes. A long, dark, forested tract separated the two farmsteads. I remember rushing through dense woods on the narrow gravel road when visiting Grandpa Martin and aunts and uncles. The Bjørlykke property had been left fallow for some time and had only a ramshackle farmhouse. Alf set up a stately dwelling.

But a man cannot exist alone or farm without help and companionship. Alf hired Astrid as a maid on his new farmstead. The two young people, living alone on the secluded parcel, sought each other's company. Soon after Astrid began her service, Alf proposed and made Astrid his wife.

Astrid grew up on the small hillside farm Liaskar. Volda, with its single street of businesses, was the community's shopping center. Alf and Astrid were married in the local *bedehus* (religious meeting house) in September 1930. Magnar was born the following year. I was born in 1934 and Svanhild in 1937. Alf and Astrid noted that Svanhild was born the same year as prince Harald, destined to become the king of Norway.

Løvoll family portrait, May 1938: Alf holds Svanhild, born while he was
away for the whaling season; Astrid stands behind Odd; Magnar at right
Photo by Borghild Løvoll Andreassen; courtesy Svanhild Wergeland

Astrid later wrote a brief account titled *"Mi historie"* (My History),
the story of her life up to her marriage. She had been employed several places from a young age, as all children were at that time, and
could not accept Alf's first request that she come and *stelle for han*
(keep house for him). He contacted her again a year later, in 1930, and
this time Astrid was free to accept. "I was there only a few months
when he wanted to marry me," Astrid relates, "and that happened."
She describes Alf as "a good and hard-working man."

Astrid describes Liaskar as "a small farm underneath the mountain." Her mother, Anne Severine Sivertsdotter Liaskar, was born
there, and in 1904 she married Odin Kornelius Aase from the island
of Andøya in the far north. Grandpa Odin would tell how, when he
began courting Anne Severine, her father, Sivert Liaskar, initially
would banish him from the farm. Odin had two strikes against him:
he was a *Nordlending*—North Norwegian—and subject to prejudice
from Norwegians farther south, and, perhaps even worse, a seaman
with the accompanying questionable reputation and long absences.
But it all worked out well. Anne and Odin moved into the log house
where Astrid's grandparents lived and were given "a small bedroom
where dad, mom, and the four small girls slept." After the birth of
their fourth child, Anne's father, Sivert, provided them a piece of land
on the small farm where Odin set up a house.

Odin was a carpenter in the Norwegian merchant fleet and often
gone for two years at a time, home for six months in between. He
generally left Anne pregnant, and one after another the girls arrived—
four in all, Astrid the second—welcoming their father when he returned. A son was born six years after the last daughter, missing the
regular two-year or so spacing in the ages of the girls. Their father's
long absences left much responsibility on their mother. "We loved our
mother so much," Astrid writes, "that when she walked all the way to
Volda to shop, we were just walking about waiting for her return."

And the homecomings of their long-absent father were joyous
events. Astrid relates that he had gifts—she recalls dolls that could
close their eyes—but once he brought a parrot. When the parrot

escaped from its cage and landed in a tree and they tried to get it down, the parrot only answered: *"Tei kjeften din, Anne Martha* (shut your mouth, Anne Martha) and laughed its ugly laughter." The worst thing was, Astrid stresses, that the bird knew how to swear, and she did not know where it had learned to do so. Grandfather Odin might say *"Hold kjeft"* (shut up), not ever to his grandchildren, but on occasion to some of his own offspring, but he never used foul language. Who Anne Martha might have been remains a mystery, as does the parrot's acquisition of profanities—though its connection with Norwegian sailors might be pondered.

Astrid grew up in a religious home "where God's word was highly respected"; her mother's unmarried older sister Anna taught them to pray also for "heathen children." Astrid pursued her own religious conviction by joining the local Salvation Army. Her strong faith characterized her entire life.[6]

During our childhood years under German occupation, Astrid from time to time took us on visits to Liaskar and Volda. There was no dock close to Bjørlykke, but one could row out on the fjord and a small coastal steamer would stop and take people aboard. The steamers transported both passengers and farm animals and had many stops, including Volda. These visits were special occasions.

Reflecting on the situation later in life, I see it must clearly have been a romantic notion for father Alf to become a *småbruker*—operator of a small farm—in Norway after achieving financial success in the United States. As Alf explained later, he pondered returning to America, and there was a fifty-fifty chance he would do so. But the economic situation both in Norway and in the United States worsened. By the 1930s, letters from friends in America told Alf of boats filled with fish, but the fish was impossible to sell. He decided to bide his time in the homeland. America became a part of life on the Bjørlykke farm, not only because of Alf's six-year sojourn there, but also because of Martin's brothers Ole, Elias, and John, and Alf's younger brother, Bendik, who in 1923 had joined his brother and uncles in America. There were "America letters" back home.

My father's sister, aunt Alvhild, took care of these precious communications. I spent much time with her, even accompanying her on the trail up the steep mountainside to the summer pastures to milk the cows and help round them up. The next morning the milk containers were taken to an aerial cable to be transported down to the road below. Aunt Alvhild yodeled to let the people waiting for the containers know they were on their way. She once related that one of these uncles had written that he had purchased a washing machine; no one could quite figure out what kind of contraption that might be. Laundry in Koparnes and Bjørlykke was washed by a housewife leaning over a washboard. America became an intimate part of growing up and entered into the conversation on a daily basis; Alf had even given the family dog the American name Buddy. In many ways America was imagined as a mighty and mysterious land. The local schoolteacher reassured his young disciples that America would rescue Norway from the occupying forces.

MY FATHER THE WHALER

The thirties were depressed times. Alf belonged to a generation of true mobility; he sought employment nearly worldwide, wherever work could be attained. Members of this generation frequently could offer only their muscle and their will to succeed. The early years in America had given Alf courage and self-confidence. Following stints as a fisherman off the coast of Norway, seal hunting off Newfoundland, and running the farm, Alf entered the more prosperous Norwegian whaling industry.

In 1984, Alf was interviewed for the Scandinavian Immigrant Experience Collection at Pacific Lutheran University, located in Parkland, a suburb of Tacoma, Washington. From Volda, his and Astrid's home after repatriating, he gave an account of how he became a whaler in the 1930s. He was offered a job on one of the large whale factory ships that went to the Antarctic Ocean; a friend with influence in the management of *Hvalfangstselskapet Kosmos*—the Whaling Company Kosmos—helped him get hired. It was a coveted position and one that paid well. The journey was long, and Alf was away from home the whole winter. His journey that winter of 1936 lasted two seasons: during the winter months, he went to the Antarctic; in summer, he worked on a ship that caught whales during Madagascar's winter season; and the following winter Alf again worked on a ship in the Antarctic. Svanhild was born in July 1937 while he was gone, and he came home only in spring the following year.

The whaling fleet was located in the city of Sandefjord by the Oslofjord. At the Vestfold Archives (*Vestfoldarkivet*) in Sandefjord in October 2016, as I did research with my daughter, Audrey, and with enthusiastic assistance from the staff, I had a strong feeling of meeting my father as a young man, separated from his family. Nearly all whalers were from the province of Vestfold and spoke a Norwegian dialect far removed from the one spoken in Sunnmøre. I wondered: Did they make fun of my father's Norwegian? How did he adjust? I tried to place myself in his situation. In the list of crew members on *Kosmos I*, Alf is identified as *arbeider* (worker). When launched in Belfast, Northern Ireland, in May 1929, *Kosmos* was the world's first specially constructed whale factory ship. In the fall of that year, with its seven newly built catchers, it reached the edge of the ice in the Antarctic.

Ten years later—after leaving Sandefjord on October 5, 1939—Alf and the other crew members on *Kosmos* headed for the Antarctic via the Dutch Caribbean island country of Curaçao and Walvis Bay in Namibia, in southwest Africa, arriving November 14. Two days later, it departed for the whaling grounds with nine catchers. After transferring the whales from the catchers to the factory ship, a team conducted the flensing, cutting the blubber and skin from the whale. The blubber was cooked into whale oil. Even this simple sketch of the demanding and complicated operation helps me visualize my father making a living under these circumstances. An interviewer described Alf's assignments: "He worked in the cannery while the boat lay in one of the ice fjords. He steamboiled the whalebones, the best oil comes from the bones. The oil was drained out until the oil

Alf worked on the factory ship *Kosmos I*.
Hvalfangstmuseet fotoarkiv, Sandefjord, Norway; courtesy Øyvind Thuresson

had some blood color, more like rose color. The oil was then filled into tanks and then given time to settle. Then the ship drove out to sea again."

The winter whaling season to the Antarctic in 1939–40 would be the last one for Alf. In a telegram to his family, he announced the date when he would be home. The German invaders beat him to it. A preserved *avregning*—remittance of salary—is dated July 19, 1940, in Walvis Bay, where *Kosmos* had anchored. A war bonus indicates that the ship was under the command of Nortraship, which administered the combined free Norwegian fleet. The ship was ordered to South Africa, and there Alf decided to join a whaling ship bound for Halifax, Canada. *Kosmos* was one of eleven Norwegian factory ships during the 1939–40 season in the southern hemisphere; the season ended with the German invasion on April 9, 1940. During the spring and summer, all except three of the eleven factory ships were anchored in port cities in the western hemisphere, with Halifax as the main base. On September 26, 1940, *Kosmos* was sunk by a German raider about two thousand nautical miles east of Trinidad.

Alf, one of many thousand stranded whalers, was granted residency in Canada for the rest of that year and moved to Vancouver, British Columbia. His return to the United States was complicated because his relevant documents were back in Norway. The issue was resolved after his uncle Elias Lowell in Everett, Washington, wrote to the state's US senator Henry Martin "Scoop" Jackson, and the senator confirmed Alf's citizenship and helped him get a visa. Alf was thus one of many men who found themselves in extended exile because of the occupation of their homeland.

Alf moved in with his uncle Ole and aunt Lina in Seattle. He resumed fishing in Alaska, for the most part on boats stationed in Seattle. The war years were spent in great agony concerning the welfare of a family he was in no position to assist. In his 1984 interview, he lamented that "except for a couple of letters, I did not have contact with my family for seven years."[7]

TOWARD A NEW LIFE IN AMERICA

In May 1945, the Germans surrendered. The Norwegian press was again under its own control, and on May 8, *Sunnmørsposten* in large headlines announced, "Germany Capitulates Norway is once again Free." On May 9, King Haakon's speech to the Norwegian people, *"Alt for Norge"* (All for Norway), got front-page attention. Universal joy was the response to German capitulation in the occupied lands.

The Norwegian flag, prohibited during the war years, was hoisted throughout the country, along with portraits of King Haakon VII, exiled in Great Britain during the war. I recall the service at Åram's local parish church and the pastor, Haakon Olaus Aarø, with great emotion declaring that Norway was again a free nation. May 17, Norway's *grunnlovsdag*—Constitution Day—was celebrated like never before. The orator in Ålesund reminded his listeners that for the

second time Norway regained its freedom in May, the first time on
May 17, 1814, and the second on May 8, 1945.

King Haakon landed in Oslo on the historically significant June 7,
the very date of his departure in 1940 and the fortieth anniversary
of the Storting's declaration of the end of the dynastic union with
Sweden. The king's homecoming became "a triumphal procession,"
as described by *Sunnmørsposten*. His Majesty was greeted by parades
in many parts of Norway, the largest one in Oslo; fifteen thousand
men in the Norwegian home front from all over Norway stood at
attention for King Haakon and Crown Prince Olav. The crown prince
had returned to Norway as early as May 13—less than a week after
German surrender—and was welcomed by, among many others, Pål
Berg, head of the Norwegian home front.

We received no news from Alf for several weeks. Was he still alive?
We sorted through difficult thoughts. We had endured much depri-
vation and hardship during the long years of occupation. Was there
to be more? The Red Cross had delivered no letters or telegrams to
us for a long time. Astrid even yielded to superstition and resorted to
the advice of a local clairvoyant, who for a small fee reassured her
that Alf was alive—the visionary claimed she could see him clearly.

Then, in June, just before school was over, we three children were
met by our joyous mother waving a telegram with the news that our
father was indeed alive and wanted us all to join him in America. He
had been out on a halibut fishing vessel off the coast of Alaska when
the Germans capitulated.

New challenges and adventures confronted the family. We were
going to America! We would join Alf, who had spent the war years
in Seattle, and become members of the Norwegian American community. There would surely be contrasting experiences to share and
consider. Later, as an immigration scholar, I explored the life and
times of people of Norwegian birth and descent in the New World.
My findings, focusing mainly on World War II, the years 1940 to 1945,
constitute a major part of the following chapter.[8]

CHAPTER 2

World War II

Norwegian Americans and the Homeland

A s AN ADULT, I pondered my father's wartime sojourn in the United States and our kin already at home there. In setting down my memories, I felt strongly that the larger Norwegian American community's response to the plight of the old homeland was very much also my own story. My research into the Norwegian American press brought a greater understanding of the response and actions of Norwegians in America—immigrants and individuals of Norwegian descent as well as Norwegians in exile. Years devoted to the study of the Norwegian American experience in its entirety, and my own residency in the United States, make all of these aspects integral and defining components of my life. For those living in Norway during the German occupation, reminders of the world beyond were frequent. Many young men fled the country to join Norwegian military units in exile or the free Norwegian merchant fleet, and my family benefited directly from the Norwegian American relief program.

Later in life, as a professor at St. Olaf College, I had colleagues and good friends who had served in the US military forces. Lloyd Hustvedt, professor of Norwegian, related intriguing tales from his service in New Guinea and the Philippines and in the American occupation army in Japan. Gerald Thorson, professor of English, had served with the US Army in France, Austria, and Germany. Each represented the Norwegian American community and had insights to share. In researching the Norwegian-speaking 99th Infantry Battalion, I had the good fortune to interview sons of men who had served in this military unit, giving evidence of the United States as a bilingual society.

The changing composition and evolving characteristics of the Norwegian American population have been much on my mind. When the "national origins" system was enacted by the US Congress in 1927, restrictions on immigration to America through the quota laws greatly reduced the flow; in its final form, effective in 1929, Norway was awarded an annual quota of 2,377. A long hiatus in the arrival of Norwegian immigrants ensued due to the altered quota system and, later the Great Depression and World War II. Members of the Norwegian American community in 1946 had immigrated in the several decades before 1930. Thus, these statistics and the big-picture history suggest that the depressed economy likely kept my father from returning to the United States. His brother, my uncle Bendik, who remained in America, told stories of the hardships he and many others endured. During the economic severity of the 1930s, those who repatriated to Norway numbered around 32,000, six times as many as those who left. Only 5,508 Norwegian immigrants are registered during that decade.

The Løvolls encountered an established and aging Norwegian American environment, one rapidly assimilating into American society. The number of Norwegian-born residents was declining quickly, from 345,522 in 1930 to 232,820 in 1940. The figures suggest a precipitous drop in the number of Norwegian language speakers in that decade. The 1940 federal census listed 344,240 second-generation individuals who claimed Norwegian as their home language, down from 658,589 two decades before; only 81,160 of the third generation made a similar claim. Another telling fact: in the 1930s, Norwegian American Lutheran congregations abandoned all efforts to give young people religious instruction in Norwegian. Some rural congregations offered options—confirmation in English or Norwegian. Lloyd Hustvedt was confirmed in Norwegian, while other siblings chose English. It was a sign of the times.[1]

A GREATER NORWAY

The concept of a greater Norway persisted. In his treatise *Vikings Across the Atlantic*, historian Daron Olson traces emigration and the building of a greater Norway from 1860 to 1945. The final chapter, "A Shared Homeland," covering the years 1929–45, shows how the early concept of a greater Norway and a Norwegian identity were actually strengthened during these years. Olson identifies the American government's official proclamation of Leif Erickson Day on October 9, 1935, and the Norwegian royal heirs' 1939 visit to America as events that rehabilitated and validated Norwegian Americans' pride in their culture following the Great War. "Thus," Olson concludes, "on the eve of World War II, the Norwegian-American self-image had been restored to its 1914 status," when Norwegians at home and abroad commemorated the centennial of the May 17, 1814, constitution. Norwegian Americans came to the aid of the occupied homeland and took part in its liberation. Following the end of hostilities in 1945, official Norway recognized Norwegian Americans' contributions. Olson makes the following point: "For homeland Norwegians, World War II had proven just how true the concept of a greater Norway really was. The contributions of Norwegian Americans had been a major factor in the liberation of Norway."

Norwegian American identity was fashioned and reinterpreted by the dynamics of the second generation and by generational transformation. In a May 2000 talk at Eidsvoll, the site of the signing of the constitution in 1814, I observed that the American-born generations had a greater concern for ethnicity than those born in Norway; for them it became to a greater degree a means of interacting with American society. An ethnic group's place and acceptance in American history and society is of paramount concern. The second generation most clearly sought to establish acceptable credentials by promoting mainstream American ideals and values as being specific to Norwegians. Its members created myths of origin and descent to show that their ethnoculture was compatible with American norms and ideals.

Chicago provides an excellent case study. In 1900, the Norwegian colony, counting only the first and second generations, numbered about forty-two thousand. Those born in America accounted for about half, among them many of the urban leaders. May 17 festivities were popular public displays of shared historical memories and myths well suited to bestow positive ethnic attributes on both Norwegian immigrants and their American-born progeny. Festivals celebrating Norway's constitution and independence enhanced the socio-historical status and acceptability of Norwegian Americans.

In central locations like Chicago, May 17 festivities continued as an identifying symbol of Norwegian American ethnicity throughout the Great Depression. In 1934, as it was reported by the Norwegian National League:

> Norway's Constitution Day May 17 was celebrated here in Chicago in good Norwegian style with a folk parade (*folketog*) and folk festival (*folkefest*). Thanks to the increasing number of children in national costume, the parade was one of the most impressive in many years. The positive fashioning and reinvention of an ethnic identity was clearly demonstrated by Pastor D. G. Ristad speaking in Norwegian, when he claimed that "the Norwegian people brought with them to this country the knowledge, understanding, and practice of the form of government Lincoln so strikingly described as a government of the people, by the people, and for the people, in addition to an ingrained respect for law and order."

Other events reinforced a Norwegian cultural heritage and connection to Norway. The spring and summer of 1939, the heirs to the Norwegian throne, Crown Prince Olav and Crown Princess Märtha, engaged in a celebratory journey from coast to coast, generating an exuberant awareness of a shared nationality and heritage. Olson sees their visit as "the high point in Norway's validation of the Norwegian-American self-image." Norwegian Americans' success clearly bolstered the idea of a greater Norway; the good fortunes, prosperity, and public regard for Americans of Norwegian birth or descent were highly important in cultivating Norway's image abroad. In studying the royal journey, I concluded, "The coast-to-coast royal visit was a historic moment with great symbolic import for Norwegians in America; commentators saw it as a reaffirmation of Norway's discovery of a Norwegian American community during the heady years following the dissolution of the Swedish-Norwegian Union."

Nordmanns-Forbundet (the Norsemen's Federation) arranged the royal visit. Nordmanns-Forbundet's founding in Kristiania (Oslo) on June 21, 1907, was directly the result of dramatic events that in 1905 created a national Norwegian monarchy and generated a fervent nationalism. Storting president Carl Christian Berner became the new organization's first president. His role in the Storting's June 7 declaration of the end of the dynastic union with Sweden made him "the country's most popular figure." Prominent Norwegian politicians, leaders in commerce and trade and in academe and the arts, and literary authors like Bjørnstjerne Bjørnson assured the federation's success. The romantic concept of "a greater Norway"—*et større Norge*—appeared regularly in diverse formulations on the pages of its journal, *Nordmands-Forbundet*, which also expressed the notion of "the emigrated Norway" and the idea of *vor egen stamme*—our own tribe or nation—to which Norwegians outside Norway also belonged.

In the initial issue, October 1907, journal editor F. G. Gade, the major figure in the federation's founding and a pioneer in cancer research, and the folklorist and professor Moltke Moe formulate the twofold purpose of the new organization: first, to reinforce a sense of nationalism at home so that Norwegians would feel part of a higher unity, and second, to make the Norwegians both at home and abroad feel more strongly their interdependence and become to a greater extent a part of each other's lives. The federation's final appeal reads: "The Federation asks for the help of all Norwegians, not only to unite the country, but to gather the bloodline (*ætt*). The Norwegian people, wherever they live in the world—provided they still feel bound by blood to a Norwegian nationality."

In writing the history of Nordmanns-Forbundet, regarding the relationship between the homeland and the Norwegian American community, I note, "In order to unite in a greater Norway the two homes of Norwegians—one in the west, the Western Home (*Vesterheimen*), and one in the east, Norway itself—a common historical narrative had to be realized."

A productive debate about how best to record the history of the "emigrated Norway" was introduced in 1904 with the publication of *Det norske Amerika. Blandt udvandrede nordmænd, vore landsmænds liv og vilkaar i den nye verden* (Norwegian America: Among our Emigrated Norwegians, our Countrymen's Lives and Circumstances in the New World) by Thoralv Klaveness. The goal was finally achieved with the pioneering volumes *Veien mot vest* (The Way West), published in 1941 and 1950, by historian Ingrid Semmingsen, initiated and supported by Nordmanns-Forbundet. "In our day and age," Semmingsen writes, "anyone who seeks can find Norwegians everywhere in the world, sailing on all oceans and living on all continents." Semmingsen's focus is worldwide, bringing together disparate Norwegian immigrant communities, but most of her story concerns Norwegians in the United States, making Norwegian Americans an integral part of Norway's history. Norwegian Americans were thus, as emphasized in my *Norwegian Newspapers in America*, finally validated as true Norwegians by the homeland.[2]

THE SECOND WORLD WAR

The German invasion and occupation of Norway in April 1940 had, as Norwegian American newsman Carl G. O. Hansen wrote, a powerful effect "in creating solidarity among Norwegian-American groups." They found a new uniting cause to champion: relief and aid to the homeland. American Relief for Norway, formed a few days after the attack on Norway, in its publicity materials pushed all groups to assist "the fair, free land of our race in the North." The aid validated, as Olson shows, the idea of a greater Norway: "The ordeal of World War II and the foreign occupation of Norway proved to be the ultimate test for the greater Norway concept. Loyalty to Norway became more than symbolic; it required real sacrifice. As a government in exile, Norway's leaders, including the royal family, upheld and put into practice the greater Norway, asking Norwegians living outside Norway to contribute financially and also through military service to the restoration of a free Norway."

World War II broke out September 1, 1939, with the Nazi blitzkrieg against Poland, and by September 3, Great Britain and France had declared war. "In the spring of 1940," writes historian Henry Bamford Parkes, "came a series of cataclysmic events which shocked the American people more profoundly than anything in their whole previous history." German forces seized Denmark and Norway in April and overran Holland and Belgium in May; the fall of France in June with a large part of the country under German occupation left Great Britain as the only remaining barrier to complete German domination of western Europe.

Great Britain was likewise the only democracy standing between Hitler's Nazi Germany and the United States. "If Hitler conquered Britain," Parkes concluded, "he would control all the eastern Atlantic and could out-build the United States in any race for military and naval supremacy." There was a growing partnership between the United States and Great Britain, with Winston Churchill encouraging Franklin D. Roosevelt to end the country's neutrality and enter the war. Meanwhile, the United States provided aid short of war. Parkes posed the intriguing question whether the American people would on their own accord break an isolationist trend and become full belligerents. The Japanese attack on Pearl Harbor on December 7, 1941, took the decision out of their hands. A united American public supported the congressional declaration that a state of war existed with Japan, and three days later Germany and Italy declared war on the United States. A single global war, merging the European and Asiatic conflicts, was thereby a reality.[3]

A NORWEGIAN COMMUNITY IN EXILE

On June 7, 1940, the Norwegian government abandoned the struggle for Norway and moved into exile in London. That same evening King

Haakon VII, Crown Prince Olav, and most of the government sailed from Tromsø aboard a British cruiser that would take them to Great Britain. Two days later, on June 9, General Otto Ruge, the Norwegian commander in chief, contacted the German High Command to request an armistice. The following day, June 10, General Ruge's representatives signed an agreement of capitulation. The struggle to regain Norwegian independence would thereafter persevere outside of Norway's borders, coupled with resistance at home. Historian Magne Skodvin praises the exceptional unity of the Norwegian resistance to the German occupation. Referred to as *hjemmefronten*—the home front—the movement included both civilian and military resistance. Many illegal organizations, including newspapers, came into existence as the resistance movement worked underground. Skodvin explains that there was one coordinated, unified civilian branch and one coordinated, highly centralized military branch of resistance, with no competing organizations.[4]

A Norwegian exile community came into being in New York and Washington, DC. Because the United States did not enter the war until December 1941, Norwegians seeking asylum for those nearly nineteen months found themselves in a nation at peace and nominally neutral. The Norwegian government in exile and the United States became wartime allies, "brothers in arms." Among the expatriates were many luminaries: Halvdan Koht, historian and Norway's foreign minister until November 1940; C. J. Hambro, president of the Storting; author Sigrid Undset, poet Nordahl Grieg, and other prominent members of Norwegian society in a variety of pursuits. Trygve Lie, foreign minister in the London government, succeeding Koht, visited New York and Washington frequently; other ministers and government officials made similar visits.

In June 1942, prime minister in exile Johan Nygaardsvold was jubilantly welcomed when he crossed the Atlantic to greet Norwegians in greater New York. His visit became front-page news in large type over several issues of *Nordisk Tidende*. The main grand event was a *stor folkemiddag*—large dinner for all people—in Nygaardsvold's honor on

Saturday, June 6, at Hotel St. George. A large assembly—more than fourteen hundred guests—enjoyed the festive meal and program. Foreign minister Lie gave a speech transmitted by radio from London. He greeted "Norwegians and friends of Norway" and anticipated Nygaardsvold's report on "how the cooperation is arranged between the two states, America and Norway, both having the same goal in this war and in many ways have so much in common." Nygaardsvold, as the last speaker among several others—including Hambro—reviewed the difficult years after the first world war, social developments, and the problems facing Norway's defense; gave a great tribute to Norwegian seamen; and emphasized that the Norwegian people had a sense of security and pride with America on their side, concluding that "on this journey I have found that the interest among Norwegian Americans for Norway in these fateful days is great and perhaps greater than ever before."

The substantial program of patriotic Norwegian music and song ended after midnight with a prayer for Norway by seamen's pastor Arthur Thorbjørnsen, who "in a beautiful and heartfelt manner interpreted everyone's deep and fervent feelings for our old fatherland and its temporary heavy fate." *Nordisk Tidende* summed up the "Nygaardsvold-dinner" by noting that the unison singing of *"Gud signe vårt dyre fedreland"* (God Bless Our Precious Fatherland) "brought to an end one of the most exceptional Norwegian arrangements in New York in living memory." Festive patriotic events reported in a national Norwegian American press gripped Norwegian Americans wherever they resided and reinforced their attachment to the old homeland.

In an attempt to Nazify Norwegian society, Vidkun Quisling's Nazi party, NS—the sole legitimate political party in Norway—declared that May 1 and May 17 were no longer observed. The Nazi party made early efforts to enlist Nordmanns-Forbundet/Norsemen's Federation in oblique efforts to contact Norwegians, especially seamen, abroad through its publications. The federation enjoyed international respect; its monthly journal, *Nordmanns Forbundet*, "which went to thousands of members around the world, could [it was believed] serve the Norwegian Nazis' dream of some kind of Norwegian-German supernationalism," according to its July 1945 issue.

The Nordmanns-Forbundet board firmly declined any cooperation with the Nazis. Writing its centennial history, *Celebrating a Century*, and following its journey on both sides of the Atlantic, and indeed in the world community, I related closely to its resistance to the Norwegian Nazi regime and to its strong engagement in spreading the news of occupied Norway to the Norwegian American community and beyond. The federation became one of many Norwegian voluntary organizations that engaged in a general protest against Nazification—which led to their administrations being replaced by Norwegian Nazis. In September 1941, a state of emergency was declared, and on September 11, Norwegian broadcasting carried the news that the federation's board and functionaries were removed from office. Nazi representative Finn Støren took over as president, or "commissary leader," and a Nazi board was put in place. The Nazi-led federation quickly lost members in America and elsewhere. As reported in 1945, "a dead hand was placed over Nordmanns-Forbundet during the years the Nazis ruled."

C. J. Hambro, Nordmanns-Forbundet's legally elected president, resided in the United States at the time of the Nazis' seizure. Through untiring actions, Hambro "gathered our emigrated countrymen under Nordmanns-Forbundet's banner to a degree never done before." With support from the organization's own commissioners, members, and friends, funding was secured to reconstitute the federation. Local US chapters and prominent Norwegian Americans strongly encouraged Hambro to establish Nordmanns-Forbundet's office and publish the journal in a free America. A board was named in New York in December 1941, and the first issue of *Nordmanns Forbundet* appeared the same month, shipping to American members as well as those in Europe, somewhat intermittently, and in other parts of the world.

In its extensive coverage, Nordmanns-Forbundet's journal bore witness to the federation's international bridge-building mission.

Prominent Norwegians in exile served on the board during the years abroad, including historians Jacob S. Worm-Müller and Halvdan Koht and the author Sigrid Undset and poet Nordahl Grieg. They spoke for both Norwegian Americans and the exile community and were joined by the influential consul Lars Christensen, who enjoyed high international esteem. Seamen's pastor Leif T. Gulbrandsen and Einar Johansen, head of the Seamen's Federation office in New York, maintained a connection to "the sailing Norway." The war and Norway's involvement in it, as editorially stated in the journal's December 1944 issue, created an extensive need for information about Norway. The details were spread to a Norwegian American audience, and also to a larger public, by *Nordmanns Forbundet* and the few remaining Norwegian American newspapers as well as through extensive speaking engagements.[5]

The exile community included the royal heirs. Crown Prince Olav alternated between America on the one hand and King Haakon and the Norwegian government in exile in London on the other; Crown Princess Märtha and the royal children—princesses Ragnhild and Astrid and the heir apparent prince Harald—found asylum in Washington, DC. When St. Olaf College awarded King Harald V an honorary doctorate on October 19, 1995, I made the point that His Majesty had himself been a Norwegian immigrant during the years of hostility, and thus knew the immigrant experience. His Majesty, sitting alongside me, nodded appreciatively.

His Majesty's mother, Crown Princess Märtha, had been at President Roosevelt's side when in September 1942 he gave his treasured "Look to Norway" speech. It generated much pride among people of Norwegian birth and descent, as did the presence of leading Norwegian politicians, cultural personalities, a commercial elite, and people in more regular circumstances. Norwegian seamen in the free merchant fleet, sailing both the Atlantic and the Pacific, when onshore in coastal cities promoted a Norwegian presence and influence along with more prominent Norwegians. These representatives were seamen on ships making regular port calls or men rescued from

On October 19, 1995, on behalf of St. Olaf College, Odd presented the
insignia of an honorary doctorate to His Majesty King Harald V;
college president Mark Edwards stands at right

torpedoed ships, even sailors who had abandoned ship. Or they were men, like my father Alf, in the Norwegian whaling operations in the Antarctic. They were all a component of a Norwegian community outside the homeland.

The Norwegian embassy in Washington, DC, represented the exiled Norwegian London government. Abiding interest in the homeland's fate increased the circle of readers for the remaining Norwegian-language news organs, published in the Midwest, on the Pacific Coast, and in the East. Because of its Brooklyn location, *Nordisk Tidende* had greater access to the Norwegian exile community and therefore a special role in informing not only the Norwegian American community but also the general American public about the adversity suffered in the occupied territory. Karsten Roedder, quoting the newspaper's editorial secretary, Niels Tjelmeland, writes, "We are involved in the extremely interesting and even somewhat miraculous situation, where we here in a Brooklyn newspaper virtually wade in Norwegian cabinet ministers and other excellencies." The excellencies, to use Tjelmeland's term, included both visiting and resident expatriated Norwegians.[6]

A NORWEGIAN-LANGUAGE PRESS

The Norwegian-language press became the conduit for leaders—resident and in exile—to communicate with and inspire the Norwegian American community. For this reason, a brief account of its historic significance should be a part of the World War II story.

Norwegian American newspaperman Carl G. O. Hansen captures his general concept of the Norwegian immigrant media: "The press—with its men and subscribers—constitute in one sense the concept that frequently designated 'the Norwegian America.' It is the frame around everything else, even after the picture has gained such strong colors and gained such impressive form that the frame seems like mere air."

Although these words appeared in 1914, in a chapter about Norwegian American newspapers until the end of the American Civil War, a major expansion of the immigrant media occurred in the subsequent decades. From 1847, with the publication of *Nordlyset* in Muskego, Wisconsin—the first Norwegian-language newspaper in the Midwest—until the present time some 280 secular semimonthly, weekly, semiweekly, or daily newspapers emerged, about 80 percent in the decades between 1871 and 1910. Even though the vast majority lasted only a short time, this figure speaks volumes about the numerical strength and impact of Norwegian American journalistic enterprise.

In all immigrant nationalities the ethnic press reflected the lives and experiences of people in motion—migration from one area of settlement to the next. I echoed historian Marcus Lee Hansen, who noted that "A significant part of history deals with mankind in motion." In American history, moving westward has constituted a persistent theme, with pioneer tales of taming the frontier and building new communities. The geographical spread of the ethnic press of individual non-English-speaking groups indicates their most important areas of settlement. In addition, the initial publication of ethnic newspapers at a new place delineates patterns of migration and settlement, as urban historian Robert Park wrote: "The distribution of the press of the various foreign-language groups locates with considerable accuracy their principal settlements in the United States, and makes it possible to indicate 'cultural areas' in which the influences of certain immigrant groups have been more pronounced than elsewhere."

Park continued: "the mother tongue is the natural basis of human association and organization." And Marcus Lee Hansen made the point that "To some extent, nearly every immigrant nationality managed to perpetuate the atmosphere of the motherland." The literary language assumed greater significance because only through the written word could immigrant populations living in many parts of the United States be united. The newspapers published in the homeland's language created a sense of national ethnic communities, among these, a Norwegian America.[7]

Hansen asserted that "A favorite occupation of the immigrant intellectual was journalism." My follow-up of Hansen's dictum: "A mobile journalistic class emerged, easily moving from one newspaper venture to another, as editors and publishers, making a living in the shifting and uncertain world of Norwegian American newspaper publishing." The Norwegian American press peaked in the years before World War I: Norwegian America's golden age. New journalistic enterprise marked the spread of settlement westward, to the Pacific Northwest. A national Norwegian American press existed.

The press was of vital importance and provided the main, for some people the only, information about the world as they adjusted to new political and social circumstances. Ethnic journals, written for the common man and woman, had distinctly democratic appeal. People who in Norway had never subscribed to a newspaper not only became avid readers in America. There was in fact an intimate relationship between newspapers and their public—evidenced in the multitude of letters from readers that filled their columns.

The Chicago journal *Skandinaven* is a good example. It was launched in 1866 and had great political and social influence. Toward the end of the century it was published in a daily and a semiweekly edition and was the largest Norwegian-language newspaper not only in America but for a time in the entire world. No newspaper in Norway even came close.

Skandinaven was one of the so-called Big Three newspapers. The other two were *Minneapolis Tidende*, founded in 1887, and *Decorah-Posten*, in 1874. These three became leading journals in the Midwest, with large circulations throughout the region and beyond, to all parts of the United States, and even to the Norwegian homeland. However, following the First World War, the Norwegian-language newspapers increasingly became supplements to an American newspaper, and there was a steady decline in numbers and circulation. The existing journals focused more on the Norwegian American community and on the homeland and over time gradually covered less general newsworthy material. Both *Skandinaven* and *Minneapolis Tidende* succumbed to the financial decline of the 1930s and the loss of subscribers, *Skandinaven* lasting until 1941 and *Tidende* only until 1935. The two journals, like the Norwegian immigrant press as a whole, were a primary expression of the resilience of Norwegian American culture—its interaction rather than assimilation with American society—and promoted a Norwegian American identity that pledged both allegiance to American citizenship and attachment to an ethnic cultural tradition. The vitality of the Norwegian American press represents one of the most remarkable and visible aspects of immigrant life and of Norwegian American history.[8]

THE PRESS AND WORLD WAR II

In *Skrift i sand*, translated as *Written in the Sand*, newspaper editor Carl Søyland describes how the German invasion of Norway in 1940 had immediate repercussions in the Norwegian American community and how it activated Norwegians in Brooklyn and brought people in the periphery of the community into the center. And in this center, Søyland explains, "was the newspaper, surrounded by the strongest Norwegian American interests, represented by individuals, churches, and organizations."

Søyland referred to *Nordisk Tidende*, which, thanks to its location in Brooklyn, had a special advantage over the other Norwegian-language journals. Søyland, with his philosophical bent, was a much appreciated and influential member of Brooklyn's Norwegian community. He was appointed editor in chief of *Tidende* on April 8, 1940, the day before Germany invaded Norway, succeeding Hans Olav, who moved on to new duties. Vilhelm von Munthe af Morgenstierne, Norway's long-serving ambassador to the United States (1934–58), announced Hans Olav's appointment as press attaché at the Norwegian legation in Washington, DC; Olav also headed the newly organized Norwegian Information Service. Morgenstierne, earlier secretary general of Nordmanns-Forbundet, eventually "knew almost the entire emigrated Norway in North America" due to his long tenure. He accompanied the Norwegian royal couple on parts of their tour in 1939. He had a good relationship with Roosevelt and influenced the president's positive attitude toward Norway. Morgenstierne engaged strongly in the fate of the Norwegian merchant fleet during the war and played a significant role in having American vessels replace the increasing number of Norwegian ships lost at sea. In recognition of Norway's efforts on behalf of the Allied cause, Roosevelt in 1942 upgraded the Norwegian legation to an embassy and Morgenstierne from minister to ambassador.

Prior to US entry into the war in December 1941, Norwegian American newspapers relied on news from occupied Norway. Newspapers and letters—censored and uncensored—as well as private telegrams from different parts of Norway made it across the Atlantic. The Norwegian Information Service thereafter became the source for news from Norway. Beyond editing *Nordisk Tidende,* Hans Olav had high credentials as a seasoned newsman; he had studied at Columbia University School of Journalism.

The Norwegian Information Service under Olav's leadership worked closely with the remaining Norwegian American newspapers. The Norwegian embassy's press and information department provided the publishers with airmailed news releases about the situation in Norway, transmitted telegraphically by the Norwegian London press office—the most important source of information about internal circumstances in the occupied homeland. The headlines and reports were highly disturbing: "Disquieting headlines—'Riots, Murder, and Arson Everywhere in Norway,' 'The Germans' Treatment of Norwegians Increasingly More Brutal,' 'Between 1,200 and 1,500 Students Arrested,' 'Eighteen More Executions,' and even 'Norway Faces Starvation'—caught the attention of the readers and created great sympathy for the people of Norway."[9]

In February 1942 the Norwegian American editors were invited to a two-day press conference at the Norwegian embassy. In attendance were seven editors, representing as many secular papers: *Washington-Posten,* Seattle, Washington; *Decorah-Posten,* Decorah, Iowa; *Normanden,* Fargo, North Dakota; *Duluth Skandinav,* Duluth, Minnesota; *Visergutten,* Canton, South Dakota; *Viking,* Chicago; and finally *Nordisk Tidende. Fergus Falls Ukeblad* and *Minneapolis Posten* in Minnesota and *Superior Tidende* in Wisconsin were not represented. These were the remaining Norwegian-language journals in the United States.

Among the several speakers was Tor Gjesdal, chief of the Norwegian press office in London, who informed the editors about the news service to and from Norway. Another speaker was Karl Evang, director of health, who accompanied the Norwegian government to exile in London and during the war played a significant role in public health for Norwegians in all parts of the world. He claimed that "the first large bright spot he had experienced when he came here [to America] in 1940, was his meeting with the Norwegian American press, which speaks out about the state of affairs—clearly and precisely." He also pointed out how immensely important Norwegian America was to people in England, like "a second kingdom behind Norway, which the Allies count on."

The remaining journals gained new subscribers from readers of discontinued newspapers, such as *Skandinaven*, but also from a growing interest in the fate of the homeland, and the fact that newspapers from Norway disappeared after December 1941. Prior to that date, the Norwegian Brooklyn colony had received a great number of newspapers from Norway, according to *Nordisk Tidende*, "thousands and thousands throughout the year." The colony housed the largest Norwegian-born population in the United States, many of whom intended to stay only a few years before returning to Norway or were "birds of passage" migrants, moving back and forth by the seasons. Port calls by Norwegian ships and the large number of colony members employed on ships and in related occupations preserved the connection to Norway. There was a special "nearness" to the homeland. When newspapers no longer arrived from Norway and news of Norway in American newspapers proved inadequate, people turned to the Norwegian American press. *Nordisk Tidende* benefitted greatly, more so than any of the other Norwegian-language journals, increasing its number of printed copies 100 percent during the war years.[10]

The excellencies referred to earlier contributed regularly to the columns of *Nordisk Tidende*. Competing journals, like *Washington Posten*, might complain about their geographic disadvantage; however, Hans

Olav reassured them that the embassy press office gave no prefer-
ence to *Tidende* and that all journals got the same news at the same
time. Olav also assured the collective Norwegian American press that
the embassy press office made an effort to prevent Norwegian officials
from giving special interviews to *Nordisk Tidende*. As they traveled
throughout the country on speaking tours, these same government
officials were interviewed by *Tidende*'s competitors, though the Brooklyn paper's advantages could not be ignored; from time to time the
officials' commentaries and those of other Norwegians in exile were
reprinted from *Tidende* in the columns of Norwegian-language journals throughout the United States. *Visergutten*, at that time published
in Canton, South Dakota, and other Norwegian-language papers in
1941 referenced from *Tidende* in some detail Hambro's speech in New
York about Norway and Nazism; also noted was the German execution of six Norwegians.

In a history of *Nordisk Tidende*, Karsten Roedder makes a substantial list of the newspaper's contributors. The names and concerns of
a few exiled columnists give a sense of the drama and individual
engagement associated with wartime journalism. Roedder describes
Dr. Karl Evang as the most productive article writer and thereafter C. J. Hambro, portrayed as "one of the bright names." The
theme of their chronicles dealt mainly with the homeland under
the occupation. The columnists included Norwegian cabinet ministers in exile like Trygve Lie and minister of finance and later of
defense Oscar Torp, who "brought both strength and authority to the
newspaper."[11]

The Norwegian war correspondent Lise Lindbæk became a close
associate of editor Søyland. Her *Tusen norske skip* from 1943, translated as *Norway's New Saga of the Sea*, deals with the contributions of
Norwegian seamen during the war. Her experience and education
gave her a deep understanding of Norway and the gripping wartime
drama it endured. In an interview with Søyland, she reflected on her
eight-month American tour, giving more than "100 lectures about
Norway in American Clubs and on the radio in the western states."
The local Norwegian American journals—from the Midwest to the

Pacific Coast—joined *Tidende* in reporting on her journey. She describes the Norwegian presence with enthusiasm: "Washington is perhaps the most Norwegian of the 48 states, with mountains and fjords and fish and boats and forests. It is no wonder that it is swarming with Norwegians, and they are content to the nth degree. Everything reminds you of Norway, but the dimensions are greater and the possibilities for the individual are greater. . . . Every year, a halibut fleet of 3,000 fishermen leaves Seattle for Alaska and the Aleutians, and at least 90% are Norwegian."

Lindbæk's depiction of Seattle, with Norwegian singing societies, theaters, churches, and a variety of other Norwegian associations and events, brings my thoughts to my father Alf Lowell, who certainly engaged in the halibut fisheries and was an interested and well-informed socially active person. When interviewed in 1984, Alf related that he had joined a Sons of Norway lodge both in Juneau and in Seattle; activities included speeches, dances, celebrations, and parties. And Alf worshipped in Lutheran churches. He also subscribed to *Washington Posten*; after returning to Norway permanently in 1966, he received it as a gift from a friend in California; by then it had become *Western Viking*. Alf might likely have attended Lindbæk's lectures in the city, and those of the many other Norwegian speakers, who found heedful and sympathetic American and Norwegian audiences.

NORWEGIANS IN EXILE

These regular speaking events by prominent, knowledgeable Norwegians in exile, attended in large numbers, created much interest and concern for a Norwegian homeland. Hambro and Koht both made well-reported tours to spread information through extensive speaking engagements. In 1940, the poet, novelist, and dramatist Nordahl Grieg escaped to England on the same ship as the royal family; his anti-fascist stance had made Norway a dangerous place for him. Grieg became a part of the government in exile. On his brief sojourn in the United States, his deep patriotism for Norway was on full display in his talks and his poetry. Literary historian Sven Rossel considers

Grieg's poems "among the most significant written about war and the fatherland"; *"Norge i våre hjerter"* (Norway in our hearts), *"17. mai 1940. I dag står flaggstangen naken"* (May 17, 1940. Today the flag pole stands naked), and other patriotic poems were featured at May 17 and other Norwegian events. In December 1943, Grieg was killed as an observer during an Allied air raid against Berlin.

Nobel laureate Sigrid Undset was the foremost representative of Norwegian culture among the exiled Norwegians. Her literary works, most especially her trilogy of historical novels, *Kristin Lavransdatter*, reached a large American public. In *Return to the Future*, first published in English in Brooklyn in 1942, she describes the confusion and struggle during those grim April days of the German invasion and her own flight from Norway. Undset had criticized Hitler from the early 1930s; her books were banned in Nazi Germany. She could easily have become a target of the Gestapo. Her eldest son, Second Lieutenant Anders Undset Svarstad of the Norwegian Army, was killed in action in an engagement with German troops on April 27, 1940, at the age of twenty-seven. He died a week after Undset's escape from the Nazis, and she only learned of it May 11, after her arrival in Stockholm, Sweden. She continued on to Soviet Russia, then Japan, and across the Pacific Ocean to Hawaii and California, then by train to New York. "Now it is only across America," she writes, "that the road leads back to the future—that which we from the European democracies call the future."

In her first interviews with an American journalist, Undset challenged him regarding US hesitation to enter the war. She tirelessly spread her anti-Nazi message in word and print and pleaded Norway's cause and that of Europe's Jews; she was appalled by anti-Semitism and in her effort to save the Jews engaged in both secret and open agitation. She lived in Columbia Heights, Brooklyn. The fall of 1940 and winter 1941 she made an extensive coast-to-coast speaking tour. A letter to her sister Ragnhild Undset Wiberg in Stockholm, Sweden, dated October 23, 1940, recorded that she had already given twelve lectures. While she possessed a broad and varied English vocabulary, her distinct Norwegian accent and occasional mispronounced words could make it difficult for her American listeners to understand her. But her message was clear, and at universities she felt her presentations were accepted and received the greatest response. The universities represented an essential forum as they set the tone and formed local opinion. In a letter to her sister dated in San Francisco, November 22, 1940, she explains: "I have now traveled high and low around in the states, and there are times when I feel that this is really a dog's life. Club ladies and women's clubs are not always very enjoyable. On the other hand, it is frequently highly enjoyable to speak at the colleges and universities. 'The question periods' following the lectures get longer and longer and the questions change substance—people over here are beginning to understand that no one can live in peace longer than the neighbor allows."

In a biography of Sigrid Undset, Sigrun Slapgard adopted the chapter title "A Lioness Goes Ashore" (En løvinne går i land) for Undset's years in America. She documents Undset's untiring activities and social life and her fondness for New York. Undset returned to Oslo, Norway, July 30, 1945. Before her departure for the homeland, Nordisk Tidende editorially praised her for having brought with her to America her own deep mooring in Norwegian history and Norwegian life. She had been, the editorial asserted, one of Norway's best advocates and ambassadors.

A substantial number of Norwegians in exile spoke Norway's cause, and they were joined by prominent Norwegian Americans and also by less-known members of the Norwegian American community. Leaders in the myriad Norwegian American societies and organizations educated their fellow members on a regular basis about the prevailing circumstances. And the pastors of Norwegian Lutheran churches, located in large urban centers, in small towns, and in the countryside, from east to west and from north to south, in prayer and sermons and calls for succor and aid reminded parishioners of the old homeland's plight. A prevalence of information and appeals fostered ethnic enthusiasm.[12]

"SPIRIT OF LITTLE NORWAY"

Historian Clarence A. Clausen, born in 1896, had a long teaching career at several universities, among these Wittenberg University in Springfield, Ohio, where he served on the faculty until he responded to a US government call to service during World War II. During the war he was a Scandinavian-area specialist for the Office of Strategic Services, the predecessor to the Central Intelligence Agency. As a highly respected professor emeritus at St. Olaf College when I joined the faculty in 1971, Clausen became my close friend and a natural source for information about wartime conditions in general and about Norwegians in particular. "If Clarence doesn't know it, it is not worth knowing" was the affectionate adage.

Little Norway (*Lille Norge*), the training camp of the Norwegian air force in Canada, became an inspiring wartime topic that created much pride among Norwegian Americans and Norwegians in exile. *Slik fikk vi vinger* (How We Got Military Airplanes) by Ragnar Wold is a personal chronicle of the Second World War and Little Norway, where he himself was stationed for some time as an instructor in air navigation. Little Norway opened as the Royal Norwegian Air Force Training Centre in Toronto, Canada, on November 10, 1940, under the presence of Norwegian and Canadian dignitaries. Canadian authorities placed Toronto Island Airport in central Toronto at its disposal. Wold describes his journey in the fall of 1941: Oslo to Ålesund, and from islands off the coast of Sunnmøre—the two most important ones Vigra and Godøy—to Shetland on a Norwegian fishing vessel, eventually making it to Liverpool and from there to Halifax, and then by train to Toronto via Quebec City. The first Norwegians had, however, arrived as early as August 1940.

Referred to as *englandsfarten* (England crossing), the traffic of refugees from western Norway across the North Sea began in the spring of 1940, mainly on local fishing boats, with Ålesund being a central point of departure. This civilian traffic ended in early 1942. German occupiers enacted a death penalty in September 1941, at the time Wold escaped, "for those who without permission . . . move to an enemy country . . . or make preparations to do so." I have distressing memories of arrests, generally of young men fleeing, and their subsequent demise at the hands of the German occupiers.

Childhood memories were movingly refreshed on October 17, 2016, when I was a guest at Godøysundmuseet (the Godøy Sound Museum) on Godøy, the island now connected with Ålesund on the mainland by an undersea tunnel. The museum exhibited World War II artifacts and photos relating to the local community, and the visit became an unforgettable and emotional experience for me. The people who so generously arranged the event stood in a circle around me, sharing stories of both bravery and deceit and responding to my queries. Among them was Magne Godøy, author of an overview of the island and its people during the German occupation. I heard disturbing tales fervently told of young men betrayed by Norwegian Nazi youth in their midst and later executed; and also of many successful crossings from Godøy to Shetland and beyond. Individual accounts gave insight into personal challenges and survival under wartime conditions at home and abroad. The men who made it across had the option of joining Norwegian military units in exile on allied soil, including the air force training camp Little Norway.

Little Norway fulfilled its mission, with Major Odd Bull as the first camp commander. It engaged in recruitment and training before its official opening. Air personnel as well as engine and chassis mechanics got their training at Little Norway. In the course of the war, more than three thousand Norwegian aircraft soldiers in all categories were trained, among these pilots, navigators, and mechanics. Major Ole Reistad was the commanding officer for the Royal Norwegian Air Force in Canada. Wold honored *"de som var med"* (those who took part) by listing their names and also the names of the air force's fallen.

The United States was not at war when Little Norway opened, and to assist anyone to conduct war was prohibited by law, as *Nordisk Tidende* reported, rejecting criticism directed at Norwegian Americans' lack of support. The newspaper could also point to the Camp

Theodor W. Simonsen trained at the Norwegian air force's
Little Norway training camp in Canada.
Courtesy NAHA

Little Norway Association organized in Minneapolis in October 1941 and given a license to collect funds for medicine, care, clothing, recreation, and other non-martial tangibles. It later merged with Norwegian Relief for Norway.

But early on, Americans of Scandinavian background acted to assemble resources to purchase airplanes in addition to those earlier ordered by the Norwegian government in the United States and sent to Toronto. The funding effort "Wings for Norway" gained great support among Norwegian Americans. Norwegians in Latin America took part as well. Leif Lind-Pettersen and his wife Carmen owned a plantation in Guatemala and at the US government's request developed a variety of quinine for soldiers fighting in the mosquito-infected tropics. On Lind-Pettersen's initiative planes with names like *El Gaucho* rolled out on the runway at Island Airport. Figure skater and film star Sonja Henie donated a whole plane, and a few others followed suit. There was a great will to sacrifice for the cause. Funds accumulated through a voluntary wage deduction by the camp's personnel; the planes their donations purchased received the inspiring name *Spirit of Little Norway*.

Crown Princess Märtha unveiled the first airplane bearing the name *Spirit of Little Norway*; for many she became the training camp's good spirit. Crown Prince Olav headed tours to Little Norway, but because of his demanding responsibilities in England, Crown Princess Märtha and the royal children more often made the trip to Toronto. The caption of a photo of Prince Harald states "the five-year-old future King of Norway, on his first visit to 'Little Norway' with Princesses Ragnhild and Astrid. Being a sweet but tough little King-to-be, he conquered all hearts at once." Political leaders like C. J. Hambro made well-reported tours of Little Norway and spread information to Norwegian and American audiences through extensive speaking engagements. Norwegian American columnists and editors visited and regularly wrote about the activities in the camp. Chapters of "Little Norway" sprang up in many cities. Camp Little Norway was the most celebrated military endeavor on North American soil.[13]

Prince Harald, then six years old, and Crown Princess Märtha petting bear cub Peik. The adventurer and explorer Thor Heyerdahl, stationed at Little Norway, acquired the bear from a lumberjack for a bottle of whiskey and taught it to be friendly to people. The crown princess and the royal children often visited the training camp.
Courtesy NAHA

RELIEF FOR NORWAY

"Help for Mother Norway!" was—*Nordisk Tidende* insisted—"the most important cause Norwegian Americans have ever had." Voluntary organizations worked to give aid to war-torn Norway. Four of the largest groups, including American Friends of Norway in New York, united with Norwegian Relief. A. N. Rygg, earlier editor of *Nordisk Tidende*, became one of its most active members, and in 1947 compiled and edited its history.

Norwegian Relief was founded in Chicago on April 18, 1940, following a planning meeting in the Norwegian legation in Washington, DC, less than a week earlier—and only three days after the German invasion. At the US government's request, the name was later altered to American Relief for Norway. Its stated purpose: "to gather contributions towards the acquisition of supplies of food, clothing and medicine for the suffering Norwegian people and Norwegian refugees, and in any way possible give them a helping hand." It became, Rygg noted, an extensive collaboration throughout the whole country, from New York to San Francisco.

Prominent Norwegian Americans headed the relief endeavor. J. A. Aasgaard, president of the Norwegian Lutheran Church of America, served as president; Arthur Andersen, founder of the Chicago public accountant firm Arthur Andersen & Co., served as the first treasurer; investment banker, philanthropist, and promoter of Norwegian Americana Birger Osland, also from Chicago, and former Minnesota governor J. A. O. Preus were among the incorporators and main supporters. Local committees were appointed in all parts of the country where there were people of Norwegian birth and descent; the first large committee covering an entire state was the one in New York. It moved into *Nordisk Tidende*'s building with Rygg as treasurer. Many more state committees with their own chairs followed. The men and women who served had before them, *Skandinaven* reported, "a task in which no one must fail."

The Norwegian Lutheran Church of America, with its 536,000 members, and the Norwegian Lutheran Free Church made appeals for support. Individual congregations in urban and rural communities solicited contributions. Secular groups were as heavily involved. May 17 observances frequently became fund-raising events for relief for Norway. Sons of Norway, with lodges throughout the land, and *Bygdelagenes Fellesraad* (Council of *Bygdelag*), with its many member *bygdelag* or societies, appealed to their memberships for aid. "Almost every group took up Norway Relief," Søyland wrote. The Norwegian American press was especially active and worked strenuously to promote the cause. As early as July 12, 1940, the board of directors of American Relief for Norway dispatched J. A. Aasgaard to send a note of thanks to the newspapers. In part it reads: "The Norwegian American press has always been at the service of every good and noble purpose among us. But never have you served a better cause than to awaken and rouse in our people a willingness to make sacrifices and to take an interest in Norway's distress in these fateful times. On behalf of the Board of Directors, sincere thanks."

The gathering of contributions progressed rapidly, according to Rygg, albeit with slow periods that led newspapers like *Washington-Posten*, *Reform*, and *Decorah-Posten* to express disappointment. Writing in *Decorah-Posten*, Carl G. O. Hansen berates his fellow Norwegians in Minnesota for being last on the list of contributing states, New York being first. Beginning in late May 1940 *Nordisk Tidende* carried "From Day to Day in Norwegian Relief's Headquarters," and May 23 reported having collected its first $50,000, which by June 13 had doubled to $100,000. Hansen wrote of Minnesotans' dilatoriness, especially noteworthy in a state with more people of Norwegian descent than any other state in the Union. The competitive spirit likely encouraged giving. And Minnesota, with an active chair and board of directors, did well in collecting money and clothing.

The process to provide aid in itself encouraged much appreciated social activity, events that would be missed once no more relief was needed. American Relief for Norway had a Women's Division, but also a substantial number of additional women's clubs and leagues (*forbund*) existed throughout the country and engaged in relief for

Norway. Many of the organizations solicited gifts and support for Little Norway, making for a twofold mission. "Thousands of Norwegian Ladies' auxiliaries went to work knitting and sewing for 'Norwegian Relief,'" Søyland relates, describing how the Norwegian neighborhood in Brooklyn teemed with activity as scores of women came together one whole day a week to work on making clothing.

Perhaps the most sensational proposition for relief was made by Andrew A. Kindem, president of the Council of Bygdelag, who proposed that fifty thousand milk cows be sent as a gift to Norway once the war was over. Mr. Kindem was thanked, but members who reviewed his proposal found it utterly impracticable. Rygg gives a comprehensive accounting of the gifts collected by individual states and also by the Norwegian Relief Fund in Canada.

During the five years of German occupation of Norway, Sweden became the gateway through which American Relief for Norway could bring its aid to the Norwegian people; aid arrived in the form of foodstuffs, including food packages to Norwegian schoolchildren and powdered milk, nearly two million pounds in all; further aid included clothing, medicine, and cash. I fondly recall the packages we received through Sweden, many originally funded by American Relief for Norway. Committees in Sweden performed remarkable and conscientious work in distributing the relief. Swedish businessman N. E. Lenander, as treasurer of the Swedish Relief Committee, was honored on a visit to New York in September 1945. After German capitulation, aid was sent directly to Norway; the destruction that retreating German forces committed in the northernmost province Finnmark received special attention. At its annual meeting at Chicago's Palmer House in April 1946, American Relief for Norway resolved to wind down all activity by October 1 that year.

A concluding assessment of American Relief for Norway was printed in *Nordisk Tidende* on May 2, 1946: "It turned into a strenuous piece of work—more than six years—but the interest has been so strong and warm that one the whole time has been able to keep it going at full speed. Today Norwegian America can take great pleasure at having been able to bring Norway considerable and necessary help at a critical period."[14]

NORTRASHIP AND THE UNITED STATES

An extensive two-volume work by Guri Hjeltnes, *Handelsflåten i krig 1939–1945* (The Merchant Marine at War, 1939–1945), is the most comprehensive scholarly treatment of the Norwegian merchant fleet during the Second World War. Drawing on her research, I suggest here how the wartime role and fortitude of the Norwegian merchant marine and its seamen influenced the view toward Norway and the measures taken in America that directly affected the Norwegian American community.

Nortraship—Norwegian Shipping and Trade Mission—was organized in April 1940 after the Norwegian government had requisitioned the country's merchant marine beyond German control. It would administer the fleet, which included about a thousand ships equal to four million gross tonnage, making Nortraship the largest and one of the most modern shipping firms in the world. Its main offices were in London and New York. Norwegian merchant ships joined the war in all waters—the Atlantic, Indian, and Pacific Oceans and the Mediterranean Sea—and at the Allied land operations. The convoys across the Atlantic had the greatest losses. According to official statistics, 694 ships were sunk by hostile action. Human losses in the domestic fleet and in the Norwegian marine included 4,600 crew members who lost their lives at sea, more than 3,000 of these in the Nortraship fleet, or about 10 percent of the 30,000 seafaring men and women in its service. "The sailors," Hjeltnes writes, "engaged in the battle where they could be of greatest use—they sailed for Norway's freedom."

The merchant fleet provided the economic foundation for the Norwegian government in exile; it was the country's most important contribution to the Allied war effort and earned Norway high esteem and praise. Maintaining the connecting link between North America and Great Britain was decisive for the war's outcome. The bulk of goods transported by Norwegian ships sailed in convoys across the

North Atlantic from ports in Canada and the United States to Great
Britain. Oil was of special significance for British warfare; Norway's
modern fleet of tank ships proved essential.

Nortraship's influence and place in America and in Norwegian
American settings is worth recounting here. The many calls Norwegian vessels made on both the Pacific and the Atlantic Coasts became
an important constituent as Norwegian Americans fostered concern
for and dedication to their ancestral homeland.

The seamen's churches played an increased role for the merchant
fleet and its crews; the motto of the Norwegian Seamen's Mission
was that it always accompanied the merchant fleet. With US entry
into the war, the station in New York gained added significance;
the church in Brooklyn was filled with sailors on festive occasions.
New York was, along with the British posts, the most important port
for Norwegian shipping. In 1940 there were no fewer than 895 Norwegian ship calls, and in 1944 as many as 1,052. Local women volunteered to prepare food and socialize with the seamen, who often had
been long at sea. Some seamen even found their future wives on such
occasions.

A substantial number of Norwegian sailors deserted their ships,
especially in the United States, where free access to leave the ship was
provided. The *avhoppere*—defectors—numbered in the thousands of,
though the exact number is difficult to determine. They found employment on land or shipped out on American vessels. And thousands
of stranded seamen rescued from torpedoed ships either remained in
the United States or signed on again. Many of these men, like my
father, were separated from their families for years. The large number of Norwegian seamen who spent a relatively long time ashore
while their ship was docked brought the homeland to the attention of
the Norwegian American community. Brooklyn, with its large Norwegian population, became a mecca for seamen. Norwegian was
spoken on the street, and there were Norwegian churches, societies
of many kinds, stores, restaurants, barrooms, and taverns where
friends could gather.

Survivors of torpedoed ships shared dramatic and bleak accounts of their heroic struggles against the unforgiving elements. Hjeltnes includes the experience of nine men, ages nineteen to sixty, who in 1942 after their boat had been torpedoed spent seven weeks on two rafts until they were rescued by the M/S *Washington Express*. Their story of survival on the high seas is thought provoking and awesome. Other similar tales of near-death experiences of seamen stranded at sea who made it safely ashore were reported in the Norwegian American press.[15]

THE VIKING BATTALION

After entering the war, the United States realized its unusual resource; it was the largest bilingual society in the world, with millions of people who had mastered English in addition to their mother tongue. These individuals also had a "secondary patriotism," as author Gerd Nyquist points out: "They fight for the United States as Americans, but they also want to do something for the other homeland, subjugated by the Germans." Their linguistic and cultural backgrounds were clearly needed to conduct warfare operations in countries occupied by Germany as well as by Japan.

I met Gerd Nyquist the summer of 1981 when I taught classes at the University of Oslo. We became good friends, and her book *Bataljon 99* (The 99th Battalion), published earlier that year, was a favored topic during those distant weeks. I learned about her own and her husband's activities in the Norwegian resistance movement during World War II. Her strong interest in defense and the homeland is present in her book about the 99th Battalion, which has gained great admiration in Norway through today.

The *Faribault (Minnesota) Daily News* on March 9, 2003, carried an interview with local resident Robert "Bob" Bjorgum, who had served as first lieutenant in the battalion. After the war he was awarded the Purple Heart. "The 99th Battalion," Bjorgum alleges, "shared something that no American battalion had ever shared before—its ethnicity." He continues, "This bond brought the men even closer than many units were." Through his son, Bruce Bjorgum, I became acquainted with the 99th Infantry Battalion Separate Educational Foundation and the people there. I was literally overwhelmed by their enthusiasm for the battalion's history and the resources and information they provided. I will limit my comments here to a brief historical survey of the 99th Infantry Battalion and how its wartime role and activities inspired a closer attachment to a Norwegian homeland.

The 99th Infantry Battalion (Separate) was constituted by the War Department on July 10, 1942, and activated at Camp Ripley, located near the city of Little Falls in central Minnesota, on August 15, 1942. Its first commander was Captain Harold D. Hanson. Requests for Norwegian-speaking volunteers were sent throughout the army. The War Department intended that the voluntary unit "shall be made up of Norwegians, of Norwegian descent first or second generation—or Norwegians who have taken out first papers to become citizens." Stranded Norwegian seamen often belonged to the last category, and many Norwegian sailors enrolled. Volunteers came from small towns and farms in Minnesota, the Dakotas, and Wisconsin, as one would expect. All had to have a working knowledge of Norwegian.

The 99th Battalion, established as a "separate" unit with no fixed connection to a larger group, regularly attached to other military units in its campaigns. The "separate" battalions table of organization called for a thousand men. Second-generation Norwegian American Captain Gustav Svendsen, a resident of Minneapolis, was assigned as the battalion dentist; the 99th was the only battalion in the European Theater of Operations to have its own dental officer. Initially Dr. Svendsen was not included when the battalion was shipped overseas to Great Britain, his son G. Rolf Svendsen related; only through actions taken by Minnesota's two senators and a congressman could he honor the wishes of the men in the 99th and rejoin the unit, giving it a full strength of 1,001 men. Svendsen was active in the Norwegian American community and served as treasurer for the Minneapolis Camp Little Norway Committee to raise funds for its operations. In 1947, King Haakon VII awarded him the *Frihetskors* (Cross of Freedom) for his work with Camp Little Norway and he received the Bronze Star for his service in the 99th during combat operation.

Because of its status, the 99th Battalion received extraordinary attention, including review by President Roosevelt on Easter Sunday 1943. As reported in *The Viking*, published at Camp Hale, Colorado, the president's "desire to review the Norwegian Battalion is a great compliment to the officers and men of this organization." The 99th truly emerged as a successful unit within the US Army. At Fort Ripley and later Fort Snelling outside Minneapolis the enlisted men trained in physical conditioning, long road marches, enhanced soldier skills, and Norwegian language classes. *Nordisk Tidende*—consistently referring to the unit simply as "The Norwegian Battalion"—describes Fort Snelling as "The Soldier's Paradise." And Doug Bekke of the Minnesota Military Museum asserts, "The Twin Cities' large Scandinavian population made sure that the men were well cared for, and many social events were organized to entertain the men when off duty."

On December 17, 1942, the battalion was transferred to Camp Hale in the Colorado Rockies. Historian David Witte writes, "for the first- and second generation Norwegians . . . Camp Hale felt like their ancestral home in Norway. The snow, the cold and a chapel in which to celebrate Christmas made them feel right at home." The unit spent much of the winter training in the mountains on skis and snowshoes and developing winter survival skills. In the spring the men received extensive rock climbing preparation.

The 99th was initially organized for a possible invasion and liberation of Norway, but its mission was revised in the spring of 1943. The battalion instead saw action on the European continent: 101 days in combat, participating in five battle campaigns; 52 men killed in battle, 207 wounded, and six men missing. The 99th Battalion joined in the D-Day invasion to fight Nazi Germany. The battalion, as summarized by Captain Charles Askegaard, was transported to Normandy, France, from England, landing on Omaha Beach on June 21, 1944. At a great sacrifice in lives, the Allies began the hard march across Europe to defeat Hitler's troops.

Dr. Gustav Svendsen and Dr. Raymond Minge, 99th Infantry Battalion,
training at Camp Hale in Colorado the winter of 1942–43
Courtesy G. Rolf Svendsen

The battalion campaigned with other military units in this march
and saw heavy action in the European theater. It engaged in the battle
for France and in attacks to secure the French city of Elbeuf on the
Seine River to obstruct German retreat. This August battle was one
of the men's first, and there were battalion casualties. Some of the
heaviest fighting of the war came in October when the battalion took
part in attacking Wurzeln, Germany, to cut the German escape route
out of Aachen. "It was," writes Nyquist, "nine days of continuous
nightmare, and the small battalion came out of it with flying colors."

The 99th Infantry Battalion engaged in the Battle of the Bulge,
December 16, 1944–January 25, 1945—the last major German offensive campaign of the war. It was launched against the Allies through
the densely forested Ardennes and with the port city of Antwerp on
Belgium's River Scheldt as a target. The 99th, as a part of a larger task

force, was ordered into defensive positions south of Malmedy, Belgium. Near Malmedy the Germans massacred a large number of prisoners of war. The Battle of the Bulge is a chapter in the war that highlights the devastation and human tragedy of the worldwide conflagration—much more than can be expounded here. The German offensive failed, resulting in a total defeat, but with heavy losses of life on both the German and the Allied sides. The Battle of the Bulge was, in fact, the largest and bloodiest battle fought by the United States in the Second World War.

While Gustav Svendsen was the only dentist to serve the battalion, a number of physicians and other military medical personnel were assigned to the unit. Captain Raymond K. Minge served as a medical doctor. His son David Minge related that Raymond Minge was born in Fergus Falls, Minnesota, and grew up in a strong Norwegian Lutheran setting with a large extended family. He joined the 99th in late 1942 at Camp Hale; his military service and the friends he made, among these Gustav Svendsen, became an important part of his life. His wartime function was operating a field hospital/triage unit at or just behind the front line; during frontline action he treated the wounded and dying. Dr. Minge's letters, published in the *Fergus Falls Daily Journal*, made his wartime experiences—"the death of a fellow doctor shot by a sniper, the Battle of the Bulge, the Malmedy massacre, fighting at bridges, country side warfare"—known in his home community and beyond. He witnessed the liberation of the Nazi death camp Buchenwald, near Weimar, Germany, and on May 14, 1945, the *Fergus Falls Daily Journal* carried an article—written before German capitulation on May 8—about his visit to the camp. Minge describes the deplorable conditions, the death of fifty-one thousand prisoners, the horrible torture of inmates of all nationalities and ages by the Nazis, the slave labor, the starvation, and the unimaginably brutal living quarters. Dr. Minge correctly predicted that "It now looks like the war is getting into its final stages."

And indeed it was. The 99th Infantry Battalion (Separate) moved to Norway to assist in disarming and demobilizing Germany's troops.

The unit arrived on June 4, 1945, and found its new home at Smestad, at a camp which the Germans had occupied. When King Haakon VII returned to Norway on June 7, the battalion stood with Norwegian and British soldiers as an honor guard, arranged on three sides of the pavilion where the king addressed the Norwegian people.[16]

PEACE AGAIN

The great rejoicing and celebrations following Germany's surrender did not mark the end of hostilities. The United States could, however, concentrate its forces in the Pacific. On August 6, 1945, the United States dropped nuclear weapons on the Japanese city of Hiroshima and on August 9 on Nagasaki. The destruction and enormous loss of lives convinced Japan to surrender, officially ending the Pacific war

The 99th Infantry Battalion made it to Norway only after war's end, arriving in Oslo on June 4, 1945, and, later, parading up the main street, Karl Johan.
Courtesy Erik B. Wiborg

on August 14. "Thus," Bamford Parkes stated, "the greatest war in history ended in the overwhelming defeat of the powers responsible for it." Japan's surrender was covered in the free Norwegian press. I still recall rumors and speculations about the atomic bomb's destructive power, even the expressed belief that the bombs turned the earth into glass.

Given the devastating effect of using nuclear weapons and the significance of Japanese surrender, surprisingly little attention was paid by the Norwegian American press. News of German surrender, the liberation of Norway, and renewed contact with the homeland had earned bold, front-page headlines. On August 9, 1945, three days after Hiroshima was bombed, *Nordisk Tidende* made brief editorial comment, focusing mainly on the atomic bomb as "one of science's greatest accomplishments." On the front page, the same issue announced in large type Quisling's indictment for treason, among other violations. The newspaper presented on August 23 an article by editor Søyland titled "Japanese 'joyous gratification (*kistefornøyelse*)' and some philosophizing on the atomic bombs that fell down on the land of the sun god"—mainly a tale of Søyland's visit to Japan and its militaristic philosophy, with no mention of the suffering and fearful perspectives of the bombing. The Norwegian homeland and its prospects overwhelmingly required *Nordisk Tidende*'s attention.

Norwegians in exile were returning to the homeland in great numbers. The Norwegian America Line's *Stavangerfjord* served as a German troopship during the war, and in the fall of 1945 it made three crossings to New York and back to Oslo with approximately five to six hundred seamen on each trip. Norwegians in exile joined the extensive Norwegian American events celebrating Norway's liberation and also many farewell arrangements before departing for the homeland. Newspapers like *Nordisk Tidende* noted that "From all parts of America where Norwegian Americans live, reports are flowing in about divine thanksgiving services and May 17 festivals." In Chicago, five thousand people marched in the May 17 parade in 1945, with forty thousand lined up along the route. Norwegians in New

York assembled in Carnegie Hall to celebrate Norway's regained free-dom. After many years in exile, Norwegians heading home found that saying good-bye to places and friends exacted its own emotional price.

In addition to the exile community returning to Norway, there was, as *Nordisk Tidende* described it, a "repressed desire to travel." The refitted *Stavangerfjord*, now a passenger ship, departed from New York on its first return voyage on June 14, 1946, with 750 passengers, 375 registered as Norwegian Americans. Other passenger lines, British and Swedish, preceded the Norwegian firm. For example, the Swedish *Gripsholm* made its first return voyage from New York with 1,427 pas-sengers on June 1, 1946. And more modern transportation made an entrance, as Scandinavian Airlines System (SAS), founded on August 1, 1946, began regular transatlantic flights in September of that year. Søyland, aboard the inaugural flight, described the journey: leaving New York on September 20 and landing in Prestwick, then Copen-hagen, and finally Oslo. For the individual passenger, as Søyland saw it, the flight was "man's triumph over matter and gravity." Aviation made Norway seem closer both in sentiment and in distance mea-sured in time.[17]

CHAPTER 3

A New Life in America

FATHER ALF was not among those making a trip to Norway but would welcome his family when we arrived in Seattle. Many of us were disappointed by this news, especially Grandfather Martin, who longed to see his oldest son. Clothing and shoes and treats made their way to Bjørlykke, but, I remember with some embarrassment, shoes and clothes tended to be too large and fit poorly. My father could not be expected to determine the size of attire for children he had not seen for many years. Still, it was something to wear that the earlier wartime rationing had not provided. Wooden clogs, not infrequently home-made, had become common footwear, and clothes, when they could be bought at all, might be made of paper burlap; even fish skin was employed in the manufacture of shoes and apparel. Happier days awaited.

The postwar years were exciting times for all Norwegians as the Kingdom of Norway adjusted to life following its liberation on May 8, 1945. The Norwegian government in exile readied itself to resume its responsibilities back in the homeland. Crown Prince Olav was welcomed to Norway's capital less than a week after German capitulation; his arrival was celebrated with gun salute. A delegation of Norwegian officials accompanied him, while the remainder of the Norwegian government and London-based administration followed shortly. On June 7, King Haakon VII and the remaining royal family landed in Oslo. Power was transferred to King Haakon the same day by the commander in chief of Allied forces in Norway, the British Sir Andrew Thorne. The United States had maintained diplomatic relations with Norway during the war. Already in May 1945, the US embassy and ambassador Lithgow Osborne were transferred from London to Norway's capital.[1]

THE FIRST STEP

Astrid and we three children found ourselves in Oslo at the newly reopened US embassy during the first year of peace to apply for visas to immigrate to America. Previously limited to life in a remote rural setting, here we were in a large city with streetcars, tall buildings, the royal palace, and the Storting, Norway's parliamentary building. It was a memorable experience. We waited to see the embassy officials on an upper floor of the Odd Fellow's building. A friendly staff shepherded us through the application process; visas were granted. Astrid's sister Sigrid and my cousin Leiv, then residents of Oslo, were our guides. There were escalators in the largest department store, a truly new discovery. We took a tunnel train on our way to the Majorstuen district and Frogner Park, site of the Vigeland Sculpture Park. The rows of muscular nude statues made me and my siblings gasp. The occupiers had praised the statues as samples of the physical strength of the Germanic people.

We returned to Bjørlykke by train across the mountains from Oslo to Åndalsnes, then out the Romsdalsfjord on a steamer to Ålesund, from there on another coastal steamboat to the small shopping center Eidså, and then home some kilometers farther out on the fjord. We young Oslo-farers had much to tell the local people, most of whom had never traveled by train or visited the Norwegian capital. We had even seen a camel when visiting the stable of a circus—too fantastic for most people back home to believe. It had been our first venture into the larger world beyond Bjørlykke—much more awaited us.[2]

ACROSS THE DEEP BLUE SEA

The voyage to America would be on the Norwegian America Line's S/S *Stavangerfjord*. This passenger ship had her maiden voyage to

New York in 1918, and in December 1939 she made her last crossing from New York to Bergen and Oslo. After serving as a troop depot ship for the Germans during the occupation, in 1946 it was refitted to accommodate three classes of passengers. On May 31 she made her first post–World War II crossing to New York, arriving on June 11, as *Nordisk Tidende* described, "new-polished and shiny gliding slowly in to pier 8 East River last Tuesday at 7:00 a.m." The newspaper in its enthusiasm listed the names of all 744 passengers, including 250 seamen.

The four of us, mother Astrid, Magnar, Svanhild, and I, had acquired berths in tourist class on the second postwar crossing of this aging passenger vessel. We would depart from Bergen in July 1946. But first: much preparation and many sad good-byes, with tearful embraces from aunts and uncles and other kin. We even arranged to have the family dog, Buddy, put to death shortly after we left. Buddy sensed that his family was leaving. As the taxi drove to the dock in Eidså, neighbors waited by the roadside to bid us farewell and wish us a safe journey. It seemed strange to leave our home in Bjørlykke. I had the distinct feeling that I would never see the place of my birth ever again.

Grandpa Odin accompanied us to Bergen. In Ålesund, we all boarded *hurtigruten*—the speedy steamer trafficking the Norwegian coast. Bergen was a new experience. We stayed at Hotel Rosenkrantz just above Bryggen, the historic German wharf. We explored the city until the day arrived for us to board *Stavangerfjord*. Docked, the large passenger steamer was a dramatic and stirring sight to behold. It was difficult to bid farewell to our grandfather Odin, who remained alone on shore as the ship departed and moved out to sea.

More than a week passed before *Stavangerfjord* docked in New York on July 10. No comprehensive list of passengers was published for this, its second crossing after the war. Life on board took up a certain routine. In writing *Across the Deep Blue Sea*, I thought back on this 1946 voyage across the Atlantic and considered the six to eight weeks required by sailing ship at the mid-nineteenth century. Historian Nils Vigeland compares voyages as well in his *Norsk seilskipsfart erobrer verdenshavene* (Norwegian Sailing Ship Trade Captures the World's Oceans): "A journey on a large, modern emigrant steamship has nothing in common with a voyage across the Atlantic on the old sailing ships that took passengers over to Quebec or other cities on the eastern coast. The emigrants were packed together onboard these small vessels about like cattle, had to do without all conveniences and suffered so much hardship that today one may ask how they endured."

The four of us Løvolls had little reason to complain. We had our own cabin below deck. The restrooms were out in the hallway; there was a chance of embarrassment if one visited at night without being fully dressed. Meals were regular events. But there was also entertainment such as moving pictures and bands that played for evening dances. A store offered souvenirs and snacks. It all represented a great novelty for us. Whenever a ship passed, most passengers stood on deck, making *Stavangerfjord* tilt as they all crowded together on one side, many leaning against the railing. One night brought extra excitement when a fire broke out; luckily it was extinguished before much damage was done. It became a conversation piece.[3]

MEETING AMERICA

The ship approached New York and again everyone sought deck space—save those who suffered from seasickness. People pointed to the Statue of Liberty, and everyone gazed at the skyline formed by skyscrapers. At age eleven I had little historical knowledge of Lady Liberty, but, as she stood in full height in the harbor, it was truly a galvanizing vision. I recall someone explaining that the colossal sculpture, a gift from France, was a national monument recognizing America's freedom and democracy. It was difficult to digest it all. We had arrived in the great America I had heard so much about from my earliest childhood. *Stavangerfjord* did not land at Ellis Island for inspection, as some had expected, but at one of the regular docks in New York Bay. Alf had arranged for an agent from Travelers Aid, who came on board and located the Løvolls. Magnar had studied English at the *framhaldsskole*—continuation school—the school year 1945–46; still, he did not have the required skill to communicate with the agent. Somehow, she made it clear that we should accompany her.

I recall the taxi drive, and a near collision that made the agent cry out loudly. The taxi stopped at a large railroad station, I do not remember which, and we were directed to a waiting room. For the first time in our lives we observed people of color and Catholic nuns in their habits. We were placed on the train to Chicago, arriving the next day at Grand Central Station, again welcomed by Travelers Aid. We spent an entire day in the city since our rail connection to Seattle did not leave until that night. The Travelers Aid representatives showed much concern for us helpless immigrants; to their surprise, we children did not relish the ice cream they offered. The agents were able to find a Norwegian-speaking Chicagoan who better explained the situation to us. Years later, as I began the research that resulted in my study of Norwegian settlement in Chicago, *A Century of Urban Life*, I spent time at Grand Central, reflecting with strong feeling on this particular phase in my own life and on the destiny of the multitude of immigrants from many lands and cultures who had entered the New Land through the Chicago gateway.

That evening, we found ourselves on the train to Seattle, the beginning of several days' journey. It was a Pullman sleeping car, and we were shown where we could sit and how to make sleeping arrangements at night. There was also a dining car, but we visited it infrequently because of language barriers, making an effort only when hunger demanded some nourishment. The service attendants, or porters, all African Americans, were most gracious and helpful. Learning that the Løvolls came from Norway, some of the attendants took a skiing pose to greet us and pointed to items on the menu one might assume Norwegians would prefer—usually a fish dish.

The changing landscape became a constant source of wonderment—so different from the land we had left behind. I especially recall how desolate North Dakota seemed as the train passed great stretches of nearly empty landscapes, frequently with only small dwellings. I would later in life discover the state's stark beauty. Crossing the Rocky Mountains, we children needled our mother about the height as we looked out at the deep abyss as the train moved up and across the mountain range; she went along with the teasing, pretending to be afraid by looking away and even closing her eyes. The train descended from the mountains without any incident, and we began the final leg of our long and adventurous journey across the state of Washington.[4]

BEGINNING A NEW LIFE

As we stepped off the train in Seattle, a group of people waved to us. A tall man walked over and placed his arms around Astrid. I did not recognize my father after a seven-year-long separation, but I let him give me a hug, as he also gave Magnar. Svanhild, not even a toddler when Alf had left, ran and hid when he approached her. Alf's uncle Ole and aunt Lina welcomed us. Their home would be our first place of residence. The family was united again. But on our very first night, we experienced some rivalry for our mother's attention and affection, which we three children had enjoyed without contest for a very long time. Svanhild was disconsolate: "Where is mom?" At Bjørlykke, the four of us had slept in the same room. Toward morning, Astrid took Svanhild along to the room she shared with our father. All worked out well as we adjusted to a new family composition and new modes and circumstances.

Now the *Lowell* family, in late summer we moved into our American home on Eleventh Avenue Northwest, only a few blocks from Whittier School, where Svanhild and I began our American educational experience. Astrid tended to the home and family while Alf made a living fishing in Alaska; his absences at times seemed long for us back home in Ballard.

Norwegian settlement in Seattle, especially Ballard, a neighborhood in the northwestern part of the city, forms the backdrop of the Lowell family's adjustment to life in America. Ballard—founded as a separate city in 1889—was annexed by Seattle in 1907. It was a new beginning for the Lowells. Leaving the familiar for the unknown

The Lowell family at their first American home, on Eleventh Avenue
in Seattle's Ballard neighborhood: from left, Astrid, Odd, Magnar,
Alf, and Svanhild
Courtesy Svanhild Wergeland

might be seen as one of the most challenging decisions a person
can make. In *The Divided Heart*, Dorothy Burton Skårdal explains
how she decided to use literary works as historical documents, "in an
attempt to preserve the depth, vividness, and complexity of individual
human lives within the broad generalization of history." Historians
might not accept her premise, asking how to trace emotion and the
secret inner life of individual immigrants. The psychological reality
of the immigrant experience is difficult to capture. Skårdal cites historian Theodore Blegen, a pioneer in social history who, in his study
of the Norwegian immigrant and social forces, views immigrant
adjustment as a dynamic process that engages the creative interplay
of European heritage and the American environment. Blegen admitted to having used some unusual sources in his inquiry, "including

the findings of linguists who have probed immigrant speech and the writings of novelists who have probed immigrant souls." In my own scholarly endeavors, understanding how immigrants accepted and adjusted to new social and cultural demands and circumstances—or failed to do so—became a major professional interest, the emotional aspect ever on my mind. My own life experience became a guide—though an insufficient one.[5]

BEGINNING SCHOOL

In a history of ethnic life in America, Maxine Seller makes the point that while adult immigrants could mingle primarily with people within their own ethnic community, children were often forced into a school situation where they felt noticeably different from their classmates. Immigrant children confronted the new society more directly than their parents. Seller concludes, "Eager to be accepted by their teachers and their peers, young people found minority status a devastating experience."

On October 22, 1946, the *Seattle Times* ran a headline above a photograph of new students from Norway: "HAN KAN IKKE SNAKKE . . . BALLARD SCHOOL HAS LANGUAGE TROUBLES." The reference "Kan ikke snakke"—cannot speak—was to Principal E. M. Towner at Whittier Grade School. It was peacetime—as evidenced by the immigrants' arrival—and this story became front-page news. Part of the newspaper account, written by journalist Dave James, is worth citing, including the botched Norwegian:

Out Ballard way it is common knowledge that fire skolebarn som gaar paa Whittier Skole de har vanskelig for og forstaa vad bestyreren Towner mener. Han kan ikke snakke Norsk.

[An editor's note translates: Four pupils at the Whittier School have a difficult time understanding what Principal Towner says. He can't speak Norwegian.]

He has been resorting to Indian sign language and making faces ever since school's opening brought to class Turid Sund, 7 years old;

Svanhild Lowell, 9; Odd (say Ode) Lowell, 12, and Torunn Ekenes, 7, all little Americans-to-be fresh over from Norway.

"They couldn't speak a word of English and I not a word of Norwegian," Towner said today. . . . "I didn't know what to do. But Mrs. [Florence] Miller, the first-grade teacher, and Mr. [Olaf] Holen, the custodian, saved the day. They could talk like natives."

On this 22nd day of October, the four transplants are stepping cautiously, a word at a time, into the great foreign language used by Americans.

From the front page of *Seattle Times*, October 22, 1946: "Four Little Norwegians Are Having a Time at Whittier School." Front, left to right: Svanhild Lowell, Torunn Ekenes, and Turid Sund; back, Odd Lowell and Mrs. Florence Miller, first grade teacher.
Courtesy Svanhild Wergeland

Entering school was a major step for the newcomers, and the newspaper article explained how they were faring: "Svanhild Lowell is in Miss Fern Litterneau's third grade room and learning rapidly. Odd Lowell, Svanhild's brother, is working like a beaver in the fifth grade. Miss Margaret Houston says children in her room have accepted Odd as their best friend."

Our brother, Magnar Lowell, was enrolled in the local middle school, James Monroe Junior High School, and not included in the *Seattle Times* report. He did well, and in the evenings shared his learning with us, his younger siblings.

Teachers had little experience in how to treat and teach immigrant children with no knowledge of English. These skills would come later when postwar immigration increased. I am most grateful to Miss Houston for the care and interest she showed for my education and acceptance by other students. Later, she wrote an article about me and what she had learned from being my teacher.

Ballard, where Whittier School was located, had a large Scandinavian population. Norwegian-speaking neighborhoods abounded, and Mr. Towner did not have to look far for whatever assistance he desired. Yet, I discovered that Norwegians in general avoided speaking Norwegian in public. For example, our father would not speak to his family in Norwegian on the city bus because people would turn and look. But as immigration expanded, Norwegian newcomers conversed in their homeland's lingo everywhere. Even earlier, Norwegian-speaking individuals were readily available in the Ballard neighborhood: "If translation is needed [when talking to the Norwegian students], Miss Litterneau can call Mrs. Miller, or Olaf Holen, the custodian, or Mrs. Adele Styve (say Stevie), the clerk, or Edwin Knutzen, the orchestra director, or Miss Rena Myhre, the school nurse. Anybody but Mr. Towner. He throws his hands in the air and gives up. In good humor, of course."

The fathers of the children featured in the article had all arrived during the war. Two, Tore Sund and Thoralf Ekenes, made it to America after their Norwegian ships were torpedoed. Alf Lowell had been more fortunate and arrived safely in Halifax on a vessel that crossed the Atlantic without incident. Each family was reunited in Seattle, a not uncommon occurrence in the first postwar years.[6]

ACQUIRING A SECOND LANGUAGE

Many old-timers became friends. They spoke a strange hybrid Norwegian that newcomers struggled to comprehend. A Norwegian *seng* was always *bedd* (bed), and the single *bil* became the plural *cars*, for instance, *carsen min* (my car); *fortau* was always sidewalk—all pronounced with a Norwegian accent. A regular greeting to guests by an immigrant speaking the Norwegian Sunnmøre dialect might be *Du får leggje kotå di på bedden*—put your coat on the bed. Linguist Einar Haugen describes the major problem in bilingualism: keeping the two languages distinct so that a bilingual in effect becomes two monolinguals. Haugen looks at the bilingual world in which the Norwegian immigrants lived and gives a historical sketch with emphasis on linguistic behavior. Examples like the ones cited above were people "behaving as social beings must," and American Norwegian, as he defined it, thus became the speech of most of the Norwegian immigrants "and their uncounted descendants."

The Lowells visited the solidly Norwegian settlement on the Stillaguamish flats near Stanwood to see a widowed relative, Oluffa Hansen Brandal, born Krabbesti in 1879; her husband, Knut Hansen Brandal (1872–1921), is listed in church records as *plassmann* (cotter). Knut had emigrated in 1891. He returned to Norway to marry Oluffa in August 1913; the following month they both moved back to Knut's residence in Stanwood, traveling over Ålesund. Hansen became their American last name. They had left from Sørbrandal, where stood the one-room country school my brother and sister and I had attended. Oluffa's brother, Martin Bjørlykke, had emigrated to Juneau, Alaska, and changed his surname to Borlick. Considering the name of my birthplace, that might also have become my last name.

Oluffa never learned English, thus was never bilingual, but she nevertheless spoke the American Norwegian to which Haugen refers.

She and her American-born children, a daughter and two sons, spoke what I experienced as an old-fashioned version of the dialect I myself spoke. Their speech was interspersed with adopted English words, declined in a Norwegian fashion, such as *barnå* for "the barn" and *chickena* for "the chickens." Oluffa's two grandchildren did not know Norwegian, and to her great sadness she could not converse with them. Oluffa died in 1955. In the world of immigrants, the linguistic isolation she experienced might not have been all that uncommon.

Learning English as a second language represents a great challenge for all immigrants. Organizations offered classes; Astrid in time attended one along with immigrants from different parts of the world. For Magnar, Svanhild, and me—Magnar having had some earlier instruction—learning English proceeded in interaction with other students and the help of patient classroom teachers. Berit K. Sjong, an immigrant from Ålesund at age eleven in 1947, tells of entering the Seattle public school system: "When I immigrated it was a whole lot different in Seattle Public Schools than what it is today [2012]. Now they have special classes and special things for kids who don't speak the English language. But they didn't have anything special when I came here. They had one of the kids go out to the hall with me and look at these little books and say 'door' with a picture of a door and so on with cat and dog."

Alf's uncles and their families had experienced the pervasive nativism of the First World War and public efforts to do away with everything that seemed foreign to English-speaking Americans. A foreign accent represented a handicap in social and occupational relations. They all consequently made English the language of the home and did not try to teach their children Norwegian. Bertha, Ole and Lina's second daughter, did, however, recall her mother scolding her in Norwegian: "*Stygg jente, tisse i buksa*" (Bad girl, pee in your pants). She enjoyed repeating the extent of her knowledge of Norwegian.

Ole and Lina were killed in a car accident in July 1947; Ole drove through a stop sign and crashed into the side of a bus, throwing them both out of the car. Another loss had occurred a few months earlier:

Alf's uncle Elias in Everett passed away in his sleep, leaving his wife, Anna, born in Hundeidvik, Sunnmøre, a widow.

We newcomers had a new set of relatives to embrace. I always thought highly of Omar, Elias and Anna Lowell's second son, born in 1918. When doing research for *The Promise of America* in 1981, I visited Anna along with Omar in a private nursing home in Everett in October. She passed away January 8, 1982, in her mid-nineties. By the time of our visit, Anna had lost the ability to understand and speak her second language—English. Omar could no longer communicate with his mother. She was delighted to be able to speak to someone who easily comprehended her quaint Norwegian dialect, happily addressing me by my father's name. Anna's plight—the loss of a second language—is sadly not all that unusual as aging and developing dementia take their toll. I was nevertheless saddened to see the schism it had created between mother and son.

In my research on language learning and language attrition and loss, I contacted two scholars, Vittorina Cecchetto and Magda Stroinska, at McMaster University in Hamilton, a port city in Ontario, Canada, who generously offered their expertise and assistance. I found greatly enlightening their discussion of how the language we grow up with is a significant factor in identity formation, closely intertwined with all aspects of our identity, and how finding oneself outside one's native land, or even within a territory where the same language is spoken but with a different accent, makes one feel displaced. In a country like Norway, with its greatly differing dialects, this experience proves true. For the person in exile, the dilemma is whether to adopt a new identity or adapt to the new environment while "trying to hold on to one's old self."

Additional factors shape our identity—age, gender, education, profession, class, and religion; loss of language does not eliminate these factors. Nevertheless, in the context of exile, language brings people together from the same linguistic background and determines group identity. This study also deals with the Lowell family's situation, where immigrants decide to speak to their children only in the language of the new country, even though they, the parents, do not speak it well. The parents hope to facilitate the children's assimilation and acceptance in the new society. But, the authors claim, immigrant parents who do not teach the second generation their native tongue deprive their children of the nuances of meaning that parents and grandparents are not able to express in the new language, and also deprive them of the accumulated wisdom and life experience that would normally be passed on from one generation to the other. Cecchetto and Stroinska see the loss or attrition of a second language as being naturally related to memory loss and to other health problems, such as strokes or certain health issues; in their study they also consider the possibility of protecting the elderly from losing their facility to communicate in the second language. The two linguists conclude "that it is definitely easier to address the problem of teaching immigrant children the language of their parents when they are small than to address the lack of communication within the family later."[7]

THE POSTWAR IMMIGRATION

In summer 1946, as great numbers of Norwegians in exile headed home to a liberated Norway, my mother, siblings, and I were among the nearly thousand Norwegians who arrived in the United States as immigration resumed during the first full year of peace. Norway made a smooth transition to peacetime conditions; because of military occupation, there had been no massive uprooting of people. No paralyzing refugee problem or dire need due to material destruction produced the overseas exodus. Viewed in a longer historical perspective, that exodus may be understood as an extension of an older tradition of immigration.

The postwar overseas movement was never very large. It gained some momentum during the first years but peaked in 1952 with an annual emigration of 2,968 Norwegian citizens. Norwegian emigration showed a regular decline from decade to decade: in the 1950s, 22,935 Norwegians were admitted to the United States on immigrant visas, and in the 1960s, only 15,484. The Immigration and Nationality

Act of 1965, effective July 1, 1968, reduced visas for Western Europe, which meant a great drop for Norway: in 1969, only 434 were issued, down from 1,574 the previous year. Thereafter, to the present time, annual immigration to the United States from Norway declined, with the greatest reduction occurring after 1992. The postwar immigration, 1946–2010, of people holding Norwegian citizenship totaled fewer than 60,000. By the end of the last century it became clear that a long and extensive Norwegian tradition of going to America largely belonged to the past.

Norway's economy rebounded faster than predicted following the great downturn it suffered during the German occupation. The Marshall Plan helped spark economic recovery. The decision to emigrate was made against a backdrop of differing and shifting social and economic circumstances. Such macro causalities must be kept in mind, but, as I emphasize in my analysis of the overseas movement—in *The Promise of America*, published in 1984, and also in *Across the Deep Blue Sea*, published in 2015—the resolve to emigrate was for the individual a matter of personal choice. The individual motives and personal situation that influenced people to seek a better life beyond the homeland must be taken into account. One person might be the decisive voice for an entire family, as was the case for the Lowells. In *The Promise of America*, I emphasize that, regardless, individuals responded with forethought to the forces and circumstances that encouraged emigration: "In a survey of the emigration the human factor may easily disappear in numbers, tables, and graphs; statistics only indicate the dimensions of the movement. It is therefore important to bear firmly in mind that the resolve represented for the individual a personal decision."

Despite economic progress, Norwegians for some time had to deal with a scarcity of commodities and, in the main urban areas, a persistent housing shortage that lasted into the 1970s. As I researched the postwar emigration, a random survey of postwar immigrants from coast to coast conducted in the 1980s revealed that a large number of the respondents listed ready access to affordable housing as a major advantage of living in America. They also stressed as important considerations greater freedom in the broadest sense, an ethos of equal opportunity and rewards commensurate with effort, and an antipathy toward the highly regulated social-democratic welfare state being built in Norway. And for many, personal ties often yielded an incentive to take advantage of the greater prosperity overseas.

Economic growth persisted in Norway, and was especially noticeable from the mid-1960s. Discovery of North Sea oil and gas in the 1970s guaranteed substantial future prosperity. By the early 1990s, Norway's annual per capita gross national product surpassed that of the United States. Norway rose to the status of one of the world's most prosperous nations. This higher standard of living influenced individual decisions about emigration, and indeed, the fact that no large-scale emigration occurred suggests a general acceptance of and faith in the postwar economic and social system that evolved. It might also reflect, as I discovered on my sojourns in Norway and especially in generations growing up in a more affluent Norway, a changing and less favorable view of American society and ideals.[8]

A POSTWAR NORWEGIAN AMERICAN COMMUNITY

Immigrants arriving in the United States after World War II generally looked to traditional regions of Norwegian settlement, though they were influenced by the economic situation when deciding on a location. The more recently selected areas in the Pacific Northwest and New York State received large numbers of new immigrants at the expense of the prime regions of early Norwegian settlement in the Upper Midwest.

In the postwar years, a welcoming and engaged Norwegian American population eagerly awaited the arrival of newcomers from an ancestral land whose wartime distress had aroused their emotions and generosity. Coming from Norway during the first full year of peace, we experienced the interest and welcome, perhaps even curiosity, that met Norwegian newcomers. The Norwegian American community consisted of people whose roots back home might be decades old. In 1950, the US federal census listed 202,294 residents of

Norwegian birth, a number that sank to 97,243 twenty years later, evidence of an aging immigration generation. By the year 2000, the federal census listed only 43,876 persons born in Norway. In 1970 there were 517,406 Americans of Norwegian or mixed parentage. As many as 12 percent, nearly 12,000, of the 97,243 Norwegian-born US residents and 9.4 percent, close to 50,000, of the second generation lived in the state of Washington. First- and second-generation Norwegians concentrated in Seattle, Everett, and surrounding neighborhoods, and to a lesser degree in Tacoma. In small communities in the bays and secluded inlets of Puget Sound, such as Poulsbo and Stanwood, a Norwegian presence was clearly dominant.

The Norwegian American community in Ballard was not an isolated ethnic enclave but a central destination for Norwegian Americans in the region. Because Ballard was my first home in America, I have special reason to devote extra time in recording its history. Recollections and impressions from my years there are vivid. Ballard's centennial history, beginning in 1888, provides some light-hearted insights alongside a historical narrative of its founding and growth. There was an influx of Scandinavians—in 1910 accounting for 62 percent of the foreign-born population, Norwegians being by far the largest Nordic contingency. "For years," the story goes, "jokes circulated in the region about the mixed Norwegian speech 'Ballard-Norsk'"—which could still be heard when we arrived. Churches, social and fraternal organizations, and singing clubs reflected a Norwegian dominance.

In 1940, Norwegians were the largest ethnic group in Seattle; the Ballard section in the northwest had the largest concentration. Because of the early arrival of Norwegians, and other Scandinavians, in the city's formative years, they influenced its character beyond their numerical strength. I recall that nearly all of the family's friends and acquaintances were either from Sunnmøre or Nord Norge—North Norway. Later, in a scholarly study, I write, "The scenery of Alaska and the west coast of the mainland United States is strongly reminiscent of the coastal districts of Norway. Many Norwegians were attracted to these parts of the continent; the landscape, as well as familiar modes of livelihood in lumbering and fishing, added to the region's appeal." I concluded that the immigrants transferred a Norwegian coastal culture to the Pacific Coast.[9]

Alf supported our family through extended absences off the coast of Alaska. I sensed that as welcome as he made us feel, there nevertheless was a transition in accepting the financial burden our presence represented. His uncle Ole and aunt Lina, with whom he had spent the war years, were excessively frugal, Lina suggesting to Astrid that she should add water to the milk. Mother protested that she had not even done that during the war. Lina Aure Ness Lowell came from the community of Langevåg, located across the fjord from Ålesund. In her childhood and youth the Norwegian dialect referred to as *halvemål* was still spoken; it left out "h" as the initial sound in front of vowels and added "h" where it did not belong. It was difficult to understand her Norwegian speech, which in addition to its peculiar localism was spiced with American words and terms.

Alf's return from the fishing banks were joyous occasions; we, his family, welcomed him as the fishing vessel docked. There was much news to share from both sides. The Lowell family shortly moved to a larger house on Earl Avenue. A couple of blocks north lived Amanda and Casper Nesset and family, all close friends, and immigrants from the 1920s; like my father, Casper made a living in commercial fishing. Their son Kenneth became a lifelong friend. I asked him to share some of his impressions about our early meetings. How indeed does one adjust to new and strange circumstances? "My first meeting with Odd and his sister," Kenneth writes, "was a bit awkward. I think they were having some culture shock and didn't know how to react to all the changes they suddenly were experiencing." But, he explains, "When Odd learned that I could speak some rudimentary Norwegian, we seemed to hit it off and Odd's shyness started to disappear."

Kenneth recalls a number of incidents, including the time the two of us nearly ended our lives riding together on his bicycle down the long and steep road after leaving Woodland Park Zoo. When the

brakes suddenly stopped working, a dramatic crash involved construction debris—wood planks, rocks, concrete. "We flew across the
busy road flying above the traffic below us," Kenneth recalls, "and to
my great surprise landed right side up." Kenneth believes that divine
intervention saved our lives, as "the good Lord had other plans for
us." Kenneth has had a successful career in banking, retiring as vice
president of Washington Mutual Savings Bank in Seattle. He also
recalls a story that suggests my personal growth as I adjusted to the
demands of life in America: "As time went by both families stayed in
touch and it became clear that Odd's personality started to evolve.
It was clear that Odd was a good student. I remember Odd asked me
to go to a beach close by called Golden Gardens. I thought that Odd
just wanted to go there for some fun. However, it turned out that he
was on a mission to gather some examples of marine life for a report

A Lowell and Nesset family outing. In front, Odd at right next to Kenneth
Nesset; Svanhild holds a cup. In back, at right, a Nesset relative, Paul Alme;
Magnar second from right; Astrid behind Svanhild; Alf stands farther back.
Courtesy Kenneth Nesset

he was doing at school. It wasn't hard to see that Odd was headed for an academic career."

The active Norwegian American community was revived and reinforced by the postwar arrivals. Norwegian services at Denny Park Lutheran Church, just north of downtown Seattle, served by Pastor B. T. Gabrielsen, himself an immigrant from Rogaland, attracted many newcomers and visiting sailors. I recall people talking of the church as a marriage bureau; ensuing weddings seemed to support the claim. It was all a part of an active ethnic environment that included picnic gatherings at places like Green Lake and Woodland Park, close to the Seattle zoo. While the women cleared up after the picnic, the men regularly escaped into the back seats of the cars to enjoy their beer. It was bad form to drink in front of women and children, but no one really seemed to notice.

In my studies of the postwar period, I identify a celebratory ethnicity. Defining ethnic identity through public festivals has a long history in Norwegian urban settlements. *Syttende mai* (May 17) festivals, celebrating Norway's Constitution Day (*grunnlovsdag*), became the foremost public display of Norwegian ethnicity—an integral part of Norwegian folk life. The ethnic revival of the 1960s and 1970s brought back celebrations in many communities where they had been discontinued, but even in Seattle there was a renewed festive vigor. As grand marshal in 1999, I, with wife Else, headed a large and enthusiastic May 17 procession through the streets of Ballard; I gave an oration to an interested audience. In 2008, Elliott Barkan described the scene in Ballard: "Norwegian Americans of all ages have been regular participants in the *Syttende mai* parade—along with many women in traditional national costumes or *bunader*, come rain or shine." These celebratory events present a constructed festival identity, an American celebration, that reflects life in a multicultural country, distant from Norway's grand nationalistic commemorations.

By 1952, we had returned to Norway and thus were initially deprived of the ethnic revival of the 1960s, which was much in evidence when I arrived back in the United States with my young family in 1967. Even during my earlier sojourn in Ballard there were popular outdoor events arranged by local Sons of Norway lodges or other Norwegian organizations, including the annual *Syttende mai* festivities at Norway Center toward downtown Seattle; there were speakers like Senator Henry "Scoop" Jackson, a liberal politician who invariably reminded his audience of his proud Norwegian heritage, thereby securing their vote; and I also recall outspoken Kristine Haugen, active in Norwegian American cultural and organizational affairs. These speakers likely did not engender much interest in younger attendees; later in life when I became acquainted with the world-renowned linguist Einar Haugen, I was impressed to learn that Kristine Haugen, the person I had met as a teenager in Seattle, was his mother. And ever present was *Washington-Posten*'s publisher and editor O. L. Ejde, a major figure in the Norwegian community; like other newspaper offices, his became an important center for the local community and beyond. Ejde notes nostalgically that "in and out of this office since 1917 have wandered most of the thousands of Norwegians who live in Seattle, in other towns and cities in Washington, and in neighboring states." The newspaper became a fixed orientation point in the lives of Norwegians on the coast.

The school years passed and, having mastered English, Magnar, Svanhild, and I excelled in the classroom. I was at times teased for being the "studious guy" and for not doing well in sports and athletics. There was always the *odd* name to call attention to. I have frequently analyzed my shyness and sense of insecurity at that stage in my life. Being a newcomer in a foreign society, the move from an isolated farmstead to a bustling city—all contributed to my sense of loneliness and inability to fully adapt. At age eighteen, Magnar graduated from Ballard High School as an honor student; Svanhild and I moved along to junior and senior high school. Then, a devastating accident struck the Lowell family and totally altered our prospects and hopes.[10]

LOSING MAGNAR

Magnar was truly a conscientious big brother and a role model. He had the enviable qualities of being gifted both intellectually and in practical affairs. A growing private library required space in the bedroom we shared. And, we discovered after his passing, he had taken out a life insurance policy with his parents as the beneficiaries. He worked part-time as a grocery clerk all through high school so that he would be financially independent. In 1950, he had saved a sufficient sum of money to make a trip back to Norway. On his return, Magnar was full of praise for the country the family had left behind and the loving grandfather, aunts, uncles, and cousins who had welcomed him. Magnar even pondered the possibility of returning to the homeland.

Plans for a college career were at the top of his agenda. To finance his education, Magnar decided to work for a while as a tuna fisherman on the fishing vessel *Attu*; Alf was part owner and proud to have achieved that rank. Magnar and I assisted in preparing the boat to head for the fishing grounds.

The Lowell family in their second home, on Earl Avenue in Ballard. Svanhild is seated in front of Magnar, Alf, and Astrid. Odd took this final picture of Magnar.

Magnar talked excitedly about his experience catching tuna off the California coast. I will never forget the last night I shared the bedroom with my brother. Magnar wanted to talk about the trip that lay ahead, but I, perhaps a bit envious and also likely tired, to my everlasting regret deprived him of an audience and fell asleep. Early the next morning, Magnar, Alf, and Alf's brother, Uncle Bendik, boarded the *Attu* at Fishermen's Dock in Ballard—as it turned out, a final farewell for Magnar and Bendik.

On October 9, 1950, Svanhild and I were taken out of our respective classrooms and transported home by a family friend. As we entered our house, Astrid, her voice breaking, informed us of the unbelievable tragedy that our brother had been washed overboard and drowned. The Lutheran minister was there, a couple of family friends, and press people. Pictures were taken, and Alf had also been contacted. The next day, "the United Press told the tragic story of the loss of . . . Magnar Lowell, 19, and his uncle, Ben Lowell, 47."

High seas were running off the California coast, and many small vessels were in trouble. . . . The 75-foot *Attu* was turning to head for a spot where birds were hovering over the water. Magnar and his uncle Ben had gone aft to prepare the gear. A heavy sea struck. It filled the cockpit and washed them overboard.

Ben disappeared. But Alf Lowell saw his son struggling in the water. He yelled to him to grab a trolling line. Magnar did, and his father managed to haul him to the stern of *Attu*. But because of the weight of the youth's watersoaked clothing, and the rough seas, he could not lift him aboard. The father quickly rigged a line with knotted handgrips, and yelled to his son to grab it. The youth tried, but his strength had ebbed. He went down.

Bendik left behind his wife, Liv Sandvik Lowell, and daughter Astrid, age two. She was known as "Little Astrid" to distinguish her from her aunt. Alf lost his brother and oldest son on his forty-ninth birthday. For years the day could not be observed. He arrived home by air from Eureka, California. And the press reported, "In her neat modern home at 7044 Earl Ave. N.W. Alf Lowell's wife Astrid, waited with their other son, Odd, 16, and daughter, Svanhild, 13, for his arrival back home." Magnar's drowning at age nineteen was a boundless loss that had lasting and profound consequences for the Lowell family. To this very day I continue to grieve the death of a brother I admired above anyone else. My dedication for *The Promise Fulfilled*, published in 2007, reads: "I have cherished the memory of my promising, intelligent, and determined big brother and sorely missed him throughout my life."[11]

CROSSROADS

Ballard First Lutheran Church on Sixty-Fifth Street was considered the fishermen's church, celebrated annually in a fishermen's festival. This status, and Alf's many congregant friends, likely explains why the Lowell family, though not members, attended services there. O. J. Haavik,

"Little Astrid," daughter of Liv Sandvik Lowell and Bendik Lowell, seated on the steps on Earl Avenue. At the age of two she lost her father at sea.

who spoke with a heavy Norwegian Nordfjord accent, had served as pastor since 1921, and the church was consequently called "Haavik Church." From time to time, services in Norwegian were held alongside the regular English-language ones. In 1948, Haavik was succeeded by Pastor A. F. Anderson.

When Svanhild and I began the two-year confirmation preparations, Pastor Anderson was in charge. Magnar had been confirmed in Norway. I have always been conscientious in my studies, and I likewise prepared diligently for the weekly sessions. On confirmation Sunday in the spring of 1950, after I had answered difficult questions correctly, Pastor Anderson turned to the congregation and smiled: "See what we can do!" Mother had made a special confirmation dinner.

It was a happy day and time. In my spiritual convictions, I did not question the teachings of the Lutheran faith, although later I would. Astrid was a loving and caring mother, and I felt close to her. Her concern included our Christian upbringing, and both Svanhild and I occasionally accepted her invitation to join in worship at the Scandinavian American Pentecostal church Philadelphia in Ballard. In 1951 we all attended more than once when Billy Graham filled a large stadium during his evangelistic crusade. Graham stressed a belief in the resurrection of both the saved and the lost, the former to eternal life and the latter to damnation and eternal punishment. Being brought back to life simply to be banished to everlasting torture was a terrifying vision, one that for me was totally impossible to believe or to comprehend. Could Graham himself truly envision it? Would he ever fathom his own condescension on one hand and self-righteousness on the other? Those who sought salvation were asked to stand and accept Christ as their savior. As a baptized and recently confirmed Lutheran Christian, I felt bewildered by Graham's exclusive message and by the great number of people who rose to accept his call.

My discomfort with the religious path I was being pulled onto would only escalate. I had great empathy with the grief and self-reproach my father Alf endured after his oldest son drowned; like Norwegian men of his generation, he struggled with showing true emotions. There might even have been some tension between Alf and Astrid; after all, she had safely cared for Magnar and the other children during his seven-year absence. At first, Alf was not capable of returning to fishing. The Philadelphia congregation was at that time erecting a new place of worship. Alf volunteered and gained social contact and spiritual nourishment while working on the construction. Alf was a religious person, though more in the Lutheran mainstream than Astrid. While my father was a person of fortitude, his new association saved his sense of well-being and gave him strength to eventually resume his career on the stormy ocean. It also appeared to strengthen the relationship between husband and wife.

In 1951, Astrid and Alf converted to the Pentecostal faith and withdrew Svanhild from her confirmation preparation; they all became members of Philadelphia. The self-conscious and timid young person I was can never quite bury the chafing memories of the day I witnessed my parents and sister being baptized by immersion. I was surrounded by people praying for me to join my family; the pastor even stepped forward to wave me toward him. It was a fearful moment in my life. Looking back, I was proud that I had been able to withstand the pressure to convert. At home that evening, I was surrounded by a family praising God and making me feel—however unintentionally—condemned to eternal damnation. I finally left the dinner table to cry alone in my room.

Another event likely had as much to do with my abandoning all religious association for some years. An evangelist who claimed he could determine whether someone was destined for heaven or hell simply by looking at that person was visiting Seattle, and I agreed to accompany my mother and sister. After a provocative, rousing sermon on afterlife, focusing on eternal bliss contra an eternity of torment in hell, during which people cried in anguish, everyone lined up in front of the evangelist. When Svanhild and Astrid approached, he welcomed them to eternal glory. I was next, and he must have noticed my reluctance and discomfort. The visionary raised his hands and loudly shouted: "I see hell fire, I see hell fire!" The other people in line gasped. I was pushed to my knees so that hands could be laid on my head in prayer. But I had already been condemned to an eternity in hell. As an adult, I cannot understand how any rational human being would ever subject a vulnerable teenager to such a degrading ordeal. A year or two later, at age eighteen, after other painful inducements to convert, I, more in protest than as a considered or even fully grasped conviction, declared myself an atheist.

In my twenties I modified my stance and found a comforting tenet and relationship to the beliefs I had left behind. My atheistic declaration may be seen, at least in part, as a youthful rebellion, but it also signified a turning point in my life. I remained a member of the Lutheran church, but, while appreciating its age-old musical and ceremonial traditions and charitable ideals, I placed a distance between myself and especially its judgmental and exclusive Bible-based teachings. After lengthy agonizing and contemplation, I came to define myself in a broad sense as a believer in humanistic ethics and values, which I feel incorporate the positive Christian teachings of my childhood. This conviction honored my lifelong sense of empathy for my fellow mortals and boosted my acceptance and respect for all faiths— Christian and non-Christian. I find great comfort in the thought that human beings do not need the promise of heaven or the threat of hell to observe the Golden Rule in Matthew 7:12: "So whatsoever you wish that others would do to you, do also to them." My conviction holds that a benevolent humanity possesses, as the American Humanist Association states, the inherent "capacity and responsibility to lead ethical lives of personal fulfillment that aspire to the greater good of humanity," and to do good and to show empathy and solicitude for the welfare of fellow wanderers on earth.[12]

CHAPTER 4

Back in the Homeland

A New Adjustment

A S   A   S C H O L A R of migration and a student of the human pilgrimage through life, I have drawn on and been energized by my
own story. The personal and family experience, the years spent on both
sides of the Atlantic, and the opportunity to observe the cultural and
social processes of adaptation provided a most valuable insight and
exceptional resources to draw on as I developed my larger views
on immigration in lectures, articles, and monographs. Our return to
Norway, even though we intended to stay for only one year, presented
another mountain to climb. Norway had become a foreign country; I
had become "the American." The decision to visit the old homeland
grew out of our struggle to accept Magnar's death and a sense that
association with family in Norway might be a healing experience. Alf
was returning to fishing after efforts to make a living on shore; one of
his ventures had been ownership of Shoreline Motel. In the summer
of 1952, Astrid, Svanhild, and I traveled to New York by Greyhound
bus; from there the journey back to Norway was on the Norwegian
America Line's grand newly built ocean liner MS *Oslofjord*, with room
for more than six hundred passengers.[1]

REPATRIATION

The liner docked in Bergen and from there we, the Lowells, took
the coastal steamer to Sunnmøre. I felt that I had come to a foreign

land—the landscape and even the people I met seemed like new and different encounters. It all presaged a time of acceptance of and adjustment to circumstances that from the outset appeared confusing and even curiously unfamiliar. Later in my scholarly career, I explored the lot of repatriated Norwegian Americans as well as their impact on the social and political life of Norway itself. Much is left to discover.

It is easy to point to national figures, as I do in *A Century of Urban Life*. Martin Tranmæl was present in Chicago in 1905 when socialists and agitators formed the militant Industrial Workers of the World; when he returned to Norway, he brought its activism and syndicalistic philosophy, which gave vitality to the Norwegian labor agitation as well. Konrad Knudsen, introduced in *Norwegian Newspapers in America*, is another example of a repatriated Norwegian who gained strong political influence in the homeland. Knudsen, an immigrant from Drammen, as editor of the Norwegian-language *Social-Demokraten* in Chicago in 1920 joined forces with the Communist faction in Chicago's Scandinavian Socialist Federation; this faction favored joining the Third Communist International. Knudsen shortly thereafter returned to Norway, where he held various positions within the Norwegian Labor Party; with Tranmæl, he influenced the party's radical move left and its adoption of the Moscow Theses in the early 1920s— the only social-democratic party in western Europe to do so. Knudsen represented the Labor Party in the Storting from 1937 until 1957.

Less obvious are the many men and women who resettled in rural areas, bringing with them practices from American agriculture. L. DeAne Lagerquist's fine study *In America the Men Milk the Cows* explores how Norwegian American women, who identified strongly with the Norwegian Lutheran church in the Upper Midwest, between 1850 and the years after 1900 made the move from traditional Norway to modern America. The intriguing title suggests a new social norm also for the men, and is valid to a much later date. In Norway, milking cows was a woman's job, but some of the men returning to a family farm in the homeland engaged in milking and assumed other barn chores. They might have been ridiculed by the men who had stayed home. My father told me about one repatriated farmer in Sunnmøre who was teased for doing women's work when he took on such tasks.

Official measures indicate that between 1891 and 1940 as many as a quarter of the emigrants to America after 1881 resettled in Norway. These statistics seem high and are unreliable. In any case, return migration was a function of labor migration; people sought employment as foreign guest workers, intending to return when they had saved enough money. Many changed their minds and settled in America. Alf's experience is a telling example of the repatriated worker— and he was only one among the many thousand homeward-bound immigrants. They influenced all aspects of Norwegian life: politics, culture, the economy, social mores, world view, and many other areas in society. Residences and agricultural buildings throughout Norway are visible reminders of the traditions and new impulses brought across the Atlantic by Norwegians returning to their native land. Norway's great novelist Knut Hamsun also spent years in America; his writing was clearly influenced by his sojourn there.

There were as well, especially from the southwestern part of Norway, the "birds of passage" migrants: people who found work in America and commuted back and forth on a seasonal basis. It is an interesting manifestation of labor migration. As recorded from the island of Karmøy on Norway's southwestern coast, fishermen took part in the fisheries on the East Coast of America and then returned for the next year's herring fishing in Norway. Bay Ridge district in Brooklyn in greater New York eventually became the largest urban colony of Norwegian-born people outside Norway—in part thanks to "birds of passage" migration but also the result of many calls by Norwegian ships and the numerous members of the colony who worked in shipping.

There are several offshoots from the Norwegian community in Brooklyn. In the Massachusetts whaling town New Bedford and even more so in Fairhaven across the bay is a thriving community of Norwegian scallop fishermen. Most have roots in Karmøy. The first Norwegian fishermen came from Brooklyn in the 1920s; in the following decade, many came from the outer regions of Karmøy. They benefitted from the easy access to market. As recently as the late 1950s and early 1960s, following the failed herring fishing off the coast of Norway, many fishermen from Karmøy moved to the New Bedford area to engage in the profitable, but also perilous, scallop fisheries.

In February 2001, I was invited to address an audience in Åkra on the island of Karmøy about my research on the New Bedford region for *The Promise Fulfilled*. In Fairhaven, research associate Terje Mikael Hasle Joranger and I interviewed Ellen Skar, who had immigrated from Karmøy together with her husband in 1963. In my talk at Åkra, I related Skar's story and played a recording of the interview in her local Karmøy dialect interspersed with American words and expressions. She related that many recent immigrants returned to Karmøy after the discovery of oil. My listeners were people with connections to America, many of them repatriated Norwegian Americans who had spent many years there. Likely no other place in Norway has more residents who themselves or through nearest family have experienced America more closely than on the island of Karmøy (with the possible exception of Lista; see below). A woman read a poem she had composed on the occasion of my visit. People in attendance displayed a true feeling of "nearness" to America.

In the study *Det amerikanske Lista* (The American Lista), ethnologist Siv Ringdal paints a stirring portrait of a district in Norway that has been significantly transformed by repatriated Norwegian Americans. Lista is a long peninsula along the Listafjord in the province of Vest-Agder on the southern coast of Norway. Ringdal's story—a well-crafted case study—is "about the relationship a windblown little peninsula on the south coast had with a large continent hundreds of miles away."

Focusing on the individual and everyday life on both sides of the Atlantic, Ringdal shows how the labor migration to America from the late 1890s until the late 1960s affected this rather remote region, also within a Norwegian context. Contacts abroad were numerous beginning in the 1850s, when sailing ship traffic and shipbuilding flourished; the coastal region of southern Norway thrived economically. Not until toward the end of the nineteenth century, when sailing ships were displaced by steamships, did emigration to America gain strength. Thousands of people immigrated to America, mostly to the East Coast and the Norwegian colony in Brooklyn. Many shuttled back and forth or spent months or years there before returning home. In 1920, one-third of Lista's population resided or had lived in America; in the postwar period, about a thousand in a population of less than five thousand are registered to have gone to America. To illustrate the close relationship, Ringdal gives the following example: "When people in Lista said 'Are you home?' or 'Have you been to town?', it was America and New York, not Oslo, Kristiansand or Farsund they were talking about."

America became a part of everyday life even for children, and as adults they would easily decide to seek their luck there and then return to Lista: "For nearly eighty years, the labor migration persisted between the community and the States, something that left its mark on growing up and family life, house construction, home furnishing, thoughts and attitudes." And these migrants brought with them a mixed Norwegian speech. They might be *konfjusa* (confused) rather than *forvirret* and ask the dry-cleaner to *kline* (clean) rather than *rense* a suit. For anyone who has lived abroad, the change is easy to appreciate. The material influence—built on American dollars—became greatly visible. During the years between the wars and in the postwar era, repatriated Norwegian Americans decided to build "America houses," as Ringdal describes them, after types of houses they had seen abroad. Their distinct difference from the traditional local houses made them stand out in the landscape. They re-created "The American Kitchen Dream," with American kitchen furniture as well as large white refrigerators, even dishwashers, and other electric appliances—all requiring 110 voltage. After the Second World War the so-called *dollarglis*, a fancy American automobile, might be one of the most important possessions Norwegian Americans had, either when visiting the homeland and then perhaps selling the car or when returning permanently. A final quote from the book sums it all up: "Lista is an adventure all to itself—the farms lie there edged by rocks, exactly as said in the geography book, and on the narrow roads drive the wide American cars—for almost everyone at Lista has been, or will go to America."

The story of repatriation can be considered nationwide. Ragnar Standal looks at the municipality of Ørsta in Sunnmøre and discusses how immigrants who returned home made lasting impressions and how those moving back to the farming communities transferred new insights in agriculture, new houses, and new equipment. In the article "Report on The Returned Emigrant Project," Knut Djupedal relates the 1986 launch of the project, an enterprise I had first suggested when speaking at a history seminar at Høvikodden, south of Oslo, at the end of July 1984. Its underlying premise is that "returned emigrants represented an untapped primary source of emigration history, one that was fast disappearing as returnees aged and passed away. Therefore, returned emigrants should be interviewed as fast as possible." Djupedal, who ran the project beginning in 1988, worked on it with other interested scholars. A book-length summary of their findings would be widely appreciated.

In a chapter titled "Norwegian Immigration and Women," published in *Norwegian American Women* (2011), I give evidence of striking characteristics in regard to women immigrants:

Women were more likely than men to settle permanently in the new land, even though women—in the youth labor movement that developed in the postbellum decades—also had a temporary residence in the United States in mind at the outset. They intended to return to Norway after accumulating resources abroad; in many cases, of course, men returned to meet obligations on family homesteads, so their sojourn in America might be considered a means to pay off debt on the home place.... An improved position in gender relationships and new social networks, might at least in part, have influenced women's decision to settle permanently rather than returning to Norway, as well as marriage and American-born children—perhaps the most significant reasons to stay.

As we Lowells returned to Norway, we were warmly welcomed by family on both the maternal and paternal side. Even so, painful memories surfaced from the war years, during which family ties were occasionally less important than making a profit on the black market.[2]

A HOME IN VOLDA

Our family planned to stay in the small village of Volda for one year. Svanhild attended middle school, and I enrolled in the local gymnas, somewhat like a junior college. We readopted the Norwegian surname Løvoll. Initially, the students viewed me with some curiosity; I remained the American—the outsider. The fact that the Norwegian language had two written forms, *bokmål* (based on reformed Dano-Norwegian) and *nynorsk* (New Norwegian), had totally escaped my recollection, likely through lost interest. *Nynorsk*, drawing on normalized forms of Norwegian rural dialects, gained official equal status with Dano-Norwegian, the later *bokmål*, in 1885. All students had to choose one for their Norwegian *hovedstil* (principal essay). The first day of class the Norwegian lektor—the highest ranking gymnas teacher—went from student to student asking which language they would use. When he came to me, I in all innocence and to everyone's great merriment answered "English." Without looking up, the lektor simply muttered in *nynorsk* lingua: *"Eg set ned nynorsk"* (I will put down *nynorsk*). We were in a *nynorsk*-oriented area of Norway.

I struggled to master the two literary forms; the greatest problem was differentiating between them. The course of study, the so-called English line or curriculum, required knowledge of three non-Norwegian languages: English, German, and French. I had taken German in high school, but the study of French was new to me, as it was for all the other students. The French lektor employed the direct method of teaching. I recall him standing in front of the class and pointing to his head and repeating, *"la tete, la tete."* Unexpectedly, a student blurted out, *"kålhaud"* (cabbage). The lektor's method had failed miserably, the term *kålhaud* or *kålhue* having the added derogatory meaning of "blockhead" or "fool."

It was a difficult year in many ways, as I worked hard not only to compete with fellow students, who had many advantages, but also to be accepted by them. At times they were inclined to make fun of me. One student stands out in my memory as being totally supportive and coming to my defense. Alf Johan Hustad showed maturity and the capacity for empathy and viewed me simply as a fellow student, not "the American." Alf Johan and I met again in the early 2000s and kept in touch. In October 2006, when I was invited to give a few lectures at the University College (*Høgskolen*) in Volda, Hustad came all the way from his home in Vestnes in Romsdal to see me again. The visit was warm albeit brief, but it did include an update on our respective life experiences. We continued to exchange letters; the last one from Alf is dated December 11, 2008; he succumbed to cancer sometime thereafter.

The 1952–53 school year became a long road with many adjustments. My formative years had been spent in a different environment, making it difficult for me to accept the unfamiliar milieu. I also might have made a greater personal effort. As the year proceeded, other students became my friends, though I was never fully accepted by them as being Norwegian.

The summer of 1953, as Astrid, Svanhild, and I were planning to return to Seattle, we looked into the possibility of traveling via Great Britain. Then a letter arrived from Alf that radically changed all our plans. He wrote that he had always wanted to return to live in Norway in retirement and asked that we not move back to America. He would join us later. The decision was difficult to make and certainly life-changing. Astrid eventually communicated back that she would agree to repatriate only if Alf made the move at the same time. She had been without a husband for long enough. Alf would turn fifty-two in the fall and was still a long way from retirement. Moving to Norway would require making a living there. Alf accepted the condition and promised to join his family in Volda.

Accepting my father's decision entailed a difficult process for all of us. *We would become repatriated Norwegians.* How would we adjust to the life ahead of us? In writing these recollections, I asked my sister, Svanhild, to share how she felt about this major change in our lives. "I had 'forgotten Norwegian,'" she volunteered, "and in the beginning it was difficult to keep up with the classroom instruction." We wished to return to what had become our normal way of life. In October 2016, Svanhild wrote: "I was disappointed when we did not return to the United States after the year was over, but were going to settle in Norway. From the age of nine until fifteen, I lived in the United States. These are important years in development and attachment to places and people. One might say that I grew up in the United States."

Did Alf ever regret his decision to retire to Norway? He answered that very question in 1984. Astrid nearly fell off her chair when she heard her husband claim that he had regretted the decision every day. Perhaps his regular sojourns in America inspired a longing for the United States, his adopted country. Astrid assured Alf that she would have returned to America with him on a minute's notice; she had adjusted well to life in America, even taking English classes for immigrants. Attachment to life in America had been fortified as well by two visits to Seattle, in 1957 and in 1963; the last sojourn for six months. She and Alf rented an apartment in familiar Ballard. In doing research for *The Promise of America*, I interviewed some of my father's fishermen colleagues. As we sat in a circle, it struck me that my father should have spent his senior years in Seattle, associating with people who shared his experience on the sea and could talk about good times and bad times in the fisheries.

No one he would associate with in Volda could visualize Alf's working years. His account of the room-sized king crab pots was hard for many to take seriously. Crab pots in Norway were quite small. Alf had been engaged in the king crab fishery off the coast of Alaska.

To benefit both American and Norwegian readers, I include in *The Promise of America*—initially published in Norwegian in 1983 as *Det løfterike landet*—images of a ship heading for the king crab grounds with crab pots on deck as well as of a halibut fisherman, who greatly resembled my father, pulling in the catch with a line. Alf was never one to show emotion or give great compliments, but upon reading my account of fisheries on the Pacific Coast, he turned to me and said, "You know, Odd, this is not too bad for someone who has never fished." It has remained the highest praise I could ever imagine.

But the decision to live in the homeland had been made back in 1953, and I never saw my father change his mind once it had been made up. A large house of American design was erected in Storgata 21. At a time when two-story houses in Volda were being built with only a simple facility in the basement consisting of a stool and a basin, my father's house had bathrooms on all floors, including the basement. It impressed the contractor and his workers.

In the spring of 1955, I took the *examen artium*—university entrance exam—after completing the three years of study at Volda gymnas. I maintain a very positive view of the educators' classroom performance and their engagement as mentors. Astri Gundersen, lektor in English, was well prepared and consistently professional in conducting her classes. Lektor Sivert Høydal, who taught mathematics, showed great patience with those of us who were less than gifted and always took time to stop and talk when we met outside of class. I do seem to recall that on the last day before the final public university entrance exams he let out a heavy sigh as he wished us well. And who could blame him? To his credit, our entire class passed.

The Løvoll family—all four of us—had by then moved into our new comfortable residence. As was the case in Lista, the kitchen had a large white refrigerator, a kitchen range, and other appliances purchased in America and transported to Volda, all requiring 110 voltage. Alf found employment in, among other pursuits, the herring fishing operations, but he felt he could better support his family by working in America. We adjusted again: Alf would return to the king crab and halibut fisheries and divide his time between Norway and America, an arrangement that would continue until he retired in 1966.

On his returns via ocean liner, Alf might bring along a used American automobile, generally purchased in New York before boarding. At that time, automobiles were strictly rationed in Norway, and people eager to buy an American car made for a profitable enterprise. But then the authorities reprimanded my father for having imported automobiles too frequently. He consulted a local lawyer, who offered the surprising advice to simply ignore the directive, as the authorities in question were too occupied with other responsibilities to pursue the issue. Alf never heard from them about the matter again, but he discontinued transporting automobiles across the Atlantic.

When my father was still importing cars, my mother, my sister, and I might meet him as the Norwegian America Line's grand trans-Atlantic passenger liner docked in Oslo. When it was the so-called *Julebåt*—Christmas ship—arriving before the holidays, our reunited family might drive in winter conditions from the Norwegian capital to Volda, making for pleasant memories. In Alf's absence, Astrid was again the one in charge of house and hearth.[3]

THE LOVE OF MY LIFE

Nothing more significant has happened to me than finding my lifelong partner and the love of my life: Else Olfrid Navekvien Løvoll. She became the mainstay in my life and in my professional career.

I met Else at the Hotel Alexandra in Loen in inner Nordfjord the summer of 1956. The large, upscale tourist hotel is located in the spectacular landscape of western Norway; the glaciers at the Jostedal Glacier National Park (Jostedalsbreen Nasjonalpark) are only some kilometers away. Else worked as assistant to the chef, and I was employed as night porter. At the end of my shift, before retiring to my room I would enter the kitchen area and enjoy a cup of coffee and the freshly baked biscuits Else had made. Else was twenty and I a year older. As we became acquainted, we would bicycle through the lovely countryside toward the glaciers. In the evening, before my night duty called, we sometimes danced in the hotel's ballroom. Over the summer, Else and I became good friends and appreciated each other's company. Else grew up on a small farm in the Bryggja community in outer Nordfjord, high up from the fjord. She accepted me for who I was; my history did not become a barrier, as it did from time to time when I was introduced with the caveat "American" attached to my name.

In the fall, I entered the two-year training at Oslo Teachers' College to qualify as a public educator, a decision I greatly regretted in later years. The school had little to offer in terms of my developing scholarly interests. I should instead have followed my friends' lead and entered university studies at the University of Oslo. Lectures on educational issues and student teaching did, however, provide knowledge and practice that would benefit later student relations and classroom performance. And, naturally, I made many new friends. I completed my training and was certified to teach in the Norwegian public educational system.

What truly made the two years in the Norwegian capital important to me was not my schooling but Else's company. Else and her older sister Torun found employment in domestic service and moved to Oslo. Else and I spent as much time together as possible, though our limited finances did not permit anything extravagant. Oslo is a great theater city, and we cultivated our shared interest in dramatic performances at venues including the National Theater. As a college student, I got tickets at half price. We generally purchased the least expensive seats, but quite regularly one of the attendants would invite us to sit closer to the stage. One performance that stands out is Henrik Ibsen's *Peer Gynt*, with Toralv Maurstad playing the leading role. The son of actors Alfred Maurstad and Tordis Maurstad, Toralv is a leading performer and considered the greatest interpreter of *Peer Gynt*. Toralv Maurstad was a friend of Else's family and regularly visited his father's birthplace, Bryggja.

Else had performed in the local youth society's plays in her home community. Her father, Peder Navekvien, had hoped to become an actor, but as an only child on the farm, home duties prevented him from realizing his dream. He was likely inspired by his friend Alfred Maurstad, who became one of Norway's premier actors on stage and in film. Peder's talents were on full display when he served as master of ceremonies (*kjøgemester*) at weddings and at other local events.

One winter, Else and I enrolled in a dance class, and on rare occasions we spent an evening at an establishment like Humla in downtown Oslo over a glass of beer and with the opportunity to dance. A walk through the city and a cup of coffee with cake—preferably napoleon pastry—were more typical activities. Or a stop at Gildevangen, the restaurant of Sunnmørslaget—the society for Sunnmørings in Oslo—where on Thursdays members could enjoy the local Sunnmøre dish *raspeball*, potato dumpling and pork.

Oslo was a peaceful and safe city during those years. I remember the funeral procession of King Haakon VII in late fall 1957; he died September 21, and many heads of Europe and other dignitaries marched behind the royal casket on the way from the palace to the Oslo Cathedral. Else and I were among the masses of observers lined up on either side of the route to watch the impressive retinue. By today's standards there was a striking lack of security; the police officers' role was simply crowd control.

As time passed, Else and I fell in love and entered the lifelong romantic stage of our relationship. Our engagement rings are dated March 23, 1957. We felt we needed to mark our betrothal. In celebration, we invited my friend from the teacher's college Knut Johansen (Leira), who later served as my best man, and his date to the elegant Frascati Restaurant. It was a memorable evening. Our total bill came to about one hundred kroner, or some fourteen dollars. The amount appears ridiculously insignificant in the 2010s, but in 1957 it represented 20 percent of my monthly budget. The following day, Knut could not sufficiently express the strength of his feelings for his date. But life can be cruel: as we were walking down Oslo's main street, Karl Johan, we saw Knut's date in the arms of another man. Our conversation turned into a quiet reflection on how unfair and unpredictable human existence is.

On March 30, 1958, Else and Odd exit the church in Volda
to begin their life together.

The wedding was scheduled for March 30, 1958, so Alf could attend before leaving for the fisheries in Alaska. I was twenty-three and Else twenty-two years old. The magnificent Lutheran edifice in Volda was the site of the marriage ceremony. Else had made her own wedding gown and looked spectacular as she and I slowly moved up the long aisle to the front of the sanctuary. The Lutheran pastor gave a sermon on Eros and Agape, love both human and divine.

Photos from the glorious event captured its warmth and family linking between the Navekviens and the Løvolls. Mother's congratulatory words summed it all up: *"Du fekk deg ei god kjerring, du Odd"* (You got yourself a good wife, Odd). Else and I established a near and supportive relationship with our respective in-laws, sharing family events and occasions. Guests at the wedding included our parents and my maternal grandfather Odin.[4]

The parents of the bride and groom: from left,
Peder and Anna Navekvien, Astrid and Alf Løvoll

TEACHING IN ARNA

I had to continue at the teacher's college in Oslo, and Else would wait in Volda for my return; some lonely weeks followed for the new-lyweds. That summer, Else and I finally had a brief honeymoon in the mountain cabin of my childhood by a little lake filled with small trout. We enjoyed hiking, fishing, and simply spending time together alone.

In the fall I became an itinerant teacher of English, serving three rural school districts in Arna, which in 1972 merged as a borough into the city of Bergen. But my continued education was on my mind; I had high hopes of moving beyond my situation. The University of Bergen might be one avenue forward.

English was at that time taught in the sixth and seventh grades, the two final years in the existing elementary school system. I enjoyed my position, moving by bus and ferry from one school district to the next. The young students appreciated having an American as their English teacher. I reassured them that I would teach "proper" English; in order to be certified, I had to adopt English pronunciation. Later, I thought the British accent had ruined my American speech. Today, with the dominance of US television programs, American pronuncia-tion is unavoidable and the "strict British" requirement is no longer enforced. Television did not enter Norway before the 1960s.

The best part of the day was coming home to Else, who waited with a good meal and a loving embrace. Evenings I would read aloud—generally classical novels by Norwegian and non-Norwegian authors—while Else occupied herself with handiwork. Later we would discuss the narratives. The first year, we lived in a residence for local teachers in Grøtnesdalen on the island of Osterøy. The second year we rented a one-bedroom facility across the fjord on Garnes, with direct railroad connection to Bergen. Family members lived in the capital of West Norway: Else's aunt Bertha, her mother's sister, and my aunt Dina, my father's sister.

Tante Dina was a remarkable person. She was single and worked as a housekeeper in wealthy homes, at times being made aware of the great social distinctions within Norwegian society and her own place in it. She had great concern for her nephews and nieces. Tante Dina never forgot a birthday, and her Christmas gifts were truly special. Even during the German occupation, Tante Dina managed to distribute holiday presents. They were stored in Grandpa Martin's place until Christmas Eve, when children with high expectations fetched them. The tradition created many happy memories.

The third year, Else and I moved a second time. Teaching English was considered an intermediate and transitional position. I applied to teach at Fana *høgre almenskole*, the gymnas and middle school in Fana, located in a suburban district of Bergen with the intriguing name Paradis—paradise. The wealthy district is home to large shipping firms. The fall of 1960, Else and I with daughter Audrey Merete, born in June of that year, moved to Paradis and lived on the second floor of a private home. Teaching at this level at a large school became a new challenge for me. I had also enrolled at the university to study Norwegian language and literature. I earned my university degree in 1961.

Christmas 1960 had been spent with my parents and sister in Volda. With a baby in our care, Else and I decided that our living conditions in Paradis were unacceptable. Else and Audrey stayed with proud grandparents Alf and Astrid while I returned to the Fana gymnas to complete the academic year and my university studies. Then I landed a position at Volda gymnas and middle school beginning the 1961 fall semester. Having achieved the academic title *adjunkt*, I would teach English, Norwegian, and history. As a teacher of Norwegian language and literature, I couldn't help but consider my missteps in Norwegian only some eight years earlier as a student at the very same school.[5]

FAMILY LIFE

Reflecting on 1960 and residence at Garnes, I consider the joy as well as some concern Else and I experienced when becoming parents. Alf and Astrid exhibited tangible anticipation and love when they learned about the blessed event. The first-time grandparents-to-be paid a visit before Alf again crossed the Atlantic, by then by airplane. He was amused when he witnessed the visibly pregnant Else clearing snow from the long path I would take home when returning from work. "Poor Odd cannot be expected to wade in snow" was how Alf warmly teased us.

The baby was due in June, and Astrid came to Garnes to be present and to help. As a young father-to-be, I had great sympathy, even a sense of guilt, when considering what my lovely Else would endure giving birth. My mother simply reminded me that it was the role all women had. "But Mother, I am not talking about all women, but about my precious wife," I replied. When birth was at hand on June 26, I sat in the waiting room of the clinic in Indre Arna, holding a large bouquet whose flowers began to fade over the many hours. Finally, I was allowed in to see my Else. I hugged her and said I was sorry for what she had endured. She simply smiled at me. Then the nurse brought in the newborn Audrey Merete. She was lovely, a princess indeed, and I loved her immediately. She was baptized in the magnificent Lutheran edifice in Paradis.

Our prince Ronald was born in Volda three years later, May 10, 1963. Astrid and Svanhild were spending time with Alf in Seattle during Astrid's second visit to the Pacific Northwest after the move to Norway in 1952. I again experienced great concern for Else's well-being. The midwife in charge at the hospital had little patience with the regular calls I made to inquire about the labor, which had been induced and was thus prolonged. "We will call you when there is something to relate," she responded brusquely. When the call eventually came, I was briefly informed that it was a boy and Else was doing well. I annoyed the poor midwife by asking her to repeat the news. For a second time I was a proud father. No role has been more cherished and rewarding for me than as a parent, with its many responsibilities and the joys of moving together through the successive stages of our children's lives, from childhood to youth to adulthood. I feel greatly blessed.

I was able to devote that entire summer to my family, which would not always be the case as I proceeded with my university studies and research. It was a good summer. We spent much time simply taking care of newborn Ronald and spending time with three-year-old Audrey, outside during the day and reading to her at bedtime. And there were also some adjustments. Audrey had naturally been doted on by caring grandparents as well as by parents and aunts and uncles. Now there was competition as the new addition received greater attention. Ronald was baptized in the Volda Lutheran church where his parents had been married.[6]

LIFE IN VOLDA

Ronald, Audrey, Else, and I moved into a small apartment at the lower level of the house Alf built in Storgata 21. Grandparents were just one floor up, and Svanhild had her own space on the third level. Our small but growing family resided under one roof.

We regularly visited the Navekviens' modest farm in Nordfjord. Else's father, Peder, passed away in 1962, before Ronald's birth the following year, but her mother, Anna, remained at home. A seamstress and experienced cook, Anna had regularly been responsible for preparing the meals at the large weddings and other events where Grandpa Peder had been master of ceremonies. They constituted a great team. I had a close relationship with my in-laws. Peder had strong genealogical interests, cultivated folk traditions in music and storytelling, and studied the Viking presence in Nordfjord in the Middle Ages. He sang *stev* (folk verse) and folk ballads broadcast on national Norwegian radio. He also converted to using New Norwegian, and once he and I visited the home—then a museum, just outside Volda—of the creator of this written form of Norwegian, Ivar Aasen (1813–96). Peder was full of stories and anecdotes about this self-taught philologist, best known for having assembled from dialects an alternative written standard to the Dano-Norwegian of his day. His popular nationalistic poem *"Mellom bakkar og berg ut med havet heve nordmannen fenge sin heim"* (Between the hills and the mountains by the ocean has the Norseman made his home) is one of the most widely known. From 1998 to June 2007 the first two stanzas were engraved on all Norwegian driving licenses; for some, especially in western Norway, it became like another national song, alongside the national anthem. Aasen was also a playwright, and his creative work displays a patriotic love for the Norway he envisioned.

Else's brother Rolf and his wife Rigmor, by then the proprietors and owners of the Navekvien farmstead, were generous and welcoming hosts to their siblings and nieces and nephews, who arrived from places like Bergen or Oslo and might spend their vacations on the home turf. Kin who lived closer by, such as in Volda and other communities in the western reaches of the country, made shorter visits. Audrey and Ronald learned much about farm life; Audrey once nearly crawled underneath the cow when her uncle Rolf was milking it. Else could relate stories Grandpa Peder had told about the *hulder*, the wicked siren, who lived underground in the elevation just behind the house. The tales fueled the imagination.

In Volda, Astrid, Alf, and Svanhild had joined the Pentecostal church Eben-Eser. When Audrey was about four years old, we accepted Grandma Astrid's suggestion that she should attend Sunday school there. Else and I thought it would do her no harm. On one visit to the Navekvien farm, Rolf had butchered a calf and nailed the hide to the outhouse to dry. The following Sunday, as told by the Sunday school teacher who happened to be my student, she had—incredible as it might seem—asked the toddlers in her class if they knew what happened to people when they died. No one responded. But suddenly it dawned on Audrey and she raised her hand: "They are nailed to the outhouse." So much for that lesson.

We soon decided to take Audrey out of this particular Sunday school setting. There was the issue of *åndsdåp*, spiritual baptism, which was considered essential for salvation; thereafter followed baptism by immersion. Grandparents would boast of when their grandchild had this experience; youngsters must have been under heavy pressure to be baptized by "the Holy Spirit." There was also

Celebrating *Syttende mai*—May 17—in Volda:
from left, Ronald, Else, Svanhild (behind), Audrey, and Astrid

the *tungetale*, speaking in tongues. Else and I respected all religions but felt uncomfortable in the Pentecostal milieu. We were also concerned that the leaders of the congregation took advantage of Astrid and Alf in their fund-raising. And we were deeply saddened to learn that Astrid had expressed worry that she might not meet her son in heaven. According to Pentecostal teaching, being a member of the Norwegian Lutheran State Church apparently did not advance one to eternal life. I was regularly prayed for in *pinsekirken*—the Pentecostal church.

But life was good in Volda. Astrid was warm, generous, and supportive and enjoyed spoiling her grandchildren. Audrey regularly checked the menu upstairs and down before deciding where to have dinner; grandparents eagerly enjoyed her company. Both Audrey and Ronald spent much time in the company of grandparents and aunt. Else was active in the upkeep and financing of a day care located across the street. When the weather was good, we took the children on long bicycle rides—Audrey sitting behind me and Ronald behind Else—with perhaps a picnic stop along the route. We also hiked in the great outdoors and skied in the winter—Else would beat me by a mile. Christmases were celebrated in Grandpa and Grandma's living room after a traditional West Norwegian Christmas meal—*pinnekjøtt*, boiled potatoes, and *surkål*—in the dining room. Audrey might play Santa Claus, asking as she entered: *"Nokre snille born her?"* (Any nice children here?). It was a joyful family event. Our many friends, both for the children and the grown-ups, produced a rich social life.[7]

TEACHING

The gymnas and middle school were separate institutions, each with their own *rektor* (principal), but they coordinated their teaching assignments. With my experience from the big-city school, I was initially overly strict in the much smaller environment of Volda, but quickly realized that student behavior was not an issue and relaxed. Indeed, I was not that much older than my students. May 17, 1965, the graduating class made me an honorary member, and I marched with

On May 17, 1965, the graduating class made Odd an honorary member,
waking him at 5:00 AM and placing the student cap on his head.

the students in the *Syttende mai* parade wearing the compulsory student cap. Later I learned that people had wondered whom that older student might be.

On a recent visit to Volda, in October 2016, I met a number of my students from the 1960s. The local newspaper *Møre* carried a story about the gathering. In its 2016 Christmas issue, the Volda journal printed an even longer piece titled *"Ein historikar si reise"* (An Historian's Journey) about my time as an educator in Volda, 1961–67, and my work on this book.

One of the students I met in October 2016 was Gunnar Botn. I recall him as a young student who always placed himself in the back of the room and did not speak very much during class. As a teacher I consistently worked to involve the students as much as possible. Once, when advising this young man, I suggested that if he always placed himself farthest back, he would not get very far in life. He clearly took it to heart. As a visiting professor in 2006, I spoke at the University College in Volda, and a man sat smiling in the front row. After my lecture, he introduced his wife and himself and thanked me for the good advice I had given him those many years ago. He was my long-ago student Gunnar Botn. A letter in *Møre* facilitated our meeting again in 2016.

The group of students reflected on the years when I was their teacher. Gunnar described me as "a pleasant and good teacher." But, he admitted, "I flunked his first-year English class," and conceded that it was fully deserved, as he was more interested in motorcycles and young women than studying. He took the class a second time and did well. He had enjoyed meeting me in 2006. "And I got to show him," Gunnar continued, "that I too can sit in the first row." He added that his economic life had benefitted from his knowledge of English.

Spending the evening with a group of my students from a generation ago, and learning about their personal and professional lives, was a moving experience for me. As I listened to their comments, I especially appreciated hearing, "You treated us all equally and we saw that you wished the best for us." I reflected on the Norwegian educational system of that time and my own place in it; there were great demands on the instructor, who was mainly judged by how well the students did on national exams. I listened patiently to colleagues boasting of their graduating students. This Norwegian competitive spirit surfaced in another way: when the major winter sports competitions were broadcast, instruction might be suspended so that teachers and students alike could listen to the reports with excitement and nervous anticipation.

We teachers wandered between the two institutions, the gymnas and the middle school, to meet with assigned classes. To boost my modest salary, I volunteered to teach extra classes, especially in Norwegian; these required the additional work of correcting essays and thus were not favored by my fellow instructors. Even so, I never rose above thirty thousand kroner, less than five thousand dollars, in annual salary. On top of the Norwegian classes, instruction in English came with its own requirements, and history mainly focused on the country's past, with some attention given to "the world beyond Norway." It was a six-day school week at that time. On my way home Saturday afternoons, I stopped at the flower shop to purchase a bouquet for my Else.

There are more memories from the years in Volda than there is space to relate. I remember fondly once when there was a heavy downpour as I was getting ready to leave the school for home and I had no umbrella. As I opened the door, there stood five-year-old Audrey, dressed in a raincoat and southwester, teasingly holding up an umbrella as she said, "Here you are Odd Lova," not quite mastering the last name. Father and daughter had a fine walk home in the rain.[8]

UNIVERSITY STUDIES

My educational goal at that time was to earn a *cand.filol.* degree in the humanities, with history as the major field of study; it would move me up to the rank of *lektor* as a teacher in gymnas or even university. I have been an avid reader all my life. Teaching history, I assembled a personal library in addition to those works available in the school or public libraries. Among the books that especially roused my interest were the two volumes by Ingrid Semmingsen, *Veien mot vest. Utvandringen fra Norge til Amerika 1825–1865* (The Way West: The Emigration from Norway to America, 1825–1865) and *Veien mot vest. Utvandringen fra Norge 1865–1915* (The Way West: The Emigration from Norway, 1865–1915). As I perused Semmingsen's account of migration, its causes, the adversity individual immigrants experienced, and their adjustment to a foreign land, I saw my own immigrant experience. She became my primary inspiration as I established myself as an authority in the field of Norwegian immigration. Her body of work is a national treasure.

Semmingsen held the distinction of being the first woman to attain the rank of professor of history at the University of Oslo and gained recognition as an authority on Norwegian immigration to the United States. Over the years, Ingrid and I established a close friendship. She was frequently a houseguest in our home in Northfield, Minnesota; I was also her houseguest on the Bygdøy peninsula west of Oslo. In 1990, Ingrid celebrated her eightieth birthday in Northfield; Else and I arranged for a dinner at the elegant Schumacher Restaurant in nearby New Prague, where she was feted by some of her many friends. Our connection dated to the spring of 1978, when Ingrid and I cooperated on a graduate seminar on Norwegian immigration. Professor Øyvind Gulliksen describes it in *Klassekampen*, October 3, 2014: "The spring of 1978, [Odd] taught together with Ingrid Semmingsen at the University of Oslo. It formed the basis for a long cooperation between them. Together with Semmingsen, Odd laid the foundation for interpreting the migration to the United States, both as an experience for the individual and for groups of people. He maintains that it was when he read her books that he discovered himself as a migrant."

In the 1960s, however, I was a neophyte who harbored a deep interest in history in general, and specifically in the saga of Norway as a major emigration nation, losing multitudes of its citizens to overseas migration. I enrolled in the summer courses offered by the University of Oslo and took my *grunnfag*—basic exam—in 1966. The summer of 1966 was one of the warmest on record; I arrived in Oslo bemoaning that my family would remain in Volda the entire summer. I was invited to occupy a room with friends, but a few days after my arrival, they informed me that they would be out of town for the duration and suggested that I bring my family to Oslo. It was truly a happy moment to welcome my family at the Oslo airport, Fornebu. Audrey and Ronald came running to hug me. "It was so far down, Dad" was Ronald's reflection on his first flight. The summer was delightful, with swimming in the large pool at the Vigeland park, exploring Norway's capital, and spending time together in our own apartment. And I even passed the exam.

The next step up in history would be *mellomfag*—intermediate exam. I studied the curriculum while teaching and signed up to take it in May the following year. The two days of written exams were followed by an oral examination. There, I encountered Ingrid Semmingsen for the first time; she was one of two examiners. One of the questions related to the so-called *formannskapslovene*—executive committee laws—which in 1837 established local self-government in Norway. I must have given an unacceptable response. When the second examiner moved on to the next question, Semmingsen stopped him with the words: "The candidate appears to have some new points of view on the law. Let us continue." It was a painful moment, though I did get my degree. Later, as a university professor and Ingrid's friend, I reminded her of the incident and suggested it was not very kind of her. We were both humored by my predicament.

In 1979, the year after my joint classroom work with Ingrid, to her great sorrow and heartbreak, her husband Rolf Ingvar Semmingsen passed away. He was a most patient and supportive spouse, giving Ingrid time and encouragement to pursue her career and scholarly achievements. He played the same role in Ingrid's life as Else did in mine; my studies, research, and scholarly publications owed much to Else's constant support and loving advice. After a time of mourning, Ingrid resumed her research and publication.

University of Oslo colleagues: from left, Dorothy Burton Skårdal,
who taught American civilization, Odd, and Ingrid Semmingsen, pioneer
in the study of Norwegian emigration

I recall one pleasant occurrence when we met for lunch at the restaurant Tostrupkjelleren in downtown Oslo. We talked, as we generally did, about our common scholarly field of interest. For some reason, we began complaining about all the lost source material. Just imagine all the documents, letters, and legal records that had not been preserved for one reason or another. Then we looked at each other, having reconsidered our gripe, and laughingly uttered: "Thank God for everything that has been lost." We agreed that if everything had been preserved, no book would ever have been completed—researchers would be stalled in the eternal examination of unending source material. It was a thought worth preserving.[9]

CHAPTER 5

America Calling

A Family Odyssey

IN THE COURSE OF my twenties, I increasingly sensed that the return to Norway had deprived me of a more rewarding life experience. I was certainly happy as a husband and father and harbored a deep love for and devotion to my family. There were rewarding and happy moments throughout my early adulthood, and friends and kin to enjoy and spend time with. The annual *lektorlagsmøter*—meetings of the society of secondary school teachers—allowed Else and me to cultivate each other's company. One of these meetings, with lectures and various other programs as well as social activities and a dance, was held at Alexandra Hotel, where we first met, inspiring happy reflections. Sad occasions, like Grandpa Martin's death, unfolded, too; I attended the funeral in Bjørlykke in 1956 and, as the oldest grandson, gave a deeply felt tribute to my much-loved paternal grandfather.

Grandmother Astrid and Aunt Svanhild happily cared for Audrey and Ronald when Else and I on rare occasions attended events outside Volda. The summer of 1962, we visited Oslo for a short time. We drove back to Volda via the picturesque Østerdalen—the extended valley to the east—but thoughts of little Audrey, then two years old, made us cut our journey short. We arrived back home a day before scheduled, eager to see Audrey and expecting her to jump for joy. We had even brought gifts. As we walked in, she was busy with her grandma and aunt and nonchalantly waved, greeted us with a "Hi," and returned to what she had been doing. She clearly had not missed Mom and Dad very much. She was in good company.

Grandfather Alf finally retired to Norway in 1966 at age sixty-five. He showed affection for his grandchildren now that he had the opportunity to spend more time with them. Audrey enjoyed sitting on his lap and sharing his dinner; he lifted Ronald up above his head and they both chuckled. Festive meals brought the extended family together. Alf had built a large boathouse on the fjord and regularly went fishing. Astrid's delicious fish cakes were frequently on the menu when the Løvoll family sat down at the table together.

THE NORTH DAKOTA DESTINATION

My restlessness and a strong desire to return to the United States, at least on a trial basis, introduced yet another turn in a wished-for situation—the Løvoll family members residing close together. With Alf finally retired, that would surely have been an ideal arrangement. Else and I discussed at length my feeling of stagnation in my career and the belief that better opportunities existed elsewhere. I also felt that the family should have returned to the United States in 1953 instead of settling in Norway. In my mind, America, and especially Seattle, had the appeal of coming home. There were constant reminders, such as my father's annual crossing and return with stories of familiar places and people, regular visits from friends, including my childhood friend Kenneth and his parents, and my mother's and sister's visits to America—all brought with them to Norway exciting experiences and pictures to share. The United States remained a close reality. But for Else, America was an unknown and foreign land. Always supportive, she promised that she and the children would accompany me to America. I promised that if, after one year, they were unhappy about the decision, we would all return to Norway.

Else always faced challenges forthrightly, and she immediately enrolled in a correspondence course in English. I contacted several institutions in America and also individuals like Professor Knut Gundersen, who taught Norwegian language and literature at Luther College in

Decorah, Iowa; he informed me that the University of North Dakota in Grand Forks was seeking someone to teach Norwegian. He recommended me to Professor Arne Brekke, a new member of the department of foreign languages at UND, who invited me to join the department as his colleague in the Norwegian section.

My young family and I traveled to the US embassy in Oslo to secure our immigration documents and undergo medical examinations. We found ourselves in front of a solemn-looking woman to respond under oath to a substantial list of questions, covering such topics as whether we were members of the Communist Party or were anarchists. I had to raise my right hand to swear on behalf of Audrey and Ronald. When we came to Ronald, I saw him as the four-year-old he was, running around and climbing on chairs; when his relationship to anarchy became the issue, I was not quite able to respond seriously. The embassy officer looked at me sternly and inquired, "Do you think this is funny, sir?" It was of course her job to take it all in earnest. "No," I responded, holding my arm high, "my son is neither a member of the Communist Party nor an anarchist." We were approved and could return home knowing that our path to the United States was clear.

Icelandair would take us to New York via Keflavik. On the day of departure, Alf and Astrid accompanied us to Ålesund. As we stood on the deck of the ferry taking us to the airport on the island Vigra and the two grandparents were still on shore, it truly dawned on Audrey and Ronald that they were not joining us. An emotional response followed as they waved good-bye. Audrey and Ronald still recall this deep image from their childhood. It took some time to comfort them, especially since Else and I were also dealing with strong feelings. Had we made the right decision?

The many new impressions and activities as we continued our journey created an absorbing distraction, and we had much to talk about. The flight from the Oslo airport Fornebu landed at night in Keflavik, Iceland, where we changed aircraft. In the morning we touched down at the large John F. Kennedy International Airport in

At John F. Kennedy International Airport in New York the summer of 1967.
Ronald, four, holds a bag filled with Matchbox cars he received from Grandpa
Alf. Audrey, seven, takes in her first meeting with America.

New York. We lined up to show our passports and visas to the immigration officer. He looked long at the documents, and with some obvious disbelief, speaking like a true New Yorker, gave the following advice: "You know, sir, we have better places in this country than North Dakota."

But Grand Forks, North Dakota, was where we were headed. We waited for some hours for the flight west. Audrey and Ronald seemed quite relaxed and amused themselves by looking around in the large waiting hall. Finally we boarded the plane to Minneapolis, from which we took another plane to the Grand Forks airport. My new colleague, Arne Brekke, welcomed us as we entered the receiving hall at the airport. It had been a long journey, in distance as well as in the new reality we would experience. But we had finally arrived at our intended destination. Our new life in America would begin. We met our yet-to-be-discovered place of residence with much anticipation.[1]

NORWEGIAN NORTH DAKOTA

North Dakota has the highest percentage of persons per capita claiming Norwegian ancestry. "The history of the United States," North Dakota historian Elwyn Robinson emphasizes, "has been to a large extent the history of the westward movement." He relates how two great Dakota booms, the first from 1878 to 1890 and the second from 1898 to 1915, ended the frontier as European settlement of the state was by then complete. By 1910 the majority—51 percent—of the state's farmers were foreign-born. They had come because of the opportunities the new country offered; immigrants found land for homes and made a living in agriculture. By 1914, Norwegian farmers could boast of owning 7,868,140 acres of North Dakota's fertile land.

Norwegian migrants flooded into the territory and state during the two boom periods and took part in the conquest of the broad grasslands. Norwegians preferred land in regions with forest but found they had to adjust to the prairie landscape. The prairie seemed overwhelming and threatening; a constant wind soughed across the plains, gathered strength, and in winter blew into terrifying blizzards. Many

Norwegians moving west were American-born and may have had greater ability to adjust. But perhaps not by much. Robinson writes, "Even the older Americans, the native-born among the settlers, shared the feeling of strangeness and loneliness on the great open grassland. . . . And all, foreign-born and native alike, shared hope and courage." My initial captious reflections came to mind, when in 1946 I had crossed the nearly empty prairies with my mother, brother, and sister. In 1967, as we made our home there and learned to appreciate the state and its people, my family and I could still not quite accept the prevailing strong prairie winds. Resident North Dakotans also complained. Both Audrey and Ronald recollect being fascinated by the flying tumbleweed on the flats between our housing and the university buildings.

The very first Norwegian pioneers moved to the North Dakota side of the Red River in 1869, marking the beginning of permanent Norwegian settlement in the state. They came in great numbers in the 1880s; indeed, it took on the proportions of a large-scale folk migration. People described it as "Dakota-fever," analogous to the so-called America-fever that had brought the immigrants to Canada and the United States in the first place. North Dakota gained statehood in 1889. In 1900, Norwegians made up 25 percent of North Dakota's population—nearly seventy-five thousand. The second boom beginning at that time brought about a new rush of Norwegians from older settlements or directly from Norway; ten years later, there were an additional fifty thousand Norwegians. Until the 1920s, Norwegians constituted the largest ethnic group in the state. In 1990, 29.6 percent, or 189,106 individuals, identified themselves as primarily or secondarily Norwegian. North Dakota thus retains in percentage of population its status as the most Norwegian state in the union.

Norwegians settled most densely in the valleys of the Red River and its tributaries to the west, a rich agricultural region. As early as 1880, Traill County in North Dakota was 74 percent Norwegian. In Griggs County, Norwegians constituted half of the population. Norwegians became numerous in many other areas, founding towns including Fargo, Grand Forks, Hatton, Mayville, and Hillsboro. The region became a New Norway, taking on a Norwegian flavor still much in evidence.

My young family and I met this America and adjusted to it. We lived in Grand Forks, incorporated in 1881, the third largest city in the state, located on the western banks of the Red River of the North. We initially resided in university housing in this friendly urban community. We noted that bus drivers consistently greeted us and welcomed us aboard; shopping was pleasant. Our neighbors on one side were Cuban refugees, Modesto and Onelia Del Busto and their children, Maria and George. We became good friends. Modesto had served in the administration of the authoritarian government of President Fulgencio Batista, toppled by Fidel Castro in 1959, and had fled to the United States. Modesto taught Spanish at the University of North Dakota and would be my colleague. We had lively, friendly conversations, his conservative convictions at times clashing with my own liberal beliefs.

We were welcomed by many eager to meet a newly arrived Norwegian family. In time we explored the Norwegian settlement areas, but even before then we gained insight. When a repairman with what sounded like a Norwegian accent visited us, I asked if he spoke Norwegian. His answer in the same brogue: "Not a word." He was of Norwegian extraction and spoke with a settlement accent, simply how people spoke English. I was later to visit not only old Norwegian settlements but also those of Russian Germans—a large ethnic group in North Dakota—to learn more about ethnic linguistic developments. But some American-born Norwegians had mastered the ancestral language. We came across these in a small town like Hillsboro in the nearly solidly Norwegian Traill County. And when the *Grand Forks Herald* quoted a representative in the state legislature uttering a few sentences in Norwegian to make his point, we had a sense that the Norwegian immigrant past was not all that distant.

To the new arrivals, the Red River Valley became the New Normandy. The statue of Rollo, the Duke of Normandy, unveiled in

Fargo in 1912 on the occasion of the millennium of his ascendancy in 911, carried the motto, "Over this land we are the lords and masters." The Norwegian American elite responsible for this and other markers of a Norwegian American presence in the Red River Valley might have wished to claim these words as their own. Certainly Herman O. Fjelde, a prominent Norwegian-born physician described as "the father of Norwegian monuments in the Red River Valley," and other community leaders manipulated their cause to create unifying ethnic symbols and pride in heritage by showing "the strength of the Norwegian race."

In time we visited the Norwegian memorials erected in the small towns of the Red River Valley. Special events called attention to them. In June 1939, Crown Prince Olav had placed a wreath on the obelisk made of Norwegian granite (unveiled in Fargo on May 17, 1904) dedicated to the author and poet Bjørnstjerne Bjørnson—the composer of Norway's national anthem. But we were in a new and different place; settling in required our immediate attention.

We soon invested in a new automobile. Else took evening courses in English, but even before mastering a second language, she passed the test for a North Dakota driver's license. And the school year was set to commence. Ronald would have a year to adjust, but Audrey would enter first grade. Else and I were concerned when we took her to school the first day. I decided to meet her on her way home, but as soon as she saw me, she crossed to the other side of the street. Audrey clearly wanted to be independent. She has always had a good ability to adjust to new environments, but of course she was different from the other schoolchildren, had different clothes, and did not yet know English. She was initially teased by her American classmates, but she had English tutors at school, learned the language quickly, and made many new friends.[2]

UNIVERSITY OF NORTH DAKOTA

The University of North Dakota in Grand Forks was established by the Dakota Territorial Assembly in 1883, six years before statehood.

Following World War II, North Dakota's flagship university expanded in a variety of research enterprises and undertook a steady effort to improve the faculties, not to mention recruit better-qualified students. Robinson points to what he described as "old deficiencies," such as faculty salaries remaining below average for institutions of the same class, thus keeping staff members' training level below average as well. The university is currently considered one of the top academic and research institutions in the northern Midwest.

I had been hired to teach Norwegian language and literature; in time I was also invited to offer courses in the history department. In 1967, the University of North Dakota had a student body of about eight thousand; enrollments have increased much since then. In 1891, North Dakota's state legislature passed a law requiring the teaching in perpetuity of the Scandinavian languages—or SCANDINAVIAN LANGUAGE, as the act's title had it—at the University of North Dakota, which, as my colleagues insisted, had always been interpreted as Norwegian, and which surely also was the aim and understanding of the Norwegians advocating the requirement. To them, *Scandinavian* signified Norwegian. Immigrants from the three Nordic countries regularly referred to their nationality as Scandinavian. The statute had been pushed by Norwegians in Fargo as early as 1884, when they had petitioned the appointment of one of their "race" to the faculty of the state university. The university regents opposed the law. When the act was passed in 1891, only 10 of 129 students at the university were of Norwegian origin and Lutheran by affiliation. The Norwegian minority demonstrated political clout; Norwegian would be taught for years to come.

When I embarked on my academic career at the university, Richard Beck was the senior scholar in the foreign-language department. He was of Icelandic background and had taught Norwegian at the institution since 1929, retiring in 1969. He was an active and inspiring scholar and a most pleasant person. Arne Brekke had joined Beck in 1962; he and I were the university's two instructors in Norwegian. Teaching Norwegian as a foreign language was a new assignment for me, and I solicited advice from Beck and Brekke. Einar Haugen's *Beginning Norwegian* was the textbook assigned the students. Since both Brekke and I were *vestlendinger* (West Norwegians), Brekke from Sogn and I from Sunnmøre, the students were exposed to pronunciation influenced by West Norwegian speech. Later in my studies, I learned that a "high Norwegian" pronunciation had developed among Norwegians in America, first in the church and then in colleges and seminaries. Because pastors and educators for a long time came mainly from western Norway, the "formal speech" among Norwegian Americans, based on a Dano-Norwegian linguistic tradition, had a strong West Norwegian flavor. Brekke and I were simply keeping up an established usage and tradition. I enjoyed my time with the students, in the classroom and also when we met outside of class. Most of them were of Norwegian background and some have retained a friendship with me.

A new instructor of Norwegian at the University of North Dakota was big news in the Norwegian American community. Not long after classes began the fall of 1967, I received a visit from two gentlemen who wanted to inspect and give some advice to the newly appointed professor. They were Peder H. Nelson and Orville Bakken, both from the heavily Norwegian small town of Northwood, North Dakota— both perhaps a bit eccentric in their Norwegian disposition. I got to know them well in subsequent years. Nelson was born at Hadeland, Norway, in 1900, and immigrated to America in his twenties. He had filled the space under his bed with clippings from as well as entire issues of Norwegian American newspapers. He was much involved in the *bygdelag*—old home societies—and edited *Brua* (The Bridge), Hadelandslaget's magazine, as well as Hallinglaget's *Hallingen* (The Halling). Bakken preferred, as he said, *"å svalle på halling"*—to chatter in the Halling lingo—even though one of his grandmothers was born in America of Norwegian parents and the three other grandparents had all emigrated. On July 4, his vintage Ford would fly the American and Norwegian flags and display on the side, in large letters, *Hilsen fra Hallingdal* (Greetings from Hallingdal). Bakken's case might seem somewhat unusual, but in visiting small towns and rural communities, we Lovolls regularly met North Dakotans who spoke a Norwegian ancestral tongue.[3]

VISIT TO SEATTLE

One of our major goals during that first academic year in Grand Forks was to make a visit to Seattle. The largest city in the northwestern United States, Seattle is located on six hills overlooking Elliott Bay, an arm of Puget Sound, and has Lake Washington along its eastern border. Seattle forever remains my hometown in America. Ballard neighborhood, the location of the family's first US home in 1946, was a very special destination. We busily contacted family and friends, all in western Washington State. Svanhild came to Grand Forks to join us on our pilgrimage; it was only the first of her regular visits across the Atlantic.

We set out on the long drive—a journey of exploration and nostalgia—in our red VW Squareback. We took the southern Interstate 94 route west and the northern route back home in order to experience and see as much as possible. We spent much time soaking up the scenery; mountainous Montana was especially breathtaking. In Billings, we picked up Interstate 90, and farther west at Livingston we decided to head south to Wyoming and explore Yellowstone National Park—which became a highlight on our way west. As we parked, Ronald recalls, two bears came up to our car. A photo shows us standing in front of Old Faithful geyser as it erupted. America was an exciting adventure.

We made it back across the steep mountain incline to Interstate 90, which would take us to Seattle, but first we had to cross more of Montana and Idaho, with stops at places like Butte, Missoula, and Coeur d'Alene; then our route brought us to Spokane, Washington, and across the state to Seattle on the Puget Sound. Much had changed since my teens. The Space Needle, a new landmark in the Pacific Northwest, was visible from a distance; we ascended its observation deck and enjoyed a ride on the nearby monorail. The freeway system along Elliott Bay was unfamiliar, as were new highways in other parts of the city. But we found Fifteenth Avenue, which we could drive to Ballard and our old haunts—mine and Svanhild's. There was our home on Earl Avenue, where we had lived for some years. A few blocks farther north on Earl lived Amanda and Casper Nesset. We would be their houseguests. I had returned to a place close to my heart. Ronald recalls the peach tree in the Nesset backyard and permission to pick one.

Our time filled with social activity; family and friends were eager to entertain us and meet the new members of the family: Else and Audrey and Ronald. I was eager to show them places I felt closely attached to—our two separate residences in Ballard, even the Shoreline Motel my father had owned for a year, which we passed on our way to visit relatives in Everett and Marysville. We saw the schools Svanhild and I had attended, and we made purchases on Market Street, Ballard's main shopping center. We did not miss visiting Woodland Park Zoo high up in the Phinney Ridge neighborhood; we spent time at the Pike Place Public Market in downtown Seattle. Literary critic Roger Sale said, "For many people the Public Market *is* Seattle, its one great city achievement, the place they love most, the place they take visitors first."

We stopped at the locks that connect Lake Union and the Puget Sound, and at Fishermen's Dock, a few blocks south of Market Street in Ballard. We all marveled as we watched the boats moving up or down from one lock to the next. I had seen my father's fishing boat *Attu* being moved out to open water in this manner.

The time came for us to depart. Else needed to return to work. My salary at the university was insufficient: perhaps an example of Robinson's "old deficiencies." Else worked for fast food establishments until she was offered a position with the university food service. She enjoyed the latter and made many new friends, among them a number of immigrants like herself. From Seattle, we took Highway 2. The one memorable stop on our way home was the Waterton-Glacier International Peace Park in northern Montana.

When founded, it commemorated the peace and goodwill between Canada and the United States.[4]

MASTER'S DEGREE

The fall of 1967, I augmented my teaching and advising responsibilities by enrolling in the University of North Dakota's graduate program. Elwyn Robinson became my main professor, mentor, and advisor as I pursued a master's degree in US history. His *History of North Dakota*, published the year before, became the absorbing text for his course on the history of the state. Reviewers applauded his work as having moved the concept of state history to new heights. Historian Michael Lansing, calling for scholars to engage in new interpretations, observed, "Alone among state histories produced in the mid-twentieth-century, *History of North Dakota* continues to be the standard reference."

The University of North Dakota had large holdings of the Norwegian-language newspapers and journals published in the state. Robinson explained that no one thought anyone would come along to look at these publications; he assumed they were destined to be largely ignored and forgotten. The two of us examined the shelves filled with the original newspapers—some not in great shape. Reading, recording, and analyzing the publications and ultimately writing their history became my commitment, all under Elwyn Robinson's friendly supervision.

The Norwegian American press provided great insight into all aspects of the private and public life of North Dakota's Norwegian immigrant community. I devoted long hours to leafing carefully through the individual papers—not on microfilm or digitalized—and taking extensive notes. There were still editors and journalists I could interview. I was able to correspond with close to twenty individuals, men like Odd Charles Lunde, editor of *Normanden* (The Norseman) in the late 1930s. In a letter from 1968, Lunde admits that "There was little glory in working for the Norwegian-American press." His English-language column, "As I see it—by ODD," was widely read. I found it both entertaining and informative. A general move toward English during the years of Lunde's editorship was motivated by a wish to reach potential subscribers not versed in Norwegian.

My research at Luther College, in Decorah, Iowa, and at the Norwegian-American Historical Association (NAHA), housed at St. Olaf College, in Northfield, Minnesota, became an important part of the story. Luther College has the most extensive collection of Norwegian American publications; among other North Dakota journals, it possesses the best-preserved files of *Normanden*, the largest newspaper. On my way back to North Dakota, I stopped in Northfield and acquainted myself with the NAHA archives. I dined with Thora Bjork, wife of Kenneth Bjork, NAHA's editor, who was attending a meeting out of town. At Archer House Hotel in downtown Northfield, Kenneth unexpectedly announced his presence. As a gift, he gave me a copy of Carlton Qualey's *Norwegian Settlements in America*. Our meeting established a productive, cooperative relationship that would have a decisive influence on my scholarly career. And it was the start of a close friendship between our two families.

I earned my master's degree in January 1969. My thesis carried the title "History of Norwegian-Language Publications in North Dakota." Shortly thereafter, Bjork invited me to submit an article for *Norwegian-American Studies*. I felt honored and recognized as an emerging historian of Norwegians in America. In the 1970 article, I outlined and interpreted the history of the Norwegian-language press in North Dakota.

The first newspaper was *Red River Posten* (The Red River Post), established in 1878, and the last one *Visergutten* (The Errand Boy), discontinued in 1955, only a few months after *Normanden*, begun in 1887, stopped publication in December 1954. The second major Norwegian newspaper in North Dakota was *Fram* (Forward), published 1898–1917. There were many journalistic undertakings, but most papers were short-lived. They all took part in the state's public life, were predominately Republican, and generally supported the liberal-progressive faction. Prohibition was a dominant concern; the state constitution included a prohibition article, championed by newspapers with titles like *Afholds-Basunen* (The Temperance Trumpet). Up to World War I, and perhaps a decade or two after, the Norwegian newspapers were leaders of a regional Norwegian American community. My final assessment of the press: "[The newspapers] helped to explain the nature of the problems facing the immigrants in a semiarid grassland, an area dominated and exploited by out-of-state interests. They guided their readers in pursuing a better life, and gave them a sense of direction and solidarity."[5]

MINNEAPOLIS

We were by 1969 established in Grand Forks and had moved to larger and more comfortable living quarters. Audrey was well adjusted in second grade and Ronald was completing his first year of schooling. We had joined the Gyda Varden Lodge of Sons of Norway. Audrey learned traditional Norwegian dances in the lodge's folk dance group. When King Olav and his entourage visited Fargo, North Dakota, the spring of 1968, the Grand Forks folk dancers provided some of the entertainment.

I was working out plans to earn a doctorate, a requirement if I wished to continue my career at the university level. A long letter from Kenneth Bjork became a deciding factor. Bjork joined the history faculty at St. Olaf College in 1937; in 1960, he succeeded Theodore C. Blegen as managing editor of the Norwegian-American Historical Association—a position he held on top of his professorship. Bjork's reputation in the field of immigration history will likely rest most solidly on two books. In *Saga in Steel and Concrete: Norwegian Engineers in America* (1947), Bjork interprets the significance of "a migration of skills" and the role of technical and financial leadership from abroad in the development of America's great and productive economic system. In *West of the Great Divide: Norwegian Migration to the Pacific Coast, 1847–1893* (1958), Bjork discusses such sociological subjects as class divisions within the Norwegian group and their bearing on settlement and adjustment. The book amounts to a reinterpretation of

St. Olaf colleagues and friends: Kenneth O. Bjork, left, professor of history
and NAHA's second editor, and Lloyd Hustvedt, professor of Norwegian
language and literature and NAHA's executive secretary
Courtesy NAHA

migration within the United States, based on the thesis that a people
once uprooted found it easy to keep moving. There was a continuous
process of migration.

In his letter, Bjork detailed how for several years Bygdelagenes
Fellesraad (the Council of *Bygdelag*) had pushed to have NAHA publish the history of the movement it represented and offered to cover
publication costs. He had made the obvious response that publication costs were not the issue but rather finding an interested and
qualified scholar and providing the needed resources for research and
writing. The Fellesraad finally agreed with Bjork. On his recommen-
dation, the Fellesraad history committee in 1969 invited me to write
the history of the *bygdelag*; Bjork advised me to consider the invitation seriously. Else and I discussed the unexpected offer, which she

encouraged me to accept. I immediately engaged in researching the *bygdelag* movement.

On May 2, 1970, I gave my first report to Bygdelagenes Fellesraad at its annual meeting in Minneapolis. As Else drove me to the railroad station in Grand Forks, I felt great closeness and gratitude to her as she wished me well. My meeting with the members of the Fellesraad was most encouraging, but to my surprise, when I first greeted them in Norwegian, I learned that many of those present did not know the ancestral tongue—at least not my modern version. In my report, I reminded the members that the first annual report of their own history committee had viewed the job as too big to handle, which, I admitted, made me feel a bit apprehensive; I thanked the history committee for their confidence in me. I outlined the history of the *bygdelag* as I saw it. It was all well received. I got to know the two men who would play a major role in the project: O. I. Hertsgaard, known as "Hallingkongen," the Fellesraad's president, and the secretary, Thor Ohme, an immigrant from Hardanger in 1909. Samuel Bergaas, an immigrant from Lindås north of Bergen in 1930, and also on the Fellesraad board, became a special friend and encouraged me greatly in my research.

In the summer of 1970, the Lovoll family moved to Minneapolis. I had submitted applications to the University of Minnesota and been accepted in the department of history and also the department of Scandinavian studies. I became a teaching assistant for the latter; the TA salary and financial support from the Fellesraad would cover living expenses.

We decided to make a brief visit to Norway in early summer. Colleague Arne Brekke owned Brekke Tours & Travel, and we booked tickets on one of his charter flights to Oslo. We enjoyed a most happy reunion with family. Alf cited the established measure of success in America: "How soon a visit to the homeland was possible." He thought we had done well. But in the age of aviation, our return visit could hardly be compared to the complexity associated with overseas travels of an earlier age.

Returning to metropolitan Minnesota, we moved into a pleasant duplex on Nicollet Avenue in South Minneapolis, which Hertsgaard had arranged for us to rent; he and his wife Laila lived across the street. As in North Dakota, Minnesota and Minneapolis exhibit a strong Norwegian association. Ivar Aus, pastor at Mindekirken, the Norwegian Lutheran Memorial Church, invited us to join the congregation. This church and the Memorial Church in Chicago are the only two churches still using Norwegian as a primary liturgical language in America. The congregation in Minneapolis was formed in 1922 in response to the rapid abandonment of Norwegian in favor of English among Norwegian Lutheran churches at that time.

We made friends among the members, many of whom were post–World War II immigrants. There was a clear distinction between more recent arrivals and the prewar ones, as well as with members of Norwegian descent. A separate club for young newcomers, Kontakt, had been formed shortly after the war. *Nordisk Tidende* explained that the newcomer club emerged quite naturally "in the city where Norwegian culture in America is oldest and the split between it and the most recent arrivals greatest." We joined Kontakt, which at the time still called itself "a youth society." In our thirties, Else and I were surely among the youngest members. But the early contrast to old-timers was quickly abating. Only Pastor Aus and wife Hulda spoke Norwegian to us. The common language for all had become English, even at the church coffee following the service conducted in the Norwegian language. The Norwegian liturgy included prayers for the protection of the Norwegian royal family, but life in America expanded the prayer to include the president of the United States.

Among the postwar arrivals there was also a social distinction. The more prosperous and technically trained immigrants gathered in such elite groupings as the Norwegian-American Technical Society. When I had occasion to speak to the Technical Society, a member introduced himself as having been my student when I served as an itinerant English teacher in Arna. The world is truly a small place! Men likely did not join Kontakt but might seek membership in an exclusive Norwegian male luncheon club like Torske Klubben.

Audrey and Ronald attended Page Elementary School, a few blocks from our residence. They had mastered English quickly; their friends and ours, in Grand Forks and Minneapolis, were, after all, mainly limited to English. In Minneapolis, we lived close to slopes along Minnehaha Creek for winter sledding and we could skate on groomed rinks. Minnehaha Falls, on the banks of the Mississippi, was a popular destination for picnics and for such events as Norway Day, a feting of heritage. At home we spoke Norwegian to each other but switched to English when Norwegian American friends visited. To get to school, Audrey and Ronald had to cross the heavily trafficked Nicollet Avenue. Whenever possible, I guided them across the street and met them on their way home. They talked to each other in Norwegian. But then one day when I met them, they were conversing in English. And English became the language of our home.[6]

DOCTORAL STUDIES

My doctoral studies began the fall semester of 1970. A year earlier, Kenneth Bjork had introduced me to immigration scholar Rudolph J. Vecoli, who would be my academic advisor in the history department. His first impression was that I appeared shy and reserved; I likely felt a bit insecure and overly impressed by the situation. But Vecoli and I became friends, and such relationships are essential to finding success in academe. I came to admire and respect Vecoli as a scholar, mentor, and friend, and still consider myself Vecoli's student. He once remarked about me: "Although he was always respectful and modest, I soon learned that in spite of the young Lovoll's formal demeanor he was a genial and gregarious person with a clever sense of humor. To his intellectual work, he brought a high degree of self-confidence, determination, and intellect."

Beginning in the 1960s, the rapid growth of the "new social history" replaced the theme of consensus dominant in American historiography in the immediate postwar era. Consensus historians primarily emphasized the stability—and therefore continuity—of the American experience over the centuries. Historian John Higham saw consensus history as engendered by postwar insecurities and an urge to define America and establish its distinctive character—the pursuit of national identity.

Social history became the new orthodoxy in historical writing, leading some consensus historians to feel marginalized. The principal interpretations of American history that had emerged in the 1950s were insupportable and, in Higham's words, had been "brushed aside." Vecoli greatly influenced the new social history and immigration and ethnic history. In 1964, then thirty-seven years old and assistant professor at Rutgers University, Vecoli published the article "*Contadini* in Chicago: A Critique of *The Uprooted*," which changed the field of immigration history in the United States. Vecoli takes exception to the immigration history classic and Pulitzer Prize–winning *The Uprooted* and challenged its author, Oscar Handlin, a distinguished Harvard historian who is credited with establishing the legitimacy of immigration history. Handlin writes within the assimilationist scholarly tradition, which Vecoli fundamentally argues against in his article, rejecting the notion that immigrants to the United States left their customs behind and sought to assimilate quickly into mainstream American society. Instead, the Italian *contadini*—peasant farmers— "clung tenaciously to their traditions and developed strategies to retain their heritage and resist pressures to embrace the American social and economic system."

My doctoral dissertation on the *bygdelag* and my later scholarly works owe much to Vecoli's perception of the immigrant experience, discussed in his graduate seminars and lectures. I pursued my studies at a hectic pace, with courses in historiography and historical method and lengthy interpretive papers and book reviews to submit. My fieldwork became a rewarding family enterprise as the summer of 1971 was totally devoted to visiting the *stevner*—reunions—of as many *bygdelag* as possible.

An American *bygdelag* is a society of immigrants from a particular settlement, group of settlements, or some general district, fjord, or valley in Norway and of their descendants in America. These societies manifested Norwegian regionalism on American soil and a deep consciousness of local origin. Peculiarity of speech—the multitude of dialects—most clearly set boundaries. When people used the same local vernacular, there was an immediate feeling of kinship; the nature of the home community in itself left an indelible imprint; every glen and peak and rushing waterfall held significance. Members of these groupings developed a deep attachment to and love of the Norwegian home community and its traditions.

Valdres Samband, formally organized in 1902, was the first society; thereafter came Telelaget and Hallinglaget, which became national organizations. By 1913, all national *bygdelag* had been organized— thirty-one in all. The movement spoke for retaining regional identity at a time when a common Norwegian American group feeling was apparent. Controversies arose between Norwegian urban civic and cultural groups, especially in Minneapolis and St. Paul, and the *bygdelag* with their largely rural membership. But national loyalty was not lost; members vigorously asserted their patriotism. Basically, the *bygdelag* sought recognition of their rural culture as equal to the national culture expressed in urban settings. Frequently the Lutheran clergy provided leadership, giving the movement a pious character. In his article on the *contadini*, Vecoli maintains that the Italian peasants had no patriotism for the Kingdom of Italy. Their strong attachment to their native village, termed *campanilismo*, suggested "that the world of the *contadini* was confined within the shadow cast by the town *campanile* [bell tower]." Members of the *bygdelag* might instead engage in arguing which local group was most genuinely Norwegian; a public debate on this issue took place between immigrants from Voss and Trøndelag, each group claiming to be the true Norwegian.

The annual reunions, or *stevner*, were the most important events; they functioned primarily to satisfy social needs. They re-created the home community in an idealized form; there was a feast with local food dishes and people in *bunad*. Some of the societies, like the Setesdalslag and the Hallinglag, had folk dance groups. My family and I toured the reunions. On June 5, we visited the Sognalag in Lodi, Wisconsin; on June 11, the Hardangerlag and Nordhordlandslag in Sioux

Falls, South Dakota; on June 12, the Møre og Romsdalslag in Monte-
video, Minnesota; on June 19, the Nordlandslag in Duluth, Minnesota; on June 26, the Hallinglag in Bemidji, Minnesota; and so it went
on. Audrey and Ronald patiently endured it all. At one of the *stevner,*
I told them that if they would sit and listen quietly, they could leave
when I talked. As soon as I was introduced, everyone to their good
amusement heard a boy's high-pitched voice, "Audrey, Dad is going
to speak; we can leave."

In my talks, I referred to the competitive spirit and pride of the
society I was visiting, as each *bygdelag* held glowing opinions about
their own Norwegian locality and the people who hailed from
there. I reviewed the movement's history. Early on, the *bygdelag*
reunions reflected the heyday of dialect use, but by the 1970s programs were conducted in English. I gathered interviews and distributed a questionnaire. My family and I made friends everywhere.
President Hertsgaard attended many of the meetings. In Valdres
Samband, I remember the warm welcome and assistance extended
by Carl and Amy Narvestad. I visited many individual *bygdelag* in the
years to come.

Much of the summer of 1971 was spent preparing for the comprehensive doctoral examination that would let me submit my dissertation.
Having successfully cleared that obstacle, I continued with my research and writing. In June 1973, following a most friendly defense
of my thesis, "A Study in Immigrant Regionalism: The Norwegian-
American *Bygdelag*," I was granted my doctoral degree in American
history with immigration as my field of specialization and a minor in
Scandinavian studies.[7]

OUR HOME IN NORTHFIELD

By then we were living in Northfield. In 1971, Lloyd Hustvedt, chair
of the department of Norwegian at St. Olaf College, offered me a
one-year teaching position, the idea being that I would then return
to the University of North Dakota. I commuted from Minneapolis, a
distance of some forty miles. Hustvedt taught Norwegian language

and literature and served as executive secretary for NAHA. He had been born and raised in Sogn Valley in Goodhue County, Minnesota, not far from Northfield. Even though it was his grandparents who had immigrated, his first language was Norwegian, and it continued to flavor his English. Sometime during that academic year, Hustvedt asked if I would consider accepting a tenure-track position. St. Olaf College, with its close connection to Norway, and NAHA, whose history now was quite familiar to me, had great appeal. I happily accepted, securing a promise that I would be able to offer courses in history in addition to Norwegian. Later, I also taught in the history department, and beginning the fall of 1992 only in that department.

In June 1972, a house on Linden Place in Northfield became the Lovoll family's new home. We already had many friends in the town known for the "Defeat of Jesse James" and made many more. Lloyd and Ester Hustvedt became our good friends, as did colleagues Olaf and Juta Millert, refugees from Estonia; their experience, so different from ours, broadened our insight into the postwar migration.

Shortly after we moved into our new home, Else's sister Torun, her husband Edvin, and their children Wenche and Erik arrived and spent some weeks with us. Then, for the first and only time, my parents, Alf and Astrid, paid us a visit. I had injured my back on moving day; by then I had had surgery for a ruptured disc. But I recovered sufficiently to show them around, and even accepted a dinner invitation from our Minneapolis friends Lois and Lawrence Hauge and drove to a fine restaurant some distance away. We enjoyed my parents' visit greatly and were sad to see them leave.

Audrey and Ronald enrolled at Sibley Elementary School. Northfield is a college town—home to Carleton College and St. Olaf College; the colleges have a positive educational influence on the public school system. Audrey showed an interest in music by taking piano lessons. Else found a job in the food service at Carleton College, offering a good supplement to my compensation at St. Olaf. Her added earnings had allowed us to invest in our new home.

Early mornings, I accompanied Else to work to prepare the breakfast meal—helping crack eggs to fill large containers—and then
returned home to get our children out of bed, prepare breakfast, and
take them to school. Occasionally, a speeding freight train hindered
me from crossing the tracks on my way to St. Olaf so that I was a
little late for my morning class. New faculty like myself were often
assigned early class periods, sparing the more established professors.
Still, it was a wonderful time for us all, with great prospects and a
sense of security.

In November 1974, the four of us were each "admitted as a citizen
of the United States" by the US District Court of Minnesota at a
ceremony in Minneapolis. We were likely the only Europeans, or
certainly the only Norwegians, among the hundred or more new
citizens. We rose to pledge allegiance to the United States and reject
all other national fealties. The judge also rose, and before completing
the ceremony said: "There is a Norwegian family seeking citizenship.
And in Norway people go to the polls and vote. Norwegians have a
lesson to teach us." We all raised our hands and made the ultimate
pledge and were declared to be US citizens. Our name was now officially registered as Lovoll.

We began taking annual trips to the North Shore of Lake Superior, where we most often stayed at Split Rock Cabins, with a view of
Split Rock Lighthouse. Ivar Aus and family had introduced us to the
allure and beauty of the North Shore; it remains our most appreciated summer destination. We spent time on the beach picking agates
and sometimes enjoying a picnic. We feasted on Superior herring
and other freshwater fish. Split Rock State Park had hiking trails to
explore, and there were places and small towns along the shore to
visit, with tourist shops and other attractions. Evenings ended with
a bonfire, fueled by wood the four of us had gathered—tree limbs,
branches, and other materials, mainly washed ashore as driftwood.
Norwegians, coming directly from Norway or from the fisheries of
New England and Lake Michigan, played an important role in developing commercial fisheries along Lake Superior's shore, extending
from Duluth to the international boundary at Pigeon River. The

elderly father of the owner of Split Rock Cabins, an immigrant from Nordland, was full of good stories from the fisheries in Norway and in America.

Else's mother, Anna Navekvien, traveled with my sister, Svanhild, the summer of 1974 to pay us a visit. We were delighted to show her where we lived and thrived. Coming from the hilly and mountainous west coast of Norway, she looked out over the flat Minnesota landscape and expressed in great wonderment: *"Ein må sjå det for å tru det"* (One has to see it to believe it). Nineteenth-century Norwegian migrants no doubt reacted the same way when they first viewed the seemingly infinite prairie scenery.

We took Anna and Svanhild on a tour to visit immigrants from Anna's home area. Marta and Per Heggedal had emigrated from Bryggja, Anna's and Else's community, in 1950. At the time of Anna's visit, they lived on their farm in Roseau County in northern Minnesota; Badger was the small town where they shopped. We discovered that the American-born owner of the grocery store was fluent in Norwegian. Marta and Per visited Norway regularly. Per was accused of telling *en amerikaskrøne*—an America fib—when he related that his fields were so large that he had to hire a plane to spread fertilizer. People on the small and steep Heggedal-farm back home in Norway could not imagine it. But there it was when we visited: a small plane flying as close to the ground as possible, fertilizing the field.

In my work as a historian, I have consistently accepted the premise that if you have a person, you have a story. Sigurd Lovold is a case in point. We visited him in the small town of Center in western North Dakota, a region of the state with heavy German settlement. We shared his name, derived from farms in Åheim in southern Sunnmøre, but we were not related. Sigurd had called us when we lived in Grand Forks, and he and his wife, Dorothy, born Woehler, had visited us and we had reciprocated. Dorothy was of German heritage and had learned German growing up, but upon marrying Sigurd, she took on a Norwegian identity, wore a *bunad,* joined Norwegian American societies, and took part in Norwegian American events. In my research, I regularly met non-Norwegian women who adopted

The North Shore: a place close to the Lovoll family's heart.
TOP LEFT. The family's first visit, Gooseberry Falls, 1971
BOTTOM LEFT. Helge, Audrey, Kristian, and Martin visit from Norway, 1996
TOP RIGHT. Margit, Else, and Ronald, 2003
BOTTOM RIGHT. Else and Odd, 1999
Photos by Hans Magnus Aus, Odd Lovoll, and Ronald Lovoll

their Norwegian husband's ethnicity and often became more Norwegian than him. Deciding to be ethnic or not, as well as which ethnicity, is an individual choice. Marriage remains a significant avenue for "converting" to a new ethnic culture. Because of the vibrancy of Norwegian American ethnicity, its open ethnic boundaries, and its welcoming invitation to join a Norwegian fellowship, many people of different ethnic backgrounds or whose ethnic origin is not clear or celebrated become active members. In *The Promise Fulfilled*, I categorize an ethnicity that regularly attracts converts or recruits as an *enlisting ethnicity*. Dorothy is a good example of a convert, or even a recruit, by marriage.

When only seventeen in 1925, Sigurd answered pleas from his aunt and uncle to come to America to help on the farm in Oliver County, North Dakota; Center was the county seat. Sigurd related the following: "When we were kids, all the stories were about Americans. People who had immigrated to the States and were back to visit gushed about the easy life compared with that in Norway. For young boys, there was one thought: 'If only I could go to America.'" Sigurd sailed into New York harbor and saw the Statue of Liberty; he was processed through Ellis Island. Norwegians he encountered at the railroad station helped him make it to North Dakota and his uncle's farm in four days. After about six months, his uncle died, bringing Sigurd new responsibility. Sigurd attended the local one-room schoolhouse to learn English and also to learn about the new country. He stayed on with his aunt and eventually bought the farm: "We had one person who could talk Norwegian, teaching me how to farm for two weeks. And then I was on my own." He persevered and in 1944 married Dorothy. They raised their four children on the farm. He made his first trip back to Norway in 1948, after twenty-three years in America.[8]

THE SESQUICENTENNIAL OF NORWEGIAN IMMIGRATION

In 1925, Norwegian Americans celebrated the centennial of the first Norwegian group immigration, the dramatic voyage of the sloop

Restauration in 1825. The festivities lasted from June 6 to 9; in Minnesota, the main celebration took place on the fairgrounds between Minneapolis and St. Paul. Reverend John Atwater and his sister Jane, children of the "sloop baby," Margaret Allen Larsen, born during the Atlantic crossing, spoke to the gathering. President Calvin Coolidge attended to honor the Norwegians' festival, lending prestige to the undertaking and attracting great interest. The grand celebration was a magnificent expression of Norwegian ethnicity, and it was long recalled and spoken of by those who took part. I interviewed participants like American-born O. I. Hertsgaard and Norwegian-born Thor Ohme, who both expressed their pride as Norwegian Americans in the event.

Fifty years later, in 1975, the sesquicentennial of Norwegian immigration became another great ethnic moment in history, celebrated both in Norway and widely in the United States. Planning began as early as 1971; I was just one representative of the Norwegian American community to serve on the board of directors of the sesquicentennial association.

Syttende mai, May 17, Constitution Day, was the logical official opening of the celebration in Norway. The immigrant anniversary was marked in many parts of the country, including an official ceremony at the Cleng Peerson monument in Tysvær, Peerson's birthplace, honoring him as "the father of Norwegian immigration." A simultaneous ceremony was held at Peerson's grave in Norse, Texas. The central point in celebrating the 150th anniversary of Norwegian immigration in Norway took place in Stavanger on July 4, commemorating the departure on July 4, 1825, of the tiny vessel *Restauration*, carrying fifty-two Norwegians bound for America. King Olav V and other Norwegian and American dignitaries attended. In fact, many noted American guests were on hand: the Minnesota delegation included Senator (and soon vice president) Walter Mondale, Senator Hubert Humphrey, and Congressman Albert Quie. Fredrik Schoitz, earlier president of the American Lutheran Church, gave the sermon at the Divine Service in the Stavanger Cathedral. The many sesquicentennial observances showed Norway as a nation of emigrants with strong historical ties to America; the anniversary was thought provoking for Norwegians on both sides of the Atlantic.

The main events in the United States were in the month of October to commemorate *Restauration*'s arrival in New York on October 9 after an adventurous voyage of fourteen weeks. Local committees arranged celebrations nationwide, from Los Angeles, San Francisco, and Seattle on the Pacific Coast to New York on the Atlantic; a memorial plaque was placed where *Restauration* was assumed to have docked. There were commemorations in the Fox River valley, where most of the Sloopers settled in the mid-1830s. Chicago and Minneapolis joined the many cities and towns in extensive celebratory arrangements.

King Olav and the royal party arrived in New York on October 5 and departed from Anchorage, Alaska, on October 28. Following a visit to President Gerald Ford, King Olav spent three days in Minneapolis. A hectic and strenuous agenda filled His Majesty's sojourn. Else and I attended a number of the scheduled events. On Sunday, October 12, he was welcomed by Pastor Harry Cleven to a Norwegian service in Mindekirken. Later the same day, the royal party attended an event titled "Salute to Heritage" in the Minneapolis Auditorium. Norwegian explorer of *Kon Tiki* fame Thor Heyerdahl gave a long keynote address. His Majesty, sitting behind him, seemed to doze from time to time.

After Minneapolis, the king and party moved on to St. Olaf College in Northfield; their next appearance was at Vesterheim, the Norwegian-American Museum in Decorah, Iowa. Next in line was Chicago, then on to the Pacific Coast and Anchorage, Alaska, and from there homeward over the North Pole. In a gracious letter dated at the palace in Oslo, November 7, 1975, King Olav expressed his pleasure at the pride Americans of Norwegian ancestry had in their US citizenship and the high esteem in which they held their Norwegian heritage.

I had written a summary of Norwegian immigration and the plans for the sesquicentennial celebration for the Minneapolis anniversary commission. My study of the *bygdelag* movement, titled *A Folk Epic: The* Bygdelag *in America*, was released in 1975 as an official sesquicentennial publication. I also participated in the international conference "Norwegian Influence on the Upper Midwest," at the University of Minnesota, Duluth, May 22–24, 1975. Leading scholars including Rudolph Vecoli, Ingrid Semmingsen, Einar Haugen, and Lloyd Hustvedt gave insightful presentations about immigration and ethnicity. Vecoli reminded us that 1975 marked the beginning of the bicentennial of the American Revolution.

Professor Carl Chrislock, on the faculty of Augsburg College (now University) in Minneapolis and an authority on the progressive movement in Minnesota, gave an inspiring paper on "The Norwegian-American Impact on Minnesota: How Far 'Left-of-Center.'" Over the years we had become good friends. We decided to mark the 150th anniversary by offering evening courses on Norwegian immigration during the 1975 fall semester at Augsburg and St. Olaf. On Tuesday evenings I would join Chrislock at Augsburg for a three-hour class, and on Thursday evenings he would reciprocate and come to St. Olaf. The course, open to the public and including guest lecturers, became a great success at both institutions.

The year 1975 was the ninth anniversary of the Lovoll family's move to a new country, and we had become American citizens. America was our home. For nearly a decade, Else, Audrey, Ronald, and I had shared the experience of many immigrants who had chosen a life away from the ancestral homeland.[9]

CHAPTER 6

Family and Career

IN MY PROFESSIONAL LIFE, as a published historian, I am some-what of a late bloomer. I was abetted by family and scholarly friends who strongly encouraged me to pursue my academic interests. My experience with life's hopes, challenges, and accomplishments—and its misfortunes and sorrows—might have played a role in my scholarly career and my drive to fathom the human dimensions of life as an immigrant. It began as a journey of self-discovery. Reviewers of my scholarly publications frequently point out my life experience—stand-ing with one foot in Norway and one in America—which has given me a unique understanding of and familiarity with the history, culture, and social dynamics of both nations: two homelands.

The publication of *A Folk Epic* in 1975, when I still was only a young forty-year-old, initiated productive scholarly decades in my career, lasting until the present time. There were changes in my family as Audrey and Ronald moved from childhood to being adults with new interests and relationships. There was also the passing of parents, of my precious wife Else, and of friends and mentors who had played an important part in my life.

A YEAR IN THE HOMELAND

St. Olaf College offers merited sabbatical leaves. I was granted one for the academic year 1977–78. After much consideration, Else and I decided that a year in Norway would foster family relations for Audrey and Ronald, most especially with their grandparents. Audrey was seventeen and Ronald fourteen. And now I was subjecting them to the same situation Svanhild and I had faced in our teens. In hindsight, considering the challenging adjustments for Audrey and Ronald after growing up in America, and the extra responsibilities placed on Else, a summer sojourn rather than a year would have been more sensible.

We landed in Oslo on Sunday, July 3, 1977. We visited family and explored places like Bygdøy and the Viking ships before arriving in Volda, where we moved in with my parents. Ronald was only four when we had left for America, and thus his experience in returning to Norway was largely that of a second-generation Norwegian American. He was interested in Norway and grateful for a book received from his grandparents, but Norway was an unfamiliar place. At fourteen, he recorded his impressions. Below a photo of Volda, he mused: "This is where we are probably going to spend most of the year. Volda is about the size of Northfield but growing fast. About the only way of getting someplace is to go on the Folkestad ferry. It's a little weird, but you get used to it."

Transportation was essential, and in early August Ronald accompanied me to Drammen to pick up a French-made Simca. Unaccustomed to a manual gear shift, I struggled and made mistakes. My loyal son sat beside me and made reassuring and comforting comments: "You are doing great, Dad." We enjoyed the couple-day drive back to Volda.

Audrey and Ronald underwent a new challenge when they began school, Audrey in gymnas and Ronald in the middle school. Having both spent the most decisive years of their lives growing up in America, they had to adjust to unfamiliar surroundings and circumstances. Ronald claimed he felt like he had been shut out of the world since there was no news from where he had grown up. Audrey recalled Norwegian, but neither she nor Ronald had learned to write it and were of course not aware of its two official forms. Audrey was allowed to use English and did well. She told of an incident when examined in English: asked what an unmarried woman is called, Audrey answered "bachelorette" but was immediately told that the correct answer was "spinster." Audrey responded that she would never use that word because it was degrading. She otherwise thought school went fine, and she made many new friends, even becoming popular as "the new girl in town."

The situation for Ronald was different. He had an unhappy school year. He was overweight and American. During recess, schoolmates regularly taunted and bullied him, and even pushed him up against the wall. As he recalls, teachers stood by and did not seem to care. He and a girl from Iceland, the two foreign students, were regularly excused from class and waited together in an empty room for what

Fishing in the shallow Kilsfjorden off from Voldsfjorden. Grandpa Alf instructed Ronald to drop the line all the way to the bottom and then lift it up and down to catch *småtorsk* (small cod).

would be done next. When the teachers could not think of anything for them to do, they were sent home. The faculty had much to learn about accepting students from different cultures. Some of the instructors had been my colleagues ten years earlier, and I found their behavior disappointing. Ronald mentioned one exception, Torstein Tomassen, who did his best to help him and even addressed him in English, something he appreciated greatly.

Ronald spent much time with his grandparents, especially Alf, and even joined him to set fishing nets in the fjord in the evening and harvest the fish the next morning. I was often in Oslo doing research and thus left much of the responsibility of caring for two teenagers, and navigating life with parents-in-law, to Else. I commuted back to Volda regularly, and my family also joined me in Oslo, Else at times alone, traveling by small plane or by rail. Their visit before Christmas 1977 was memorable, as Ronald related: "In Oslo, we (me and dad) went to a show called Rocky Horror Show, which was pretty weird but fun. We also went to the Holmenkollen Ski Jump. . . . On the way home in our car we got into some slippery roads so we had to drive very slow, but we finally got back to Volda and were going to celebrate Christmas in four days."

In the spring semester, I was invited to give twelve double lectures on US history at the University of Oslo. Ingrid Semmingsen and I jointly conducted a graduate seminar. We engaged in long and foundational discussions about how to teach the history of immigration and settlement. Having two instructors at all times must have been a unique experience for the students. And a few times they must have enjoyed seeing me and Semmingsen not in total agreement on the process of immigrant acculturation.

The pattern of visits continued. I would make it to Volda regularly, and my family would join me in Oslo. One stay included a theater performance at Det norske teater (the Norwegian theater) on our twentieth wedding anniversary, March 30, for the Johann Strauss play "An der Schönen Blauen Donau" translated into New Norse. Ronald wrote: "It was pretty nice but a little hard to understand."

Toward the end of our stay, Ronald, then fifteen, had lost weight and felt he was being accepted by his schoolmates; as he said, "girls began showing interest in me." Audrey, as young as she was, had met Helge Syversen, a student at the local college who in time would become her husband. He was from Moss, and Audrey had visited with his parents, Else and Gunnar Syversen, when in Oslo.

Before returning to the United States, we joined the Brunæs family, Edvin, Torun, Wenche, and Erik, on a monthlong camping tour of Europe. Ronald saved postcards that document a most educational and exciting journey through the continent, with stops in places like Bremen, Paris, Venice, Cologne, and Hamburg. It was a memorable concluding activity before returning to our home in Northfield.

We landed in Minneapolis on July 29; Kenneth Bjork met us at the airport. Seeing the freeways from the air, Ronald said he felt at home, and even more so that night when he fell asleep to thunderstorms and tornado warnings. We were all glad to be back in Minnesota.

The kids were in high school: Audrey a senior and Ronald a freshman. He had lost a year in Norway and struggled to keep up, making me question the wisdom of spending so much time away from home. Helge arrived at Christmas, and he and Audrey became engaged. Else and I were fond of our son-in-law-to-be even though we felt our daughter was a bit young to make a lifelong commitment. At the end of May 1979, I accompanied Audrey to her new life in Norway. I spent time with Audrey and Helge; we welcomed my father's cousin Arthur Lowell and his wife, Suzanne, to Oslo and accompanied them on a tour of attractions. Saying good-bye and leaving Audrey behind was heart-rending.

Audrey would enter *handelsskolen* (the business school) in Volda to better master the Norwegian language and to learn occupational skills. Like her mother, Audrey faced challenges directly. In mid-June 1981, Else, Ronald, and I left for Norway for Audrey and Helge's wedding. Else had planned the reception at the Tourist Hotel in Volda before leaving Northfield. On June 27, the day after Audrey's twenty-first birthday, I escorted my daughter up the long aisle in the same church where Else and I had been married some twenty-three years earlier. As Audrey and Helge were pronounced husband and wife, it was a truly memorable occasion celebrated by two emotional families. A rewarding future lay ahead.[1]

THE NORWEGIAN-AMERICAN
HISTORICAL ASSOCIATION

In my scholarly career, no organization has held greater significance for me than the Norwegian-American Historical Association. NAHA gave me an opportunity and incentive to pursue my enthusiasm for immigration history, particularly the Norwegian and Norwegian American story. My support of and pride in the association dates from the late 1960s and grew even stronger with my direct involvement in its mission.

The Norse-American Centennial in 1925, celebrating the Slooper anniversary, inspired the organization of the Norwegian-American Historical Association; a group of people convened at St. Olaf College on October 6, 1925, and successfully launched NAHA. As publications editor, Theodore C. Blegen became the dominant force in the new learned society. The association intended to collect and write the history of Norwegian Americans free from church influence and from exaggerated piety toward the immigrant forebears. Its archives would be at St. Olaf College. The association was headed by professional historians to assure a high scholarly and artistic level. It was the first completely professional historical society founded by any immigrant group. The founders were motivated by the immigrants' desire to be accepted as an integral part of American society and history. All publications would be in the English language, which disappointed some members.

A breakthrough in the study of immigrant cultures began in the 1920s. In 1927, Marcus Lee Hansen, of mixed Danish and Norwegian background, published "Immigration as a Field for Historical Research"; the article makes a meaningful investigation of migration acceptable as scholarly subject matter. It establishes Hansen as "the father of modern historical scholarship in migration." He served on NAHA's board of editors. The association's financial support originated in Chicago. Stavanger-born investment banker Birger Osland, treasurer from 1930 to 1951 and one of the incorporators, donated most generously and often; he had a high sense of stewardship of the association's resources. The funding assured a regular publication program.

Kenneth Bjork succeeded Blegen as publications editor in 1960. Early on in my working relationship and lifelong friendship with Bjork, he considered me his logical successor in the editorship. We were asked to write the association's fifty-year history in 1975. When an automobile accident injured Kenneth and killed his wife, Thora, I wrote a draft alone. As we edited and revised it jointly, our sessions became pleasant considerations of the association's history and of the editor's responsibilities. My official tenure as the association's third editor began on May 15, 1980. On May 30 at a well-attended dinner in Minneapolis, I presented Bjork a volume in his honor that contained essays by prominent Norwegian American scholars. I chronicled him as a teacher, scholar, and friend.

The association enjoyed a remarkable reputation as a learned society. It had set high standards of selection and editorial work. My role in the editorial post thus presented a formidable challenge. As the many demands associated with the editorship became a reality, Else was always there to reassure me that it all would work out well. Highly qualified and dedicated scholars—all my trusted friends—serving on the board of publications were there to assist as well. And Mary Hove, with degrees from Smith College and Johns Hopkins University, became my editorial assistant. Much later, in her nineties, Mary described assisting me in the editing process: "When I first started, Odd may have been a little bit unfamiliar with me. He may have had some doubt about my ability. That ended very soon. I asked a lot of questions and if I didn't ask, it was that I already knew the answer. He knew that I knew what I was doing right away. The material was interesting and we worked on over 30 manuscripts.

I kept most of the books we worked on together. I would best de-
scribe Odd as a collaborator and an extremely pleasant colleague
and friend."

During the more than twenty years of my tenure, thirty-two titles
were distributed to the association's membership, about one-third
of all individual publications up to the present time. J. R. Christianson, research professor of history at Luther College and member
of NAHA's publications board, observed: "The Golden Age of the
Norwegian-American Historical Association's long and distinguished
history came in the two decades when Odd Sverre Lovoll was not
only its editor but also its most productive and respected author.
Few scholars have dealt with ethnicity in a multicultural society with
more insight."

I devoted much time and energy alongside a full-time teaching
and advising schedule to assure the continued high quality of publications and to increase the annual output. In my efforts, I stood on
the shoulders of my predecessors and enjoyed broad support from an
appreciative membership, the executive board, the board of publications, and, among many others, executive secretary Lloyd Hustvedt.
Mary Hove was indispensable in the preparation of publishable manuscripts. For one volume, when Mary had surgery and was hospitalized, my friend Debbie L. Miller at the Minnesota Historical Society
stepped in to assist in the editorial process.

Seven substantial volumes of *Norwegian-American Studies* appeared
during my editorship. One significant mission of the series related
to expanding the field of immigration history by attracting young
scholars in the early phase of their careers, though established scholars were not in any way neglected. Seven of the twelve essays in
volume 29, published in 1983, were based on Norwegian master's theses or community studies; all are devoted to the Norwegian background. Clarence Clausen faithfully translated the submissions in
Norwegian. The lead article is by Ingrid Semmingsen; she discusses
the emigrants of 1825 and their contacts with German pietists in Norway and America.

Countering criticism that NAHA was primarily a midwestern historical society, I made evident in volume 30, published in 1985, "the rich opportunity for scholarly research that Norwegian settlement in the Far West provides." Professor Terje I. Leiren, University of Washington and board member, helped to plan the volume and solicited articles from West Coast authors.

Volume 31 in 1986 was intended to provide a better balance by giving increased attention to the urban environment. In the lead article, John Higham reviews the scholarly debate about the immigrant impact on urban America. Volume 32 in 1989 pursues the immigration story on both sides of the Atlantic, with a number of Norwegian contributors. It is dedicated to the memory of Carlton C. Qualey; at the time of his death at age eighty-three in March 1988, he had served on the publications board for fifty-five years.

Volume 33 appeared in 1992—the quincentenary of Columbus's voyage of discovery. Arlow Andersen recounts the editorial opinions of the commemoration in 1892 by the Norwegian American press and found that Columbus was given his due. Volume 34 in 1995 is dedicated to the memory of Einar Haugen (1906–94) and Ingrid Semmingsen (1910–95) "in gratitude for their pioneering scholarly contributions." In the lead article, J. R. Christianson convincingly argues the important influence of Thorstein Veblen's family and his Norwegian background in his criticism of capitalism and his idea of conspicuous consumption.

The year 2000 marked the seventy-fifth anniversary of the association's founding and the 175th anniversary of the beginning of Norwegian immigration to the United States. Studies volume 35 commemorates these two historical events and recognizes those who provided editorial leadership and, as I conclude in the preface, "established the high standards of selection, writing, and editing that have won acclaim from an international community of scholars and the loyal support of a faithful membership from all walks of life."

A brief review of the Studies series suggests the scope and variety of the association's publication program. But during my time at the helm, twenty-five books also saw print, mainly monographs but also a few translated works. Manuscripts were submitted to the publications board and to me as editor to evaluate and accept or reject. In my reports to the executive board, I made a point of suggesting topics; soon I became responsible for convincing qualified scholars to do the work. I enjoyed negotiating with printers, mostly in the Twin Cities, but also in Iowa. The final act on my part was "to put the manuscript to bed" by declaring that it could go to production. Sometimes I watched the books rolling out after being bound. On my way home, I usually stopped to call Else and let her know that we had another volume ready—a gratifying moment.

Norwegian-born politician Knute Nelson (1842–1923) had long been on my list of desired subjects for NAHA's biographical series. Nelson was the first Scandinavian American politician to attain national prominence, as congressman, as governor of the state of Minnesota, and as US senator. In 1987, I invited Millard L. Gieske, professor of political science at the University of Minnesota, Morris campus, to prepare a biography of Nelson. His doctoral dissertation in political science dealt with Nelson's politics from 1912 to 1920. He began work on the biography the summer of 1988, with grant-funded visits in the fall to Voss and to Nelson's birthplace, Evanger, in western Norway. In his investigations, Gieske had as his research assistant Jostein Molde, who earlier had assisted me. Despite failing health, at the time of his death from leukemia in January 1991, Gieske left an impressive first draft of six hundred pages. His widow, Emily Gieske, graciously gave me permission to bring the manuscript to completion and have it published. In the summer of 1991, Steven J. Keillor agreed to take on the project; he brought dedication, expertise, and talent to the task. *Norwegian Yankee: Knute Nelson and the Failure of American Politics, 1860–1923,* saw print in 1995. In the preface, Keillor wrote: "I never had the privilege of meeting Millard L. Gieske, yet we have co-authored a book!" The genesis of the biography extended over a number of years, which was not all that extraordinary. Each publication has a story, from its inception to its distribution to the association's members.[2]

DET LØFTERIKE LANDET/THE PROMISE OF AMERICA

My next large scholarly work dates to the Symposium on Modern Norway at St. Olaf College in April 1980, with Erik Rudeng, Oslo University Press, giving the keynote address. He invited me to consider preparing a history of the Norwegian American experience. During the family's year in Norway, 1977–78, I had spent much time looking at the story of Norwegian immigration, hoping eventually to publish a treatise based on my research. Rudeng's suggestion was consequently most welcome. First, I needed to raise funds for a year's leave from my academic position. I applied to the Minnesota Historical Society and attended an open meeting in New Ulm on June 27, 1980. I think back on that rainy day when Else and I drove the seventy-five miles from Northfield. Russell W. Fridley, a tireless historian and the longtime director of the historical society, and the grant committee had a number of queries about the project as I stood before them. Fridley's strong support convinced the committee members to vote unanimously to award me the grant. St. Olaf College approved a leave of absence for the 1981–82 academic year. The assembled funds did not match my salary, however. On August 31, 1981, I noted on my calendar, a bit concerned, "Last salary at St. Olaf."

The goal, as assigned, was to write a Norwegian American history in the sphere of popular scholarship, one that would appeal to a general as well as an academic readership. The published work would include a substantial bibliography. My main sources consisted of published studies and were available at St. Olaf College's well-stocked library and in the library at the University of Minnesota; primary source material informed later revised editions, both Norwegian and American. Aside from research excursions to Seattle and Chicago, my work was largely confined to my office on campus. January 1982 was spent in Oslo to consult with Laila Stange, my main editor at the press.

Det løfterike landet (The Land Rich in Promises) required much reflection and contemplation to determine how I would best present and interpret Norwegian American history to give an accurate account to people in Norway. From the foreword: "Norwegian American history is interpreted as an independent historical process. . . . Identity, culture, and social life were formed by forces within the Norwegian American population itself and by the expectations from and interaction with an ethnically pluralistic America. Norwegians were, in other words, active participants in giving shape to the society to which they belonged." I reminded my readers that "the homeland's move toward modernization must not become the norm against which Norwegian American cultural developments are judged."

The book was launched at a large press conference at Grand Hotel in Oslo on August 9, 1983. The numerous newspaper reviews, all praising the book, were quite overwhelming, as was seeing it featured in bookstores throughout the city. I like to think that it met a need in the Norwegian people to connect with "the emigrated Norway," as some reviewers referred to the Norwegian American community. The following day *Aftenposten* had two separate reviews. Under the heading "Magnificent about Norwegian America," Steinar Wiik, on the editorial staff, wrote: "As a first generation Norwegian American and moreover historian at St. Olaf College, Odd S. Lovoll possesses the best qualifications to write a nearly definitive account about Norwegian emigrants. He does this with a love that is temperate in its profile—and at the same time exceedingly exciting to read."

I was by then occupied in rendering an English translation. An agreement between Oslo University Press and the University of Minnesota Press called for publication the spring of 1984. *The Promise of America* came off the press May 15; on June 10, NAHA president Lawrence Hauge hosted a book reception in his large residence in the wealthy suburb of Edina, southwest of Minneapolis. As with the Norwegian edition, the history of the Norwegian American people was warmly received and gained a large readership. A Lutheran pastor who had experienced the turmoil and dissent within Norwegian American Lutheranism wrote to commend me for my objective treatment of the many conflicts. In a review, noted immigration scholar John Higham made a special point of the illustrations, especially the group photos: "These powerful group portraits, so immediate yet so remote,

The imaginative poster advertising the "Promise of America" /
"Reisen til Amerika" exhibition at the Henie-Onstad Art Center
Courtesy NAHA

so flatly declarative yet so elusive, add a touch of wonder to the story Mr. Lovoll has insightfully, and authoritatively assembled."

The Promise of America inspired *Aftenposten* and Oslo University Press to collaborate on an exhibition that "throws light upon Norwegian Emigration to the United States from 1860 until today" at the Henie-Onstad Art Center at Høvikodden, south of Oslo. Erik Rudeng was again the driving force behind the exhibition. "Reisen til Amerika" (The Journey to America) was formally opened by His Majesty King Olav V on June 23, 1984; dignitaries from Norway and the United States added luster to the occasion. *The Promise of America/Reisen til Amerika* was considered one of the most popular exhibitions organized in Norway. On June 29, I addressed a seminar on Norwegian immigration at the art center. After closing on September 16, the exhibit toured to several cities in Norway and the United States. The Minnesota Historical Society in St. Paul displayed *The Promise of America* exhibition from June 1985 until June 1986. The summer of 1986, the exhibition traveled to Ellis Island, where it became a part of the Statue of Liberty Centennial.[3]

A CENTURY OF URBAN LIFE

A sabbatical leave was approaching, and I had a new project in mind. As early as 1975, when I wrote NAHA's history, I harbored the following concern: "If we have given inadequate attention to the rural community, our neglect of the city has been even greater. Where are the students of urban life, trained in sociology as well as history, who could give comprehensive treatment to the Norwegians in such vital centers as Minneapolis, Chicago, Greater New York, San Francisco, and Seattle?" Chicago Norwegians played a significant role in the association's founding; thus, a history of the Norwegians in Chicago was one of its early undertakings, announced in the Chicago newspaper *Skandinaven* on April 28, 1928. The initial project had failed, and by 1985 the study was long overdue.

In applying for a leave, I stressed that a work on the Norwegian urban experience as expressed in Chicago would serve to correct a strong rural bias in the historiography of the Norwegian American population. *A Century of Urban Life: The Norwegians in Chicago before 1930*, published in June 1988, became the first scholarly historical study of Norwegian Americans in urban settings. My leave for 1985–86 was granted; later in the academic year, Lloyd Hustvedt asked St. Olaf College to extend my leave for a second year, and the extension was approved by dean Keith O. Anderson. Thanks to St. Olaf's liberal sabbatical leave policy, I would have two years, 1985 to 1987, in which to complete a demanding and ambitious research and writing project.

By the end of the decade of the 1920s, Norwegians in Chicago—counting only the first and second generations—numbered some fifty-six thousand, and Chicago could, according to the newspaper *Scandia*, be seen as "the third largest Norwegian city in the world," after Oslo and Bergen. Beginnings were modest—but early. Chicago was a frontier community when the first Norwegians arrived in the mid-1830s. The Norwegian colony became the third permanent Norwegian settlement in America, after that in Kendall and one in the Fox River valley.

The pioneer Norwegian emigration was basically a rural-to-rural movement. But Chicago was the gateway and port of entry for most immigrants to the Northwest. An urban colony had its genesis in 1836 when a few families decided to remain in Chicago rather than continue on to the Fox River settlement. Among these was a family from Voss, Nils Knutson Røthe, his wife, Torbjørg, and their three children—the first of many Chicago immigrants from the region. The resident Vossings recruited people from home; by 1840, there were more Vossings in Chicago than all other Norwegians taken together. They were referred to as "Vosseringen" (the Voss Circle) and played an important role in the early history of the Norwegian enclave.

The rural-to-urban movement persisted until the 1850s, when there was a sudden surge of emigration overseas from some of Norway's cities—an urban-to-urban migration—especially from the capital Christiania (Oslo); among the immigrants were many craftsmen and artisans. The year 1848 had seen the frontier pass beyond Chicago, which was on its way to becoming the great central city of the continent.

The Norwegian immigrant community grew with and adjusted to shifting demands; the immigrants formed their own neighborhoods and prospered. The first arrivals lived close together in an unhealthy area known as "The Sands," just north of the Chicago River where it emptied into Lake Michigan. They moved across the North Branch of the Chicago River, and in the 1850s Norwegians increasingly congregated around Milwaukee Avenue and Kinzie Street. By 1860 Norwegians numbered 1,313. They continued to trek northwestward and were replaced by other ethnic groups. The more prosperous Norwegians resided in the fashionable Wicker Park neighborhood. Because of early settlement and rapid economic growth, class distinctions among Norwegians were more evident in Chicago than in any other American urban environment. None of the pioneer immigrants attained the prominence of Ivar Larson Bøe from Voss, who became Iver Lawson and realized wealth through speculation in property.

The district described by *Scandia* as "Little Norway," located in the Logan Square community north of Humboldt Park, would be the last colony before Norwegians dispersed to the suburbs. Together with Wicker Park it formed a large contiguous Norwegian area. North Avenue, along the northern edge of the park, was a major commercial thoroughfare referred to as Karl Johan—Oslo's main street. People promenaded on North Avenue, Saturday being an especially lively time. There were Norwegian saloons, restaurants, and religious groups, such as the Salvation Army. Within Little Norway were churches, and not only Lutheran; Methodist and Baptist congregations existed alongside the Lutheran gatherings. In the city, the Lutheran church competed more directly with temporal interests and adverse social conditions. In the 1920s, Norwegian ethnicity was on parade as celebratory public activities and organizational life flourished. The double purpose might have been to convince the American-born to take pride in their heritage and to make a Norwegian presence visible to Americans of all nationalities.

Understanding the complexity of ethnic life through the decades in Chicago—a city that had experienced a nearly explosive growth from its founding—would require comprehensive research. Modern Chicago took shape in the 1920s, and by 1930 the city's population was approaching 3.4 million.

As one ethnic group replaced another, Little Norway had by the 1980s become a Spanish-speaking Mexican enclave. There were still a few Norwegians in Logan Square, and the Norwegian Lutheran Memorial Church was active, and still is. Funding for my leave and research came from many quarters, and I received wholehearted assistance from many people; only a few can be mentioned here. Helen Fletre, widow of Norwegian-born painter and sculptor Lars Fletre, entered into the project with great enthusiasm. Her home in the Logan Square community was frequently my residence and main headquarters. There was also a Chicago History Committee with many helping hands; its chairman, Rolf H. Erickson, longtime comrade and friend, opened his home to me. In addition, I had two salaried and talented research assistants: Jostein Molde, a Norwegian graduate student at the University of Trondheim who with great discipline read files of Norwegian American newspapers, and Kay J. Carr, a graduate student at the University of Chicago who patiently worked through tedious census manuscripts.

Throughout the two-year research period, I regularly drove to Chicago to spend one to two weeks or more there. Much of my time was devoted to research at the Chicago Historical Society, but also at other archives and libraries, churches, hospitals, nursing homes, and other institutions and societies. Back home in Northfield, Else showed great interest in the project and in my safety as I drove the seven to eight hours each direction, sometimes in winter conditions. She accompanied me on research excursions outside Chicago, such as at the American Lutheran Church archives at Wartburg Seminary in Dubuque, Iowa. Else also took it upon herself, at times assisted by Molde, to prepare maps of the Norwegian neighborhoods in Chicago, later to be professionally drawn by a cartographer.

On July 22, 1988, we both went to Chicago, this time by plane, to attend a reception for the release of *A Century of Urban Life*; we had a great time when Else became my guide in the Logan Square community. She knew the area well even though it was her first visit. During the time given to research and writing, my consistently supportive wife not only prepared the drafts of the maps but engaged in evening discourses about what I had uncovered, people I had met, and how I would interpret it in a historical narrative. Else had a great instinct about human nature and made observations that were most helpful in my own analysis. In 1989, the Illinois State Historical Society gave my Chicago history the Award of Superior Achievement.[4]

MY PARENTS

During the years devoted to *A Century of Urban Life*, there were joyous, but also heartrending, events, situations, and changes. We were an international family, and travels back and forth across the Atlantic became commonplace. In October 1985, my mother called to let me know that my father was very ill. I got on a plane to Norway three days later and made it to Volda soon after. I stayed for a few weeks before returning to America. I spent much time at my father's bedside in the hospital and otherwise comforting my mother at her home and visiting relatives. Ronald and I returned to Norway in April; Svanhild accompanied us to Volda. Alf had been moved to a nursing home, and there was a warm reunion with Ronald. Svanhild had by then moved to Halden, and she joined Ronald in visiting Audrey and Helge in Moss while I attended a conference at Voss where I spoke about Vosseringen in Chicago and its influence on emigration from that district.

On April 23, I met Audrey and Ronald in Oslo—a memorable day. After Audrey moved to Norway, I had not had the privilege of spending a full day together with both of them.

The month before, King Olav V had bestowed the Knight's Cross of the Royal Norwegian Order of Merit for my work on Norwegian immigration, and the Norwegian consul general in Minneapolis made arrangements for an audience with His Majesty to pledge my loyalty to him as the grand master. Audrey, Ronald, and I entered the royal palace and waited in a reception room until a palace employee bowed deeply to me and asked me to accompany him to the second level. I was given instructions on how to act in the king's presence. The doors to his quarters opened, and I took three steps and bowed, and then repeated the action while King Olav stood at attention. He motioned to me to be seated. His Majesty asked all the questions, and when he learned that I had just been in Voss, his comment was: "Do you understand the Vossings? I cannot understand a word they say." His Majesty was also interested in my work as a historian. After fifteen minutes, King Olav rose and thanked me for my visit as the double doors opened and I backed out of the royal chamber, stopping twice to bow to express my gratitude. It was quite an experience.

Audrey and Ronald waited as I descended the stairs and were clearly proud of their father. We stopped at an outdoor restaurant to review the day's events and refresh ourselves. One little incident deserves to be recorded. Ronald did not wish to be seen as a tourist, so when the friendly waitress asked in English what he would like to drink, he responded in the heavy Sunnmøre dialect he had picked up the year in Norway: *"Ei skal ha ein øl"* (I want a beer). Then he conversed once again in English while the drinks were served.

We returned to Moss, where son-in-law Helge awaited us with much interest. We were joined by Svanhild and her fiancé, Kåre Wergeland. We celebrated in the Sjøboden (the boathouse) restaurant, known for its seafood menu. Ronald and I returned to Northfield a few days later.

My father passed away on October 30, 1986, and I immediately returned to Norway. Audrey and I drove from Moss to Volda across the mountains. Svanhild was already there; Helge and Kåre arrived a day later. A Pentecostal funeral service was held on November 6 in the large Lutheran church, which was nearly filled to capacity. I gave an emotional oration about a father I loved and would greatly miss.

After my return from Norway, Svanhild and I worried about our mother, who would be living alone and who was showing early signs

Audrey and Helge Syversen at their home in Moss, 1995

of dementia. Food was delivered to her, and twice a week someone came by to look in on her. I called Svanhild regularly to find out how Astrid was faring and what actions we needed to take. After long consideration, we both felt that the best solution would be for our mother to join me and Else in Northfield. In early August 1988, I went to Norway to make the necessary arrangements, including at the US embassy, and then on to Volda in a rental car. I took my mother on a visit to bid good-bye to family and friends. Some days later, Svanhild and Kåre arrived to help my mother pack; she accompanied them to Halden, where she would stay until she joined me for the flight to America. I returned to Oslo and Moss on August 16. On my calendar I noted that it was *"en vemodig tur"* (a melancholy drive).

My mother and I began our long journey home on August 29. Else greeted us as we walked up the gangway in Minneapolis—a wonderful sight indeed. We quickly realized that Astrid required more help than we were able to give. Within the month, she moved into the Odd Fellows Home in Northfield. We invited her for meals and special occasions and took her shopping. Else stopped by the nursing home once or twice every day to check that Astrid got the care she needed, and I generally looked in on my mother on my way home from the college. Svanhild and Kåre also visited when they could. My mother's mental health deteriorated, and the last couple of years of her life she frequently did not recognize me. It hurt to see this loss of dignity, and I remembered my mother's heroic perseverance and care for Magnar, Svanhild, and me during the austere and oppressive war years.

In June 1994, I was invited to speak at immigration conferences in Tysvær—the Sloopers' home community—and in Sogndal. Before leaving on June 13, I visited my mother at the Odd Fellows Home. When I asked her if I should greet people back in Norway, for a moment she understood and responded, *"Hels dei alle ihop"* (Greet them all)—the last words I heard her utter. She was much in my thoughts on my flight, and after landing in Amsterdam, I decided to call home. Else told me my mother had passed away during the night.

I returned to Northfield early in July. On July 22, I went back to Norway with my mother's urn. A funeral service was arranged in the Pentecostal church Eben-Eser in Volda, where Astrid had been a member, and her urn was placed on my father's grave.[5]

A GROWING FAMILY

Audrey and Helge visited us regularly in the summer, and we all enjoyed tours to the family's favorite vacation spot on the North Shore. Our first grandchild was due in July 1983, and Else headed to Norway to be there for the birth. I joined her the following week, traveling via a small propeller plane from Oslo to the airfield between Ørsta and Volda. Else wept as she told me that the child had been stillborn and our daughter was seriously ill with the "hamburger disease" (E. coli), caught by eating spoiled meat. An E. coli bacterial infection could cause severe anemia and kidney failure. Audrey was hospitalized in Fredrikstad, and we were greatly concerned as we witnessed our daughter's grave illness. On our agenda was also the release of *The Promise of America* at the Grand Hotel on August 9. I attended alone as Else stayed with our daughter. The following day, I tearfully bid Audrey good-bye; she was heavily medicated and not able to hear me. It was a difficult journey back home. Else returned to Minnesota on September 10—her birthday. Audrey was still weak but had recovered; she had called in mid-August to reassure me that everything would work out well.

The following years were filled with rewarding visits from Norway and to Norway and with occupational engagements in all quarters. In February 1988, Audrey called with the good news that a baby was on its way. We understood that her physician had given the green light, but Else and I were still concerned. Then, close to midnight Norwegian time on July 28, Helge called with the wonderful news that we had a grandson born earlier that day, and that he and our daughter were fine. The following month, as it turned out, I was in Norway and with Else Syversen, the paternal grandmother, had the great pleasure of being *fadder*, a sponsor, when Martin was baptized on August 28. He was a most beautiful baby. I remember him a few years later sitting on his father's shoulders when I met them at the airport for a visit at Christmastime in 1991.

Four years after Martin's birth, April 5, 1992, our second grandson, Kristian, was born. As luck would have it, I had been invited to speak at a Marcus Lee Hansen conference in Ålborg, Denmark, June 29 to July 1. I arrived in Norway to see my family and to meet Kristian. We celebrated Audrey's thirty-second birthday on June 26. I returned from Ålborg for Kristian's baptism on July 5. I carried my new grandson to the baptismal font, and as I lowered him for the pastor to sprinkle water on his head, I felt a strong pull on my pants leg. There was four-year-old Martin, looking troubled, seeming to ask, "Is Grandpa drowning my little brother?" Both Martin and Kristian were registered as Americans born abroad and were thus, like their mother, American citizens.

On this side of the Atlantic we were also blessed with grandchildren. Andrea Kristen was born to Ronald and his wife, Lynnea Larson Lovoll, at the Northfield hospital on June 19, 1987. They had been married in Bethel Lutheran Church and had a fine wedding reception at the Jesse James Restaurant—a most appropriate venue for Northfield.

They lived in Minneapolis, and their visits were frequent and much appreciated. Time and again I noted in my appointment calendar: "What a beautiful baby." Andrea spent much time with her grandparents; she was almost like a daughter as well as a granddaughter to us. We felt that even more strongly after Ronald and Lynnea separated and then divorced in 1990–91, when Andrea was not yet four years old. Else, Ronald, and I enjoyed celebrating her fourth birthday at the Edgewood Inn Restaurant with its Norwegian-influenced menu. Andrea had fun blowing out the candles.

In July 2000, Audrey, Helge, Martin, and Kristian arrived from Norway; they were soon joined by Rigmor Navekvien, the widow of Else's brother Rolf, and her husband Harald Maurstad. Andrea was staying with us until she returned to her mother, then living in Texas. We were all on hand to celebrate Ronald's marriage to Margit Paulson

The whole family—including Andrea, thirteen—was on hand when
Ronald and Margit celebrated their marriage on July 15, 2000.

on July 15. The weather was lovely, and Margit's parents, Rieber and Ginny Paulson, also Northfield residents, arranged for a large wedding reception on their ample parcel of land.

We welcomed grandson Peter Magnar, born May 16, 2002. His middle name honored my late brother Magnar. And two years later, September 6, 2004, Jon Elias was born. Ronald and family made their home in Northfield. Being a part of our grandsons' lives and watching them grow up gave us great pleasure, pride, and joy.[6]

THE PROMISE FULFILLED

The decade of the 1990s was a time filled with many activities and responsibilities for Else and me, from regular visits with Ronald and Andrea to summer excursions with family from Norway and travel to the North Shore. Many Norwegians visited St. Olaf College; Else and I regularly served as hosts. The Norwegian actor Toralv Maurstad, with roots in Else's home community, was one of our very pleasant guests in March 1994. NAHA publications demanded a hectic pace, with many significant titles coming off the press.

I was busy planning my next major project. I had negotiated with the University of Minnesota Press the possibility of a sequel to *The Promise of America*. There was much interest for a contemporary history—1945 to present—of the Norwegian American population. My plans and prospects were already in place by early 1994. I signed a contract with the press in May 1995, and St. Olaf College granted me a two-year special leave of absence, 1995–97, on generous terms.

The project would require much travel, and Else, always concerned for my safety, insisted I have a research assistant accompany me. And I wished as well to have someone assist me in such an ambitious undertaking. My good friend Professor Einar Niemi, University of Tromsø, suggested I consider Terje Mikael Hasle Joranger, who had completed his master's degree in migration history. I met Terje at a conference in Sogndal and was soon convinced that he was the person I sought. I had the distinct impression that he would not only diligently tend to assigned research but would also be easy to spend time with as we explored many parts of the United States. Terje did not disappoint.

To make our research known in all areas of Norwegian settlement, brief articles appeared in numerous American and Norwegian
American journals throughout the country. Newspapers in Norway
announced the project. I contacted far-flung friends and lodges and
societies and was greatly encouraged by the broad interest in and
enthusiasm for the research project. Grants-in-aid made it possible
to conduct the study; we connected with people nationwide. Later,
in writing the preface, I recognized a great number of people who
gave of their time, enthusiasm, knowledge, and financial support.
Nearly three hundred people volunteered to help on a local level, and
that number was multiplied many times over during our visits.

In May 1995, I tested my approach to the fieldwork among Norwegians in Tampa, Florida. Terje Joranger joined me in August. We
scheduled research excursions throughout the twelve months of fieldwork. Else patiently helped prepare our travels and patiently accepted
my extended absences. Terje and I made it to thirty states from coast
to coast. We had informants in Hawaii and Alaska.

During these months of travel, I missed my family very much. In
January 1996, I wrote to Else from Los Angeles: "I do miss you and
Andrea and Ronald. [Audrey was by then a resident of Norway.] It
will be good to get back home. In many respects it is a strange year.
We are pursuing a research goal that is difficult to define. I trust that
next year when I sit down to analyze the result of the research that
it will all become clear to me."

The Promise Fulfilled: A Portrait of Norwegian Americans Today was
published by the University of Minnesota Press in cooperation with
NAHA in 1998, with a second printing in 2007. A Norwegian translation titled *Innfridde løfter. Et norskamerikansk samtidsbilde* (Fulfilled
Promises: A Norwegian American Contemporary Portrait) came off
the press in 1999. *The Promise Fulfilled* "is a story told by Norwegian
Americans themselves through interviews and completed questionnaires, and also through the historical record as preserved in libraries
and archives." In reality, it was an experiment in social history that
marked a departure in the study of American ethnic groups: "It is a

Odd and Terje Joranger on a research trip to New York

case study that presents a comprehensive portrait of an 'old' immigrant group toward the end of the twentieth century."

I am grateful to all who completed the questionnaire and agreed to be interviewed. Many were eager to tell us their life story. One evening Governor Terry E. Branstad of Iowa called and volunteered to be interviewed; he asked that I make an appointment with his secretary. I called the next morning and talked to someone who insisted I was mistaken; the governor would never contact anyone directly. But she promised to get back to me. Ten minutes later, she called to apologize and we set up a time to meet. Terje and I had a most informative and enjoyable conversation with the governor.

Vice president Walter Mondale agreed to be interviewed and related how his Norwegian heritage influenced his political career. We met with people in all walks of life and recorded their attachment to their ethnicity. I even visited the correctional facility in Faribault, just south of Northfield, and interviewed a young man serving a life term for first-degree murder. He was a fourth-generation Norwegian American, and we had a pleasant conversation. He claimed his innocence and also his attachment to the Norwegian Lutheran values he had been taught. His American-born grandmother spoke "pretty much nothing but Norwegian," he volunteered. Our questions regularly elicited emotional responses. The interviews and the questionnaires contributed essential details to our research.

We visited societies, organizations, churches, and festivals. The fieldwork benefited greatly from Terje Joranger's talent for social history, and he contributed personally as well as professionally to the entire enterprise. In 2017, Terje observed, "During our research . . . Odd trusted my work and treated me as an equal. This positive relationship between professor and a younger scholar was new to me. Although he was the leader of the project he always made me feel comfortable, and I remember the many conversations and debriefings that we had following a long day of research. I experienced personal growth during the entire period I worked with Odd."

Our work on the West Coast was greatly aided by longtime friend Professor Terje Leiren; he assisted enthusiastically in the research in Seattle and became our guide to places like Fishermen's Terminal. Terje had also served as tour guide when Else and I had taken part in the Seventeenth of May Festival in Ballard in 1999. The Fishermen's Terminal became an important destination. In 1988 a Fishermen's Memorial was erected there as a tribute to fishermen lost at sea. The memorial aroused deep and visible emotions as I found the names of my brother, Magnar Lowell, and my uncle Bendik Lowell, and October 9, 1950—the date they were swept away—inscribed on the bronze name plaque at its base.[7]

UNIVERSITY OF OSLO

I later became Terje Joranger's academic advisor for his doctoral dissertation at the University of Oslo. He defended it successfully in

Else and Odd
(above) in 1999
at the Seattle
Fishermen's
Memorial (at
right), honoring,
among others,
Magnar Lowell
and Bendik Lowell,
lost at sea in 1950
*Photos by
Terje Leiren*

March 2008. The two opponents at his disputation were my colleagues and friends Einar Niemi and Jon Gjerde. In my congratulatory speech, I noted that in Niemi's case the circle had been completed, from recommending Terje to be my research associate to examining him as a doctoral candidate. Gjerde, a published authority on migration and on Norwegian American history, had been our contact at the University of California at Berkeley, where he was a professor of history, when Terje and I explored a Norwegian presence in the state. In *From Peasants to Farmers* (1985), which considers the immigration from Balestrand, a fjord district in western Norway and his ancestors' home community, Gjerde makes the point that the study, "like all historical inquiry, is, in part, a personal search"—a valid acknowledgment for most students of the past. We, his colleagues and friends, grieved his premature death on October 26, 2008, a great loss for the field of immigration history.

The fall semester of 1993, I was a guest professor at the University of Trondheim (later the Norwegian University of Science and Technology) and at the University of Oslo. I also spoke at a conference in Bardufoss in Troms province and lectured at the University of Tromsø at Einar Niemi's invitation. To my delight, Else stayed in Norway most of the month of September; we had a great time sightseeing and visiting family.

Lucy Smith, rector at the University of Oslo, wrote on June 22, 1995: "The University of Oslo has the pleasure of offering you a position as Professor II [adjunct professor] with employment in the Department of History and the Department of British and American Studies." The two departments, she added, had determined that "Lovoll possesses the special competence the position requires." Kjetil Flatin, director of the University Foundation for Student Life, promoted my appointment. The process had begun in 1994, and St. Olaf College gave its strong support. On October 31, 1994, interim vice president and dean of the college Kathleen Fishbeck had responded enthusiastically: "We are delighted to give our approval to Professor

Lovoll's appointment as Professor II and thereby strengthen our formal ties to Norway. We look forward to an enriching exchange of ideas between the faculties of our two institutions."

In the ensuing years I spent six to eight weeks at the University of Oslo during the fall semester. For some of these years, Else was able to join me for part of the time. We were given a small apartment at Blindern. Else would welcome me from the balcony as I walked up the hill—by far the best part of the day.

My tenure at the University of Oslo covered the years 1996 to 2005, with mandatory retirement at age seventy. In the history department, Norwegian was the language of instruction, and in the British and American studies department, English. Migration became the focus in the latter department, but I also had a lecture series on the topic in the history department. I taught courses in US history and gave lectures for students and the public. My course on the American Revolution attracted much interest; I actually had more students than my colleague who taught the French Revolution.

In both departments I led graduate seminars, which tended to delve into issues relating to Norwegian immigration and settlement, with titles like "The Immigrant Society," "Immigration in a Multi-Cultural Society," "Norwegians in the Cities—A New Frontier," and "The United States, 1877–1945." In general courses on US history, students relished when I introduced and challenged such ideas as American exceptionalism. Is the United States really more exceptional than other nations? If so, what makes it exceptional? I made an effort to convince my students, and also some of my colleagues, not to generalize about American society and culture.

I truly enjoyed advising master's students, who mainly pursued topics dealing with aspects of immigration and settlement. They did not necessarily focus on the Norwegian story; I oversaw an excellent thesis on Asian settlement on the US Pacific Coast. Idar Ree, from the Stavanger area of Rogaland, was one of the graduate students I advised; he earned his degree in 2003. He volunteered the following observation: "Odd S. Lovoll became my advisor at the University of Oslo. His patience and steady disposition and scholarly competence and broad experience inspired me as we worked together. In all the tendencies, syntheses, and theories historians seem to see in their research, Lovoll has taught me that historical research first and foremost is the story of 'completely ordinary people.' This down-to-earth approach to the subject distinguishes in my opinion Lovoll's scholarship. As an advisor, Lovoll can also be described as down-to-earth. I could have called it collaborative advising."

A major benefit of the appointment was the opportunity to spend time with my family. Martin was only eight and Kristian four when I joined the faculty at the University of Oslo; nine years later, in 2005, they were in their teens. Else was also present from time to time. The notes in my calendar are filled with visits to Audrey and Helge and the two grandsons in Moss; or they joined me in Oslo—occasionally just the boys for a day of shopping, dining, and a movie. Many events and occasions created lasting memories. But I also missed Else and my home in Northfield. We called each other daily. On August 24, 2003, I noted on my calendar: "I miss my home very much. I will be glad to be done in Oslo."

My relationship to colleagues in both departments was most pleasant, and they became my friends. I think of Professor Øystein Rian, whom I first met when I visited the University College (Høgskolen) in Bø in Telemark back in October 1977. I correspond regularly with Øystein, and every time I visit Oslo I spend a most pleasant evening with him and John Wroughton and invited friends. Over a fine meal, we discuss our scholarly interests and our lives and reminisce about those good years, now long ago, when we were colleagues in the department of history.

Other close friends at the University of Oslo are Ingeborg Kongslien, professor of Nordic literature, and Dagfinn Worren, noted lexicographer. I think back to my years teaching in Volda, where Dagfinn was my student at the gymnas. I spend much time with all these friends when in Oslo.

KING OLAV V PROFESSOR OF
SCANDINAVIAN-AMERICAN STUDIES

Over the years, St. Olaf College had received substantial gifts from the Norwegian government to establish a chair in history. As early as 1974, when St. Olaf celebrated its immigrant beginnings, Sidney A. Rand, then college president, expressed the desirability of an endowed chair in immigration history. Together with dean Jon Moline, I sought to raise additional funds, and there were many generous donors. My thought was that the person holding the professorship should also serve as NAHA's editor, with the two institutions jointly financing the position. The Kenneth O. Bjork Endowment Fund became a part of the funding. NAHA's editor would thus receive compensation for services rendered—and would be a member of the St. Olaf faculty.

The position would require half time teaching and an equal time devoted to research, to expanding the publication program by recruiting scholars to the field of Norwegian American studies, and to editing and supervising production. In 1992, His Majesty graciously consented to have the position named King Olav V Chair in Scandinavian-American Studies. I was greatly honored to be named the first occupant of the chair, which was inaugurated at a symposium and festive celebration on the St. Olaf campus on November 6–7, 1992. The proceedings of the conference were published by NAHA in 1993 as *Nordics in America: The Future of Their Past*.

I would teach only in the history department. The position was created to ensure the continued study of Scandinavian and Scandinavian American history. The title advertised St. Olaf's dedication to its Norwegian roots. On May 17, 1993, the City of Northfield recognized my appointment in a special resolution. The reduced teaching load made it possible for me to accept the adjunct professorship at the University of Oslo.

Through my career at St. Olaf, I had enjoyed teaching Norwegian as a foreign language. Students have told me they humorously enjoyed hearing me demonstrate the rounded vowels—o, ø, å, y— difficult for English-speaking people to master. These same students took my Scandinavian history, Viking, ethnic studies, and immigration courses, which carried both Norwegian and history credits. Chad Rossow, who graduated in 1992, commented on how he and his friend Joel Magrane fared in my Norwegian classes in the fall of 1989:

> Professor Lovoll would spend the next few months teaching us his native language. It wasn't until the following spring that it dawned on me that Norwegian was not as prolific a language or practical to learn as say, Spanish. It was then that I understood how unique this education in Norwegian was to St. Olaf. . . . Joel and I decided that if we were ever to put that knowledge to use we should spend some time abroad in Norway. In the fall of 1990 we enrolled in the University of Oslo through an abroad program with St. Olaf.

They traveled widely. Chad concluded: "I learned more about myself, the world, and the world's perspective on the United States— good and bad. I traveled, fell in love and made lifelong friendships that I still cherish to this very day. And it all began in the basement of Old Main in the late 80s with Professor Lovoll."

Another much-appreciated student, Michael Paulson, class of 1996, now an attorney in Sioux Falls, South Dakota, and the state's honorary Norwegian consul, contributed comments about his time at St. Olaf: "As a Norwegian Major at St. Olaf College, I had the privilege of studying Norwegian history and literature under Professor Lovoll. In addition, I was honored to work with Professor Lovoll on a number of his personal writing projects, including research for *The Promise Fulfilled* (1998). Professor Lovoll's passion for preserving the history of the Norwegian-American experience is unparalleled. My time, experience and friendship with Professor Lovoll left an indelible mark that I will forever recall with the fondest of memories."

Jeff Kindseth from Kenyon, Minnesota, now a radiology technician at the Mayo Clinic in Rochester, may have enrolled in more of my courses than any other student in my thirty-year tenure at St. Olaf. Jeff commented: "Dr. Odd S. Lovoll was noted for very organized lectures, and his enthusiasm, in addition to having genuine concern for his students. At the International Summer School in Oslo, Norway, in 1981, I experienced two additional Dr. Lovoll history courses: History of Norway, and Norwegian Emigration. The enjoyable course on emigration from Norway was especially noteworthy. I have returned on several trips to Norway, enjoying time with extended family, and taking in the scenic treasures of the country of Norway, and the origins can be traced to the inspiring classes taught by Dr. Odd Lovoll."

In retirement, I think back on those hectic years in my life and my good relationships with my students. Young people have faith in a positive future for themselves and for society in general. I have always appreciated the company of young friends. Still, the time came to consider becoming professor emeritus, and at the end of December 2000 I entered retirement.

My loyalty to and enthusiastic support of the Norwegian-American Historical Association remained strong, and there were several accepted manuscripts for my successor to publish. During spring semester 2001, I completed editing and supervised publication of a book compiled and edited by Bjørn Gunnar Østgård, *America-America Letters: A Norwegian-American Family Correspondence*. We speak of America letters and of Norwegian America letters; by my logic, correspondence among Norwegian residents in the United States might very well become America-America letters. Mine was thus not an immediate move into retirement. Indeed, the history department invited me to continue offering my January interim course "The Norwegian American Experience" for a few more years.

On May 9, 2001, a dinner was arranged in my honor, a great send-off, as NAHA's president Lawrence Hauge called it, at the Interlachen Country Club in Edina. It was a splendid affair, the large dining room filled to the last place. The history department chair, Jorunn Bjørgum, and the American and British department chair, Per Winther, represented the University of Oslo and offered congratulations. My greatest joy, however, came when Audrey, Martin, and Kristian stepped forward; they had come all the way from Norway to honor me. The

Odd with Kristian and Martin in Moss, 2005

boys, twelve and eight, recited a "Grampa-Rapp" they themselves, with assistance from their father, had composed beginning *"Vi kommer fra Norge til Amerika, og vi er her for å feire vår Grampa. Yeah!"* (We come from Norway to America, and we are here to celebrate our Grampa. Yeah!). Everyone was moved by their performance. It was the highlight of my day.[8]

SCHOLARSHIP IN RETIREMENT

My next research project, published in 2006, had a title that identified well its theme: *Norwegians on the Prairie: Ethnicity and the Development of the Country Town*. In a review, Jon Gjerde pointed to the scholarly neglect of the midwestern small town, stating, "Lovoll's richly illustrated narrative thus fills a void, and he provides us with a lively description of Benson over a century and one-half." Gjerde also mentioned my long fascination with the small town in the Norwegian American past.

I had traced the history of three country towns, Benson, Madison, and Starbuck, all located on the western Minnesota prairie. Founded as railroad towns and made up primarily of Norwegians, they served as urban centers and gathering places for the surrounding farming communities. Gary G. Erickson, a resident of Norway Lake, prepared maps of the counties where the towns are located; for Swift County, where Benson is the county seat, Erickson prepared a table, a chart, and a map showing Norwegian land ownership in 1907. In several regions of the county Norwegian farmers owned 100 percent of the land.

The Norwegian presence is still much in evidence. Many residents had their roots in the Nordfjord area in western Norway, the fjord region where Else grew up. She accompanied me doing fieldwork several times. Elderly third-generation Norwegian Americans still spoke a Nordfjord dialect transplanted by grandparents; they learned English only when starting school. Else enjoyed using her more modern Nordfjord dialect in conversations with them.

The three towns celebrate a re-invented and re-interpreted ethnic identity. Madison sees itself as "The Lutefisk Capital of the World," with annual festivities including lutefisk-eating competitions. Starbuck displays a lefse-shaped monument and claims it as the "World's Largest Lefsa"; *Lefse Dagen*, Lefse Day, is celebrated to commemorate *Syttende mai*, Norway's constitution day, May 17. Ethnocentricity is also present in Benson in a competition to see who can eat the most *klubb* (potato dumpling)—a robust peasant fare many of the people I interviewed grew up with. In the small western towns, ethnic groups could not separate to the same degree as in heavily settled Norwegian communities in the countryside or in Norwegian colonies in metropolitan areas, which operated as worlds apart from other nationalities. In the small-town environment, ethnic groups instead frequently interacted in celebrations of many kinds, including *Syttende mai*. Their identity was tied to the town—the place called home.

The book was published by the Minnesota Historical Society Press in cooperation with NAHA and distributed to its membership. Todd

W. Nichol, who succeeded me as NAHA's editor, noted in a foreword that my study "is the first full-length treatment of Norwegian Americans in the small towns to which so many of them were drawn." First published in Norway in 2005 as *Norske småbyer på prærien. En kulturhistorisk studie* (Norwegian Small Towns on the Prairie: A Cultural Historical Study), the book was seen as a Norwegian American contribution to the centennial observance of the 1905 dissolution of the Swedish Norwegian union. Both editions are dedicated to my two youngest grandsons, Peter Magnar and Jon Elias. The Denver Public Library awarded the book the Caroline Bancroft History Prize, cited as the best book published in 2006 about the history of America's westward movement.[9]

Nordmanns-Forbundet—the Norse Federation, now Norwegians Worldwide—celebrated the centennial of its founding on June 21, 1907, with a festive anniversary commemoration in Oslo City Hall on June 21, 2007. Harry Cleven, then the federation's editor, took the initiative to have its history written. He and Sigmund Holtskog are true friends, and I have been a frequent guest in their home. On one such visit, over a glass of wine, Harry broached the idea that I should consider tracing the federation's historical century-long journey and its worldwide commission in a rapidly changing international community.

After much consideration, and having cleared my schedule of other projects, I accepted Harry's invitation. Throughout the anniversary year, I published five interpretive articles in successive issues of *The Norseman*. The work required a comprehensive examination of every volume of the Norwegian-language *Nordmanns Forbundet* and the English-language *The Norseman*—an arduous but also productive exploration. Through it all, Harry Cleven was my enthusiastic and talented helper. Harry selected all illustrations and was an ever-attentive editor and respondent to my many queries. In 2009, the five essays were published collectively as *Celebrating a Century: Nordmanns-Forbundet and Norwegians in the World Community, 1907–2007*. The historical perspective of the federation's role among Norwegians at home and abroad calls attention to a much-neglected aspect of emigration history:

national attitudes toward emigrated citizens. Through Nordmanns-Forbundet, "Norway discovered its emigrated compatriots; their success whether as permanent or temporary residents in foreign lands enhanced Norway's international reputation." In the final chapter, "One Hundred Years," I reflect on the federation's celebratory tradition, its recent past, and its vision for a continued role as an international organization rooted in Norwegian ethnicity. A more complete story is yet to be told.[10]

Norwegian Newspapers in America: Connecting Norway and the New Land, published in 2010, represented my next major scholarly undertaking. Two years later, a Norwegian publisher released it as *Norske aviser i Amerika* (Norwegian Newspapers in America). My long-standing interest in the immigrant press, dating back to the late 1960s in North Dakota, prepared me for this comprehensive study. I had published articles about individual journals and frequently lectured on the immigrant press as a major source in the effort to understand the Norwegian ethnic group in America.

The newspapers were, as their mastheads occasionally noted, American newspapers printed in the Norwegian language. For some months during the fall of 2007, Vidar Bjørnsen, a student at the University of Tromsø, helped me peruse the multitude of existing newspapers, mainly available on film, and take notes. Fritt Ord (the Freedom of Expression Foundation) became my greatest benefactor.[11]

The fall of 2001, I had published an article in *Minnesota History* with the title "Canada Fever—The Odyssey of Minnesota's Bardo Norwegians." I had visited their settlement, located by Edmonton in Alberta, Canada; the Norwegian Canadian residents were invited to my lectures at the University of Alberta and at Augustana College in Edmonton.

I felt that we had neglected the history of Norwegians in Canada, although Kenneth Bjork had published articles dealing with Norwegian settlement there and at the time of his death in 1991 was working on a book on Norwegian settlement in Canada and Alaska. I have been intrigued by the history of the French-speaking Quebec province and how Quebec City and other port cities became the gateway for Norwegian immigrants in the mid-nineteenth century. In September 2012, I took the long flight to Quebec City and acquainted myself with the Old City, and with libraries and archives where I would do research. The most memorable part of my stay was the cruise to the quarantine station Grosse Isle, where all ships were required to stop and gain clearance to Quebec harbor. Visiting the cemeteries and seeing Norwegian names was quite moving. I made four more excursions to Canada, doing research in Ottawa, Montreal, Quebec, Gaspé, and Sherbrooke. I had no assistant, but everywhere I went people stepped forward to help; doing fieldwork is a good way to make new friends. I had a similar experience during five weeks of research in Norway, February–March 2013.

The introduction of free trade following the repeal of the British Navigation Acts in 1850 changed the destination of most Norwegian immigrants from New York to Quebec and other cities in the province; the Norwegian entry into the timber trade, transporting timber from Canada to the British Isles, opened the route to Canada for Norwegian immigrants at low fares. Norway became the most important foreign shipping nation in the Canadian wood trade. For most of the Norwegian emigrants the Canadian gateway was a corridor to the Upper Midwest. Individual states—Illinois, Wisconsin, Minnesota, and Iowa—undertook extensive campaigns as they competed for Norwegian settlers. It is difficult to imagine what the immigrants endured, first the lengthy voyage on sailing ships across rough seas and then the hazardous journey south, as they sought a better life away from the homeland.

Across the Deep Blue Sea: The Saga of Early Norwegian Immigrants was published in 2015, followed the next year by a Norwegian translation titled *Den lange overfarten. Tidlig norsk utvandring til Amerika* (The Long Passage: Early Norwegian Emigration to America). In a review in *Annals of Iowa*, Daron W. Olson, on the faculty of Indiana University East, observes that most historians of Norwegian immigration have focused exclusively on the final destination, while he has argued for giving more attention to the homeland, and "Now Lovoll, the sage historian of Norwegian immigration, has pointed to another neglected aspect of that history: the stepping stones or transition points along the way."[12]

LOSING THE LOVE OF MY LIFE

In writing my memoirs, no part of it has been more difficult to formulate and reflect on than the present one. I had never imagined that I would spend this juncture of my time on earth without my life partner since the age of twenty-one. *Across the Deep Blue Sea* is dedicated to the memory of my wife, Else Olfrid Lovoll (September 10, 1935–May 3, 2011): "Else was the love of my life. She gave me much joy, love, and happiness and was the mainstay in my life and in my professional career during our fifty-five years together and the anchor and rock of our family. She is greatly missed and much on my mind."

I think about the time in 1998 when she, Ronald, and Andrea visited Norway. This time I was left alone at home. Audrey provided transportation, and they had a wonderful time, reporting to me by telephone as they made their way to Else's birthplace, Bryggja. Andrea, eleven years old, could not get over the large breakfasts served at Norwegian hotels and the strange showers where you had to mop the water from the floor after use.

Else and I made our final trip together in the spring of 2003, attending Martin's confirmation in Moss on May 11. Audrey loaned us her car, and we set out for a memorable excursion. We stopped to eat in rest areas on the roadside, spent nights at hotels up the Gudbrandsdalen valley, crossed the mountains to Hjelle by Lake Oppstryn, and took in the hotel where I had worked the summer before meeting Else. We visited family farther out on the fjord, including Else's home place, and even Bjørlykke before returning to Oslo.

Else developed vertigo and could no longer travel by air. Ronald and I attended Kristian's confirmation in Moss in May 2007, but Else had to send her best wishes. Then, Kristian chose to complete his senior year, 2009–10, at Northfield High School. He stayed with Ronald and

Odd and Else, 1997

family because by then Else's health had deteriorated to the point that she was not able to care for a teenager. But Kristian spent much time with us. He adjusted quickly. Peter and Jon became like Kristian's younger brothers.

Else was diagnosed with cancer in March 2008. In the coming weeks, months, and years, she endured surgeries, radiation, and chemotherapy. Our schedule required driving to Abbott Northwestern and other health facilities in Minneapolis and St. Paul for treatment, generally five days a week. When Else underwent surgery, I stayed close by until she was released. She suffered greatly and eventually had difficulty swallowing. We still made it to the North Shore the summer of 2010, and, later that year, Else made a traditional Christmas for us all. In April 2011, we learned that no further treatment was possible. Later that month, Else suggested we take a day's tour to New Ulm; we had continued our excursions even during her cancer treatment. And this one was also most pleasant.

On Sunday, May 1, after a typical morning, suddenly Else collapsed. When the police and ambulance arrived, Else had lost consciousness. The night at the Northfield hospital will never leave my mind. I sat and held Else's hand and declared my love and gratitude. Suddenly she pressed my hand and was gone. Else lingered until May 3 and was declared deceased at 1:30 PM.

Audrey and Svanhild arrived from Norway for the funeral, which would be at Bethel Lutheran Church, where we were members. Pastor Timothy McDermott had spent much time with us to get to know Else and the Lovoll family. I asked that he not bring up Lutheran teachings about eternity, and I was most grateful to him for accepting my stand and for his inclusiveness in his sermon. Andrea gave a moving tribute to her grandmother. She reflected on Martin, age three, calling her Mammama, how she was known as the "neighborhood grandma," how she encouraged creativity and how creative she herself was, how she passed on family traditions, and how she valued hard work. Andrea concluded:

> She taught me to cook, to clean, to garden, to sew, to knit, to act, to write, to read, to memorize my times tables, and most importantly, to love and care for people unconditionally. So to Grandma, Mammama, my teacher, my best friend, my front row audience, co-conspirator in fun summer activities, the neighborhood grandma, my second mother. Thank you for everything you have given me, and everyone you have influenced. I would not at all be the person I am without you. You have made my life more special than you could know. I love you Grandma, I miss you already.[13]

REFLECTIONS

The loss of wife, mother, and grandmother Else was a painful reality for her family to accept. I received great comfort from being surrounded by my children and their spouses and by my grandchildren. Ronald and Margit and grandsons Peter and Jon were close by in

Northfield. I was privileged to see them grow up and to treasure their company. Granddaughter Andrea visited often from Texas and later moved to Minnesota. On Christmas Eve the family continued to gather at my place and celebrate with a traditional Norwegian holiday meal.

I accompanied Kristian when he returned to Norway in June 2010 after graduating from high school. Audrey turned fifty on June 26, an event celebrated with friends and family. I shared greetings from family in America and expressed how proud I was of my daughter. She had made a good life for herself in Norway. Audrey is an American citizen and speaks of the United States as my country. We communicate in English.

I visited Norway again the fall of 2011. Earlier that year, Erik Rudeng, director of Fritt Ord (the Freedom of Expression Foundation), had called to let me know that with the publication of *Norwegian Newspapers in America* I had been awarded the prestigious Freedom of Expression Tribute (*Fritt Ords Honnør*) for my contributions to the history of Norwegian America—uplifting news as I was dealing with a heartbreaking loss.

On September 6, Professor Guri Hjeltnes presented the award in the foundation's auditorium, which was filled to capacity. My lecture, "A Neglected Cultural Heritage: The Remarkable Flourishing of the Norwegian American Immigrant Press" (*En glemt kulturarv. Den norsk-amerikanske innvandrerpressens eiendommelige blomstring*), was followed by many questions and social visiting. A dinner was served for invited guests, my family included.

Erik Rudeng recently reminded me of coincidences that affect our lives, in this case his invitation by chance—after the scheduled speaker changed his mind—to give a lecture on "Norway Today" at St. Olaf College in 1980. About the reception that followed he wrote, "I found myself standing next to the then doyen of the Norwegian American historical profession, the very impressive Kenneth O. Bjork. I tried to turn our conversations towards this admittedly rather vague idea of a possible book project. He did not reject it. Then his eyes suddenly discovered a much younger colleague [Odd Lovoll] present in this very lively reception room, pointed his finger at him and said almost solemnly in Latin: *'ille faciet'* (He will make it)."

The rest, as they say, is history. Rudeng contacted me, and I secured grants and other support for the project he had suggested, which eventually became *The Promise of America*. Rudeng made a final generous observation: "Even without early economic and institutional support Odd S. Lovoll would have been able to make impressive contributions to Norwegian American history, no doubt. But maybe his early experience of success and support whetted his appetite and professionalized his publishing life, enjoyments, and outreach."

During it all, my life and my career, I had my family's support and love. They are all doing well, moving forward in their chosen occupations and livelihoods. I have indeed been blessed. New members are joining the family. Andrea and her husband, Paul Carlson, have made their home in the Twin Cities. Their visits to Grandpa Odd are truly special occasions. Kristian is engaged to Rita Johansen, and they have their own home a short distance from Moss, where Audrey and Helge reside. Martin has settled in Bergen and has found his Jeanette Grønbekk. Weddings for both couples are set for the summer of 2019.

In August 2015, Ronald, Margit, Peter, Jon, and I made a trip to Norway, the first for the two grandsons. They were especially delighted to see Kristian, and he and Rita found activities they would like. We visited Svanhild and Kåre in Halden. In Bergen, Martin became our knowledgeable guide to places on Bryggen—the wharf—with its Hanseatic commercial buildings. The boys even climbed to the top of Rosenkrantztårnet (Rosenkrantz Tower), a defense structure from the 1500s.

I was on a special mission to make a pilgrimage to my place of birth. On August 16, the five of us boarded a train in Oslo and had a spectacular journey north and across the mountains to Åndalsnes. From there we made it to Volda by bus and across the fjord on a ferry. With Ronald driving a rented car, we arrived in Bjørlykke. Cousin

Magne and Ragnhild Løvoll and family, now the owners of the Bjørlykke farm, gave us a warm Norwegian reception in their stately residence. The local newspaper *Synste Møre* reported on our visit. We
even visited the little schoolhouse I had attended. Peter and Jon
thought Grandpa had a long way to school. Vivid in my memory are
the two grandsons running around to inspect the hilly farmstead. I
tried to impress upon them that some seventy years ago Grandpa had
wandered about in the same fields and patches of land.[14]

Grandsons Peter Magnar and Jon Elias on the Bjørlykke farmstead, August 2015

Notes

NOTES TO CHAPTER I

1. Throughout this and following chapters, my own recollections, checked for accuracy whenever possible, constitute a significant source.

Odd S. Lovoll, *The Promise of America: A History of the Norwegian-American People*, 2nd ed. (Minneapolis: University of Minnesota Press, 1999), 11–18; Odd S. Lovoll, *Across the Deep Blue Sea: The Saga of Early Norwegian Immigrants* (St. Paul: Minnesota Historical Society Press, 2015), 55–58; Ragnar Standal, "Emigration from a Fjord District on Norway's West Coast, 1852–1915, trans. C. A. Clausen, *Norwegian-American Studies* 29 (1983): 185–209; Julie E. Backer, *Ekteskap, fødsler og vandringer i Norge 1856–1960* (Oslo: Statistisk Sentralbyrå, 1965), 165; "Løvoll/Lowell Slekta," privately prepared family register in author's possession; Kristofer Randers, *Sunnmøre. Reisehåndbok*, 4th ed. (Ålesund, Norway: Sunnmøre Turistforening, 1962), 1.

2. Johs. Andenæs, Olav Riste, and Magne Skodvin, *Norway and the Second World War* (Oslo: Aschehoug, 1996), 45–55, 95; Jan Olav Flatmark, *Sunnmøre i Festung Norwegen. En oversikt over tysk virksomhet 1940–45* (Lesja, Norway: Snøhetta forlag, 1994), 61, 65; *Sunnmørsposten*, April 9, 10, 15, 25, 27, 29, 30, May 3, 4, 7, June 10, 1940; Vestfoldmuseene, *Hd Posisjonsdagbøker 1939–40*.

Geir Stian Ulstein, *Våre fremste motstandshelter med livet som innsats 1940–1945* (Oslo: Spartacus Forlag, 2016), is highly recommended for its treatment of people engaged in the resistance movement. Vidkun Quisling and his misguided role during the occupation is not a topic here.

3. Guri Hjeltnes, *Hverdagsliv i krig. Norge 1940–45* (Oslo: Aschehoug, 1987), 60–62, quote 61; Joel Perlman, *Ethnic Differences: Schooling and Social Structure among the Irish, Italians, Jews, and Blacks in an American City, 1880–1935*

(Cambridge, MA: Cambridge University Press, 1988), 122; *Nordisk Tidende*, June 11, 1942; Therese Alvik, *Familien Steinfeld—Da byen gråt* (Førde, Norway: Selja forlag, 2013), 25–28, 29, 32, 43–45, 50–51, 55–67, 72–73, 74, 81–82, 83, 119, 126–28, 137–40, quotes 66, 91, 193; Kristian Ottosen, *I slik en natt. Historien om deportasjonen av jøder fra Norge* (Oslo: H. Aschehoug & Co. [W. Nygaard], 1994), 13–17, 287–98, 334–65; *Sunnmørsposten*, October 6, 24, 27, November 19, 26, December 7, 1942; Ole Kristian Grimnes, "Norge under andre verdenskrig," *Store norske leksikon* (nettversjon, hentet 2. juli 2016), published online; see also Irene Levin Berman, *"We Are Going to Pick Potatoes": Norway and the Holocaust, The Untold Story* (Lanham, MD: Hamilton Books, 2010); Guri Hjeltnes, "Fangeskipet 'Donaus' siste reis," *Aftenposten*, April 8, 2014; Ulstein, *Våre fremste motstandshelter*, 88–91; Jo Benkow, "The History of the Norwegian Jews," in *Jewish Life and Culture in Norway: Wergeland's Legacy,* ed. Ann Sass (New York: Abel Abrahamsen, 2003), 16–21, quote 21.

4. Hjeltnes, *Hverdagsliv i krig*, 116, 133–39, quotes 138, 139; *Sunnmørsposten*, May 29, 1945. The financial assistance and gifts the Løvoll family received during the war were distributed by Nasjonalhjelpen (The National Aid), an institution that during the war, 1940–45, raised funds for distribution and aid to those in need. Its most important task during the occupation was to distribute Swedish and other foreign aid to Norway. When I visited my daughter, Audrey, in Moss in 2016, she was able to get *boknasild* and made a dish I had not had since the war.

5. Haakon M. Fiskaa, *Bygdebok for Syvde sokn. Gards- og ættesoge* (Volda, Norway: Syvde Sogelag, 1974), 562–63; "Alf Lowell/Løvoll Oral History Interview, 1984," Robert A. I. Mortvedt Library, Scandinavian Immigrant Experience Collection, Archives and Special Collection Department, Pacific Lutheran University, Tacoma, WA; Leonard Lowell, "John and Anna Lowell," in author's possession. Løvoll was the name of the farm Lars Olsen Løvoll had owned at Åheim, also in southern Sunnmøre, and he retained it after buying Koparnes. A common practice would have been to adopt the farm name (*gårdsnavn*) Koparnes as the last name succeeding the patronymic Olsen. Koparnes was located in the municipality of Syvde, which in 1964 merged with the municipality of Vanylven.

6. Astrid Aase, "Mi historie," in author's possession; conversations with Odin Aase; Jakob Bjørlykke and Olav Liset, *Soga om Sande og Rovde*, new and expanded edition by Bjarne Rabben (Volda, Norway: Sande Sogenemnd, 1976), 2:23–24; Per Mork, *Morkabygd-soge. Laga av alle, for alle* (Volda, Norway: Egset Trykk, 1953), 176–77. Bjørlykke was located in the municipality of Sande. In 2002 this part of Sande was transferred to the municipality of Vanylven.

7. Mannskapsliste Kosmos 1939/40; Hd *Posisjonsdagbøker-navigasjonsdag-bøker 1939–40*; photo: http://www.lardex.net/jahre/skip%20(2)/1929kosmos .htm; Lowell/Løvoll interview; Arkivet etter Kosmos ARS-A-1052 Serie PBA: Mannskapsoppgjør 1939–40; Erling Mossige, *Storrederiet Nortraship. Handelsflåten i krig* (Oslo: Grøndahl & Søn Forlag, 1989), 108–13.

8. *Sunnmørsposten*, May 8, 9, 14, 18, 29, June 8, 11, 1945.

NOTES TO CHAPTER 2

1. Lovoll, *The Promise of America*, 37–38; US Bureau of the Census, *Sixteenth Census, 1940, Population, Mother Tongue* (Washington, DC: GPO, 1943); Backer, *Ekteskap*, 158, 184.

2. Daron W. Olson, *Vikings Across the Atlantic: Emigration and the Building of a Greater Norway, 1860–1945* (Minneapolis: University of Minnesota Press, 2013), 159–209, quotes 175, 179, 209; Odd S. Lovoll, "The Changing Role of May 17 as a Norwegian-American 'Key Symbol,'" in *Nasjonaldagsfeiring i fleirkulturelle demokrati*, ed. Brit Marie Hovland and Olaf Aagedal (Copenhagen, Denmark: Nordisk Ministerråd, 2001), 65–78, quote 74; Odd Sverre Lovoll, *Celebrating a Century: Nordmanns-Forbundet and Norwegians in the World Community 1907–2007* (Oslo: Nordmanns-Forbundet, 2009), 8–9, 10–15, quotes 8, 10, 15; Odd S. Lovoll, *Norwegian Newspapers in America: Connecting Norway and the New Land* (St. Paul: Minnesota Historical Society Press, 2010), 227, 309–10, 319–21, quote 321; Sune Åkermann, "Ingrid Semmingsen och den nordiska utvandringsforskningen," in *Migrasjon og tilpasning. Tid og Tanke*, ed. Odd S. Lovoll (Oslo: Historisk institutt, Universitetet i Oslo, 1998), 29–37; Wilhelm Morgenstierne, *Et større Norge. Fra Nordmanns-Forbundets arbeidsmark* (Oslo: Nordmanns-Forbundet, 1932). Nordmanns-Forbundet has the current English name Norwegians Worldwide, which is also the title of its monthly journal.

3. Carl G. O. Hansen, *My Minneapolis: A Chronicle of What Has Been Learned About the Norwegians in Minneapolis Through One Hundred Years* (Minneapolis: privately published, 1956), 345–46; Olson, *Vikings Across the Atlantic*, 192, quote 160; A. N. Rygg, *American Relief for Norway: A Survey of American Relief Work for Norway during and after the Second World War* (Chicago: American Relief for Norway, 1947), 10–11; Henry Bamford Parkes, *The United States: A History*, 3rd ed. (New York: Alfred A. Knopf, 1968), 648–55, quote 650.

4. Andenæs, Riste, and Skodvin, *Norway and the Second World War*, 50–53, 90.

5. Lovoll, *Norwegian Newspapers in America*, 322–23; *Nordisk Tidende*, May 21, 28, June 11, 18, 25, 1942; Lovoll, *Celebrating a Century*, 82–94, quotes 88, 90, 93.

6. Odd S. Lovoll, "Norwegians and Norwegian Americans, 1940–Present," in *Immigrants in American History: Arrival, Adaptation, and Integration*, ed. Elliott Barkan (Santa Barbara, CA: ABC-CLIO, 2013), 3:1163–64; Lovoll, *Norwegian Newspapers in America*, 322–23; Karsten Roedder, *Av en utvandreravis' saga. Nordisk Tidende i New York gjennom 75 år* (New York: Nordmanns-Forbundets, New York Chapter, 1968), 2:63–64, quote 63.

7. Carl Hansen, "Pressen til borgerkrigens slutning," in *Norsk-Amerikanernes Festskrift 1914*, ed. Johs. B. Wist (Decorah, IA: The Symra Company, 1914), quote 39; Lovoll, *Norwegian Newspapers in America*, 2–5, 9–12, 351, 373; Odd S. Lovoll, "En glemt kulturarv. Den norsk-amerikanske innvandrerpressens eiendommelige blomstring," speech given in Oslo, Norway, September 6, 2011, when awarded Fritt Ords Honnør; Marcus Lee Hansen, *The Immigrant in American History*, ed. Arthur M. Schlesinger (New York: Harper & Row Publishers, 1940), quotes 3, 140; Robert E. Park, *The Immigrant Press and Its Control* (New York: Harper & Brothers, Publishers, 1922), 237–95, quotes 5, 287.

8. Hansen, *The Immigrant in American History*, quote 137; Lovoll, "En glemt kulturarv"; Lovoll, *Norwegian Newspapers in America*, 3, 74–76, 109–12, 146–52, 272–80, quote 141. Around 1900, *Skandinaven* had nearly 54,000 subscribers for its semiweekly edition and for its daily, mainly for Chicago, 25,000 subscribers. In comparison, *Aftenposten*, Norway's largest daily, had a circulation of only 14,000.

9. Lovoll, *Norwegian Newspapers in America*, 322–33, quote 328; Odd S. Lovoll, "Preface," Carl Søyland, *Written in the Sand: Fragments of the Emigrant Saga*, trans. Rigmor K. Swensen (Minneapolis, MN: Western Home Books, 2005), xvii, quote 177; *Nordisk Tidende*, May 14, 1942; Roedder, *Av en utvandreravis' saga*, 2:18; *Store norske leksikon* (publisert på nett, 13. februar 2009), published online.

10. Lovoll, *Norwegian Newspapers in America*, 322, 323; Roedder, *Av en utvandreravis' saga*, 2:28–29, 71–72, quotes 28, 72; Knut Ringen, "Karl Evang: A Giant in Public Health," *Journal of Public Health Policy* (Autumn 1990): 360–67; Lovoll, *The Promise of America*, 267–70.

11. Lovoll, *Norwegian Newspapers in America*, 322–24; Roedder, *Av en utvandreravis' saga*, 2:28, 63–64, 72, quotes 64; *Visergutten*, November 13, 1941.

12. Søyland, *Written in the Sand*, 204–10, quotes 205, 206; Roedder, *Av en utvandreravis' saga*, 2:64, 85, 137, 161–62, 279; Lovoll, *Norwegian Newspapers in America*, 329; Lowell/Løvoll interview; Sven H. Rossel, *A History of Scandinavian Literature*, trans. Anne C. Ulmer (Minneapolis, MN: University of Minnesota Press, 1982), 188–90, quote 190; Arne Skouen, *Sigrid Undset skriver*

hjem. En vandring gjennom emigrantårene i Amerika (Oslo: H. Aschehoug & Co. [W. Nygaard], 1981), 5, 38–39, quote 39; Sigrun Slapgard, *Sigrid Undset. Dikterdronningen* (Oslo: Gyldendal Norsk Forlag, 2007), 443–44, 445, 451, 458; Sigrid Undset, *Return to the Future*, trans. Henriette C. K. Naeseth (Hastings. MN: Scandinavian Marketplace, 2001), 68–70, 73–74, quote 204, in 1945 printed in the original Norwegian as *Tilbake til fremtiden*.

Fredrik Juel Haslund, *Nordahl Grieg. En dikter og hans tid* (Oslo: Gyldendal Norsk Forlag, 1962), is an insightful interpretation of Grieg as a person and author. As a salute to the Norwegian American and Canadian American press for their efforts on behalf of Norway during the war, the Norwegian Ministry of Foreign Affairs through the Norwegian embassy's information service in Washington, DC, in 1947 invited thirteen Norwegian American and Canadian American editors to a two-month-long visit to Norway.

13. Roedder, *Av en utvandreravis' saga*, 2:31, 65–66; *Star Tribune*, May 11, 1991; *Northfield News*, May 15, 1991; Søyland, *Written in the Sand*, 180, 181–84; Ragnar Wold, *Slik fikk vi vinger. En beretning om opplæringen av luftpersonell i Canada 1940–45* (Oslo: N. W. Damm & Søn A/S, 1990), 6, 7, 8, 17–26, 37, 51, 72–73, 88, 101–30; Lovoll, *Norwegian Newspapers in America*, 329; University of Toledo Digital Repository, "Wings for Norway," War Information Center Pamphlets, Book 580, http://utdr.utoledo.edu/ur-87-68/580/; *Little Norway in Pictures* (Toronto, Canada: S. J. Reginald Sanders Publishers, n.d.); Max Manus, *Mitt liv* (Oslo: Cappelen Damm, 2009), 256–72.

Frithjof Sælen, *Sjetlands-Larsen* (Bergen, Norway: J. W. Eides Forlag, 1947), is highly recommended for its personal and detailed account of the flight to Shetland. See also Magne Godøy, *Øya og folket i krigs- og okkupasjonstida 1940–1945* (Godøy, Norway: Godøytunmuseet, 1995). From 1943 armed forces were also created in Sweden by Norwegian men who sought refuge there. More than forty thousand Norwegians crossed into Sweden during the war.

14. *Nordisk Tidende*, April 25, 1940, June 21, 1945, May 2, June 21, 27, August 1, 1946; Roedder, *Av en utvandreravis' saga*, 2:24–25, 28; Søyland, *Written in the Sand*, 177–80, quotes 178; Rygg, *American Relief for Norway*, 9–11, 12–14, 16–17, 34–41, 43–45, 46–48, 213–14, 304–9, quotes 11, 14, 15. On June 14, 1946, the Norwegian Lutheran Church of America became the Evangelical Lutheran Church, dropping Norwegian from its name.

15. Brit Berggreen, Arne Emil Christensen, and Bård Kolltveit, eds., *Norsk sjøfart* (Oslo: Dreyers Forlag, 1989), 2:213–24; Guri Hjeltnes, *Handelsflåten i krig 1939–1945. Sjømann. Lang vakt,* (Oslo: Grøndahl og Dreyers Forlag, 2. opplag, 1999), 1:12, 164, 269–78, quote 23; Guri Hjeltnes, *Handelsflåten i krig*

1939–1945. Krigsseiler. Krig, hjemkomst, oppgjør (Oslo: Grøndahl og Dreyers Forlag, 2. opplag, 1999), 2:112–14, 129–33, 164–70, 170–72, 203–5, 213–14, 219–28; Mossige, *Storrederiet Nortraship,* 108–13, 133–40, 248–51, 267–70. The two volumes were presented as gifts to the author by Guri Hjeltnes, for which I thank her most sincerely.

16. Gerd Nyquist, *Bataljon 99* (Oslo: H. Aschehoug & C. [W. Nygaard], 1981), is the only book-length account. I refer to the English translation, restricted to members of the 99th Infantry Battalion. Historian Morten A. Tuftedal gave me a copy, for which I am most grateful. Gerd Nyquist, *The 99th Battalion,* trans. Inger-Johanne Gerwig and Henrik M. Hansen (Decorah, IA: Anundsen Publishing Co., n.d.), 19–20, 25, 38–39, 41–43, 51, 54–56, 61–63, 94–99, 112–14, 125–34, 135–48, 176–90, quotes 19–20, 125; *Faribault Daily News,* March 3, 2003; Maj. Doug Bekke, "Norwegian-Americans and the 99th Infantry Battalion (Separate)," in Military Historical Society of Minnesota, *Allies* 10, no. 1 (Winter 2003); David Minge and G. Rolf Svendsen, "99th Infantry Battalion (Separate)," talk at Torske Klubben meeting, April 2, 2016; interview with David Minge and G. Rolf Svendsen, June 24, 2016; G. Rolf Svendsen, Gustav Svendsen Biography, December 2016; *The Viking,* Camp Hale, CO, May 24, 1943; David Minge, "Dr. Raymond Minge/99th Battalion," biography, November 2016; *Nordisk Tidende,* October 29, 1942, March 16, 1945; David Witte, *World War II at Camp Hale: Blazing a New Trail in the Rockies* (Charleston, SC: History Press, 2015), 98–99, 109–13, 128–30, quote 98; *Fergus Falls Daily Journal,* December 7, 1943, August 29, September 9, 1944, May 14, 1945; gift from Bruce O. Bjorgum, *The Viking Battalion: The Story of 99th Battalion (Separate),* DVD, Shybert Productions, Edwards, CO, 2013; 99th Infantry Battalion Educational Foundation, "99th Infantry Battalion (Separate)," http://www.99battalion.org/. The US War Department became the US Defense Department in 1949.

17. Parkes, *The United States,* 668–69, quote 668; *Nordisk Tidende,* May 31, July 26, August 9, 23, October 26, November 16, 1945, May 2, June 6, 13, 20, 27, 1946; Hjeltnes, *Handelsflåten,* 2:412–13; Søyland, *Written in the Sand,* 221–27, quote 227.

NOTES TO CHAPTER 3

1. Andenæs, Riste, and Skodvin, *Norway and the Second World War,* 121; Tor Dagre, "Norway's Liberation," http://www.reisenett.no/norway/facts/history/history_Norways_liberation.html; Kjersti Solberg Ofstad, Information Advisor, US Embassy Public Affairs Office, October 5, 2016.

2. See Tone Wikborg, *The Vigeland Park in Oslo: Sculpture Park and Museum in Oslo* (Oslo: Normanns Kunstforlag, 1991).

3. *Nordisk Tidende*, June 13, 20, July 11, 1946; Lovoll, *Across the Deep Blue Sea*, 100–109; Nils P. Vigeland, *Norsk seilskipsfart erobrer verdenshavene* (Trondheim, Norway: F. Bokhandels Forlag, 1943), quote 113.

4. See Odd S. Lovoll, *A Century of Urban Life: The Norwegians in Chicago before 1930* (Northfield, MN: NAHA, 1988), and Odd S. Lovoll, "A Perspective on the Life of Norwegian America: Norwegian Enclaves in Chicago in the 1920s," *Migranten/The Migrant* 1 (1988): 24–37.

5. Dorothy Burton Skårdal, *The Divided Heart: Scandinavian Immigrant Experience through Literary Sources* (Lincoln: University of Nebraska Press, 1974), quote 15; Theodore C. Blegen, *Norwegian Migration to America: The American Transition* (Northfield, MN: NAHA, 1940), quote vii; Patsy Adams Hegstad, "Scandinavian Settlement in Seattle, 'Queen City of the Puget Sound,'" *Norwegian American Studies* (1985): 55–74.

6. Maxine Seller, *To Seek America: A History of Ethnic Life in the United States* (Englewood, NJ: Jerome S. Ozer, 1977), quote 130; *Seattle Times*, October 22, 1946.

7. Einar Haugen, *The Norwegian Language in America: A Study in Bilingual Behavior* (Bloomington: Indiana University Press, 1969), 1–16, quotes 8, 15; Ministerialbok for Sande prestegjeld, Sande sokn, 1901–1917; Arkivverket, Digitalarkivet, "Emigranter over Ålesund 1878–1930"; online obituary for Oluffa Hansen, Stanwood, WA, newspaper, May 12, 1955; Vittorina Cecchetto and Magda Stroinska, "Introduction," Magda Stroinska, "The Role of Language in the Re-Construction of Identity in Exile," and Vittorina Cecchetto, "From Immigrant to Exile: Does Language Contribute to This Process," in *Magda Stroinska and Vittorina Cecchetto, eds., Exile, Language and Identity* (Oxford: Peter Lang, 2003), 13–15, 95–109, 151–61, quotes 97, 102; Vittorina Cecchetto, Magda Stroinka, and Rachel Cheng, "Communication Barriers in Aging Bilinguals," paper presented by Cecchetto, York University, Toronto, Ontario, Canada, October 3, 2008; Magda Stroinska and Vittorina Cecchetto, "The Speech Act Force of Complaints: Some Pragmatic Aspects of Language Loss in Aging Immigrants," in *Current Trends in Pragmatics*, ed. Piotr Cap and Joanna Nijakowska (Cambridge: Cambridge Scholars Publishing, 2007), 354–68; Gordon Strand, ed., *Voices of Ballard and Beyond: Stories of Immigrants and their Descendants in the Pacific Northwest* (Seattle, WA: Nordic Heritage Museum, 2012), quote 119. See also Botolv Helleland, ed., *Norwegian Language in America* (Oslo: NAHA-Norway and Novus Forlag, 1991), and Per Moen, "The English Pronunciation of Norwegian-American Words in Four Midwestern States," *American Studies in Scandinavia* 20 (1988): 105–21.

8. Odd S. Lovoll, "From Norway to America: A Tradition of Immigration Fades," in *Interpretive Essays in Contemporary American Immigration*, ed.

D. Cuddy (Boston, MA: Twayne Publishers, 1982), 1:86–107; Lovoll, *The Promise of America*, quote 23–24; Lovoll, "Norwegians and Norwegian-Americans," 3:1163–73.

9. Lovoll, "Norwegians and Norwegian-Americans"; *Norwegian-American Studies* 30 (1985), quote in preface; Kay F. Reinartz, ed., *Passport to Ballard: The Centennial History* (Seattle, WA: Ballard News Tribune, 1988), 47–51, quote 51; Lovoll, *The Promise of America*, 236–38, 243–46, 261–62.

10. Lovoll, *Norwegian Newspapers in America*, 326, 342–43; Kenneth Nesset, "Odd's Life in U.S.A. What I Remember," December 2016; Lovoll, "Norwegians and Norwegian-Americans"; Elliott Barkan, "Norwegian Americans in the Pacific Northwest: Fading Migrations but Enduring Memories," in *Norwegian-American Essays: "Migration and Memory,"* ed. Øyvind T. Gulliksen and Harry T. Cleven (Oslo: NAHA-Norway, 2008), quote 179. *Store norske leksikon*, published online February 14, 2009, defines *halvemål* and has examples like *est* for *hest* (horse) and *høy* (hay) for *øy* (island).

11. *Seattle Times*, October 10, 1950; *Washington Posten*, October 13, 1950; Odd S. Lovoll, *The Promise Fulfilled: A Portrait of Norwegian Americans Today* (Minneapolis: University of Minnesota Press, 1998), dedication page.

12. My own memories are strong; "Billy Graham Evangelistic Association Statement of Faith," https://billygraham.org/about/what-we-believe/; Matthew 7:12 (English Standard Version); the American Humanist Association, https://americanhumanist.org/.

NOTES TO CHAPTER 4

1. MS *Oslofjord* (1949), https://en.wikipedia.org/wiki/MS_Oslofjord_(1949); William H. Miller Jr., *Pictorial Encyclopedia of Ocean Liners, 1860–1994* (New York: Dover Publications, 1995), 92.

2. Lovoll, *A Century of Urban Life*, 269; Lovoll, *Norwegian Newspapers in America*, 266; L. DeAne Lagerquist, *In America the Men Milk the Cows: Factors of Gender, Ethnicity, and Religion in the Americanization of Norwegian-American Women* (Brooklyn, NY: Carlson Publishing Inc., 1991), 1–11, 57–105; Lovoll, *The Promise of America*, 38–40, 267–70; Lovoll, *The Promise Fulfilled*, 63; letter from Olav Tysdal, December 21, 2016, in author's possession; Siv Ringdal, *Det amerikanske Lista. Med 110 volt i huset* (Oslo: Pax forlag, 2002), 9–10, 16–17, 20, 22, 43–45, 46, 53–55, 131–47, 157–61, 194–95, 265–66, quotes 10–11, 15–16, 16–17; Lovoll, *Across the Deep Blue Sea*, 79; Ragnar Standal, "Gjeninnvandring til Ørsta på Sunnmøre," and Knut Djupedal, "Report on the Returned-Emigrant Project," in *Essays on Norwegian-American Literature and History*, ed. Øyvind T. Gulliksen, Ingeborg R. Kongslien, and Dina Tolfsby (Oslo:

NAHA-Norway, 1990), 2:183–85, 189–99; Odd S. Lovoll, "Norwegian Immigration and Women," in *Norwegian American Women: Migration, Communities, and Identities,* ed. Betty A. Bergland and Lori Ann Lahlum (St. Paul: Minnesota Historical Society Press, 2011), 51–73, quote 53–54.

3. Letter from Alf Johan Hustad, December 11, 2008, in author's possession; Svanhild Wergeland, statement about moving to Norway, October 16, 2016, in author's possession; Lowell/ Løvoll interview.

4. See Tim Greve, *Haakon VII of Norway: The Man and the Monarch* (New York: Hippocrine Books, 1983).

5. This section is based on personal notes and recollections.

6. This section is based on personal notes and recollections.

7. See Jostein Krokvik, *Ivar Aasen. Diktar og granskar, sosial frigjerar og nasjonal målreisar* (Bergen, Norway: Norsk bokreidingslag, 1996); Stephen J. Walton, *Farewell the Spirit Craven: Ivar Aasen and National Romanticism* (Oslo: Det norske Samlaget, 1987); and Edith L. Blumhofer, *Restoring the Faith: The Assemblies of God, Pentecostalism, and American Culture* (Chicago: University of Illinois Press, 1993).

8. *Møre,* October 20, 2016, quote; *Møre,* Julenummer 2016; interviews with students, October 18, 2016.

9. *Klassekampen,* October 3, 2014; Lovoll, ed., *Migrasjon og tilpasning.*

NOTES TO CHAPTER 5

1. My notes, personal documents, and recollections.

2. Elwyn B. Robinson, *History of North Dakota* (Lincoln: University of Nebraska Press, 1966), 131–32, 133, 157, 203, 208–10, 235–36, 246, 289, quotes 133, 289; Lovoll, *The Promise of America,* 123–25; Lovoll, *The Promise Fulfilled,* 47, 115, 208–11, 251; Odd S. Lovoll, "History of Norwegian-language Publications in North Dakota," MA thesis, University of North Dakota, Grand Forks, January 1969, 121–22; Odd S. Lovoll, *A Folk Epic: The* Bygdelag *in America* (Northfield, MN: NAHA, 1975), 199–200, 236–37; Carlton C. Qualey, *Norwegian Settlement in the United States* (Northfield, MN: NAHA, 1938), 160–61, 163–70; La Vern J. Rippley, *The German Americans* (Boston, MA: Twayne Publishers, 1976), 172–79.

3. Robinson, *History of North Dakota,* 201, 306, 312–13, 498–501, 501–4; University of North Dakota website, www.und.edu; see Wynona H. Wilkins, et al., *History of the Department of Modern and Classical Languages, University of North Dakota, 1883–1983* (Grand Forks: University of North Dakota, 1983); Curt Hanson, head, Elwyn B. Robinson Department of Special Collections, provided a copy of the Legislative Act dated March 8, 1891, titled "Teaching

Scandinavian Language at University"; Lovoll, *The Promise of America*, 212, 334; Lovoll, *A Folk Epic*, 199–200, 237; Institute for Regional Studies & University Archives, University of North Dakota, Grand Forks, ND; online obituaries for Orville Bakken.

4. Roger Sale, *Seattle Past to Present* (Seattle: University of Washington Press, 1976), 8, 53–56, 61, 62, 141, 169–70, 190, 197–98, 202–4, 251, quote 169.

5. Kimberly K. Porter, "Here's to You, Mr. Robinson," *North Dakota Quarterly* (Spring/Summer 2016): 15–17; Michael J. Lansing, "Robinson's *History*: Fifty Years Later," *North Dakota Quarterly* (Spring/Summer 2016): 18–20, quote 19; Lovoll, "History of Norwegian-Language Publications in North Dakota," quote 14; Lovoll, *Norwegian Newspapers in America*, 164–73, 317; Odd Sverre Løvoll, "The Norwegian Press in North Dakota," *Norwegian-American Studies* 24 (1970): 78–101, quote 99.

6. Odd S. Lovoll, "Kenneth O. Bjork: Teacher, Scholar, and Editor," in *Makers of an American Immigrant Legacy: Essays in Honor of Kenneth O. Bjork*, ed. Odd S. Lovoll (Northfield, MN: NAHA, 1980), 3–14; my May 2, 1970, report to Bygdelagenes Fellesraad with notes; Lovoll, *A Folk Epic*, 49, 210–11, 218; Lovoll, *The Promise of America*, 334; Odd S. Lovoll, "Norwegian-American Historical Scholarship: A Survey of Its History and a Look to the Future," in *Essays on Norwegian-American Literature and History*, ed. Dorothy Burton Skårdal and Ingeborg R. Kongslien (Oslo: NAHA-Norway, 1986), 223–39.

7. Rudolph J. Vecoli, "Odd Sverre Lovoll as Historian," in *Interpreting the Promise of America: Essays in Honor of Odd Sverre Lovoll*, ed. Todd W. Nichol (Northfield, MN: NAHA, 2002), 3–12, quote 3; John J. Bukowczyk, "Homage to the Contadini: The Influence of Rudolph J. Vecoli on Immigration and Ethnic History," *Italian Americana* (Summer 2002): 125–34; Rudolph J. Vecoli, "*Contadini* in Chicago: A Critique of *The Uprooted*," *Journal of American History* (December 1964): 405–17, quote 406; "Rudolph J. Vecoli Obituary," *New York Times*, June 23, 2008, quoted; Robert Harrison "The 'New Social History' in America," in *Making History: An Introduction to the History and Practices of a Discipline*, ed. Peter Lambert and Phillipp Schofield (New York: Routledge, 2004), 109–20; John Higham, *History: Professional Scholarship in America*, rev. ed. (Baltimore, MD: Johns Hopkins University Press, 1989), 221–24, 236, quote 236; Odd Sverre Løvoll, "The *Bygdelag* Movement," *Norwegian-American Studies* 25 (1972): 3–26; Lovoll, *A Folk Epic*, 1–5, 13–19, 117–19; Odd Sverre Løvoll, "A Folk Rally: The *Stevne* of the American *Bygdelag*," in *Norwegian Influence on the Upper Midwest*, ed. Harald S. Naess (Duluth: Continuing Education & Extension, University of Minnesota, 1976), 117–20; Odd S. Lovoll, "'Better than a Visit to the Old Country': The *Stevne* of the Sognalag

in America," in *Norwegian-American Essays 1996*, ed. Øyvind T. Gulliksen, David C. Mauk, and Dina Tolfsby (Oslo: NAHA-Norway, 1996), 3–29; Odd S. Lovoll, "The Norwegian-American Old-Home Societies," in *Hembygden & Världen. Festskrift till Ulf Beijbom*, ed. Lars Olsson and Sune Åkerman (Växjö, Sweden: Svenska Emigrantinstitutet, 2002), 117–33.

8. Lloyd Hustvedt, "Vignettes from a Norwegian Settlement," in *Nordics in America: The Future of Their Past*, ed. Odd S. Lovoll (Northfield, MN: NAHA, 1993), 189–98; Joseph M. Shaw, *History of St. Olaf College, 1874–1974* (Northfield, MN: St. Olaf College Press, 1974); Matti Kaups, "Norwegian Immigrants and the Development of Commercial Fisheries along the North Shore of Lake Superior: 1870–1895," in Naess, *Norwegian Influence*, 21–34; online obituary for Marta Heggedal; Sigurd Lovold, Legacy Program, October 15, 2010, Sons of Norway, http://www.sofnbismarck.com/tree%20dedications/Lovold%20Story%20%20October%2015,%202010.pdf; Lovoll, *The Promise Fulfilled*, 214–18. Løvold ending in "d" is the Dano-Norwegian version. A movement to Norwegianize changed the spelling to Løvoll. Not everyone followed suit, and thus both forms still exist.

9. Lovoll, *The Promise of America*, 300–303; Norwegian Information Service, Oslo, "Emigration Anniversary," undated, in NAHA archives; "Transcription of Tape Recording of the Meeting of the Central Coordinating Committee for the Sesquicentennial of Norwegian Emigration to USA in 1975, at Augsburg College, Wednesday, October 27, 1971," November 16, 1971, in NAHA archives; Norwegian American 1975 Sesquicentennial Meeting of Board of Directors, February 1, 1972, in NAHA archives; *Commemorative Publication of the 1975 Sesquicentennial Association* (Minneapolis, MN: Sesquicentennial Board, 1975), 5–7, 8–13, 15; Lawrence Milton Nelson, ed., *From Fjord to Prairie: Norwegian Americans in the Midwest, 1825–1975* (Chicago: Norwegian American Anniversary Commission, 1976), 4, 5, 25–26; Naess, *Norwegian Influence*, 106–16.

NOTES TO CHAPTER 6

1. Interview with Audrey Lovoll Syversen, October 22, 2016, and January 30, 2017; interview with Ronald Lovoll, January 29, 2017; Ronald Lovoll, mementos and comments, 1977–78; personal notes; entries on calendars.

2. Odd S. Lovoll and Kenneth O. Bjork, *The Norwegian-American Historical Association, 1925–1975* (Northfield, MN: NAHA, 1975), 14–17; Marcus Lee Hansen, "Immigration as a Field for Historical Research," *American Historical Review* (April 1927): 500–18; Lovoll, *The Promise of America*, 300–303, 330–32; Lovoll, "Norwegian-American Historical Scholarship," 223–39; Lovoll,

"Kenneth O. Bjork: Teacher, Scholar, and Editor," 3–14; Mary Hove, statement, December 9, 2016; J. R. Christianson, statement, February 4, 2017; Millard L. Gieske and Steven J. Keillor, *Norwegian Yankee: Knute Nelson and the Failure of American Politics, 1860–1923* (Northfield, MN: NAHA, 1995). For Theodore Blegen's commendable career as a historian and educator, see John T. Flanagan, *Theodore C. Blegen: A Memoir* (Northfield, MN: NAHA, 1977).

3. Odd S. Lovoll, *Det løfterike landet. Historien om norskamrikanerne* (Oslo: Universitetsforlaget, 1983; rev. ed., 1997); Lovoll, *The Promise of America*, ix; John Higham, review, *Minnesota History* 49, no. 5 (Spring 1985): 204; *Aftenposten*, August 10, 1983, June 22, 1984; *Prisma-Nytt*, summer 1984; notice from Minnesota Historical Society, St. Paul, June 1985.

The title *løfterik*, suggested by me, was an unfamiliar word even though compounded words are common, and had to be approved by the Norsk språkråd (Norwegian language council). I may perhaps claim it as my contribution to the Norwegian language.

4. Lovoll, *A Century of Urban Life*, 11–17, 35–38, 42–44, 240–49, 279; *Skandinaven*, April 28, 1928; Lovoll and Bjork, *The Norwegian-American Historical Association*, quote 64–65; Lovoll, "A Perspective on the Life of Norwegian America"; Odd S. Lovoll, "Den tidlige Chicago-kolonien og dens innflytelse på den vestnorske utvandringen," in *Eit blidare tilvere?* ed. Ståle Dyrvik and Nils Kolle (Voss, Norway: Voss folkemuseum, 1986), 176–93; Odd S. Lovoll, "A Pioneer Chicago Colony from Voss, Norway: Its Impact on the Overseas Migration, 1836–1860," in *A Century of European Migrations, 1830–1930*, ed. Rudolph J. Vecoli and Suzanne M. Sinke (Chicago: University of Illinois Press, 1991), 182–99; Odd S. Lovoll, "A Scandinavian Melting-Pot in Chicago," in *Swedish-American Life in Chicago and Urban Aspects of an Immigrant People*, ed. Philip J. Anderson and Dag Blanck (Chicago: University of Illinois Press, 1992), 60–67.

5. Notes on appointment calendars; personal records and recollections; conversations with Audrey Syversen and Ronald Lovoll.

6. Notes on appointment calendars; personal records and recollections; conversations with Audrey Syversen, Margit Lovoll, and Ronald Lovoll.

7. Lovoll, *The Promise Fulfilled*, ix–xv, 119–20, 123–25, 176–78; personal notes during fieldwork; notations on appointment calendars; Terje Mikael Hasle Joranger, statement, January 25, 2017.

8. S. Deborah Kang, "Jon Gjerde's Immigrant America," in *Norwegian-American Essays*, ed. Øyvind T. Gulliksen and Harry T. Cleven (Northfield, MN: NAHA, 2011), 39–52; Jon Gjerde, *From Peasants to Farmers: The Migration*

from Balestrand, Norway, to the Upper Middle West (Cambridge, MA: Cambridge University Press, 1985), quote xiii; correspondence from the University of Oslo and St. Olaf College, in author's possession; Martin Syversen and Kristian Syversen, "Grampa-Rapp," in author's possession.

9. Odd S. Lovoll, *Norwegians on the Prairie: Ethnicity and the Development of the Country Town* (St. Paul: Minnesota Historical Society Press, in cooperation with NAHA, 2006), xiii–xvii, 60, 192–94, 266–69, 270, quote xi; Jon Gjerde, "The Scandinavian Migration from Local and Transnational Perspectives," *Journal of American Ethnic History* (Winter 2008): quote 86; Odd S. Lovoll, *Norske småbyer på prærien. En kulturhistorisk studie* (Oslo: Forlaget Vett & Viten, 2005).

10. Lovoll, *Celebrating a Century*, 6–7, 137–69, quote 6.

11. Lovoll, *Norwegian Newspapers in America*, ix–xiii, 1–5, 349–50, 351–76.

12. Odd S. Lovoll, "Canada Fever—The Odyssey of Minnesota's Bardo Norwegians," *Minnesota History* 57, no. 7 (Fall 2001): 356–67; Lovoll, *Across the Deep Blue Sea*, 36–37, 43–46, 141, 145–50, 155–58; Daron W. Olson, review, *Annals of Iowa* (Winter 2016): 75–77.

13. Personal notes from Else's treatment; hospital records; recording of the funeral at Bethel Lutheran Church; records from Benson and Langehough Funeral Home; Andrea Lovoll, tribute to her grandmother—all in author's possession.

14. Erik Rudeng, "Coincidence and Support," February 20, 2017; letter from Erik Rudeng, February 21, 2017; *Aftenposten*, September 6, 2011; *Pressemelding*, September 1, 2011; personal notes; *Synste Møre*, July 2015.

Publications

BOOKS

A Folk Epic: The Bygdelag *in America.* A Sesquicentennial Publication. Boston: Twayne Publishers, 1975.

The Norwegian-American Historical Association, 1925–1975, Northfield, MN: NAHA, 1975. Co-authored with Kenneth O. Bjork.

Bygda i den nye verda. Dei norsk-amerikanske bygdelaga. Oslo: Det norske Samlaget, 1977.

Cultural Pluralism versus Assimilation: The Views of Waldemar Ager. Northfield, MN: NAHA, 1977. Edited.

Makers of an American Immigrant Legacy: Essays in Honor of Kenneth O. Bjork. Northfield, MN: NAHA, 1980. Edited.

Det løfterike landet. Historien om norsk-amerikanerne. Oslo: Universitetsforlaget, 1983; rev. ed., 1997.

The Promise of America: A History of the Norwegian-American People. Minneapolis: University of Minnesota Press, 1984; rev. ed., 1999.

Scandinavians and Other Immigrants in Urban America. Northfield, MN: St. Olaf College Press, 1985. Edited.

A Century of Urban Life: The Norwegians in Chicago before 1930. Northfield, MN: NAHA, 1988.

Nordics in America: The Future of Their Past. Northfield, MN: NAHA, 1993. Edited.

Migrasjon og tilpasning. Ingrid Semmingsen, et minneseminar. Tid og Tanke. Oslo: Historisk institutt, Universitetet i Oslo, 1998. Edited.

The Promise Fulfilled: A Portrait of Norwegian Americans Today. Minneapolis: University of Minnesota Press, 1998; 2007.

Innfridde løfter. Et norskamerikansk samtidsbilde. Oslo: Vett & Viten, 1999.

Norske småbyer på prærien. En kulturhistorisk studie. Oslo: Vett & Viten, 2005.

Norwegians on the Prairie: Ethnicity and the Development of the Country Town. St. Paul: Minnesota Historical Society Press, 2006.

Celebrating a Century: Nordmanns-Forbundet and Norwegians in the World Community 1907–2007. Oslo: Nordmanns-Forbundet, 2009.

Norwegian Newspapers in America: Connecting Norway and the New Land. St. Paul: Minnesota Historical Society Press, 2010.

Norske aviser i Amerika. Oslo: Spartacus forlag, 2012.

Across the Deep Blue Sea: The Saga of Early Norwegian Immigrants. St. Paul: Minnesota Historical Society Press, 2015.

Den lange overfarten. Oslo: Spartacus forlag, 2016.

ARTICLES AND CHAPTERS

"The Norwegian Press in North Dakota." *Norwegian-American Studies* 24 (1970): 78–101.

"North Dakota's Norwegian-Language Press Views World War I, 1914–1917." *North Dakota Quarterly* (Winter 1971): 73–84.

"The *Bygdelag* Movement." *Norwegian-American Studies* 25 (1972): 3–26.

"Valdres heimkjensle." *Tidskrift for Valdres Historielag* (1972): 55–64.

"The Great Exodus." In *They Came from Norway,* edited by Erik J. Friis, 10–15. New York: Norwegian Immigration Sesquicentennial Commission, 1975.

"*Decorah-Posten*: The Story of an Immigrant Newspaper." *Norwegian-American Studies* 27 (1976): 77–100.

"A Folk Rally: The *Stevne* of the American *Bygdelag.*" In *Norwegian Influence on the Upper Midwest,* edited by Harald S. Naess, 117–20. Duluth: Continuing Education & Extension, University of Minnesota, 1976.

"En utvandreragent på Ringsaker." *Heimen,* nr. 3 (1979): 149–56.

"Norwegians in America after World War II." In *Cleng Peerson Memorial Institute 1970–1980,* 21–23. Stavanger, Norway: The Institute, 1980.

"Simon Johnson and the Ku Klux Klan: Impressions from His Memoirs." *North Dakota Quarterly* (Fall 1980): 9–20.

"From Norway to America: A Tradition of Emigration Fades." In *Interpretive Essays in Contemporary American Immigration,* edited by D. Cuddy, 1:86–107. Boston, MA: Twayne Publishers, 1982.

"Foreword." In Waldemar Ager, *Sons of the Old Country,* translated by Trygve M. Ager, v–xv. Lincoln: University of Nebraska Press, 1983.

"On Being a Norwegian-American in the 1980's." *Scandinavian Review* (Winter 1985): 80–91.

"Den tidlige Chicago-kolonien og dens innflytelse på den vestnorske utvandringen." In *Eit blidare tilvere?* edited by Ståle Dyrvik and Nils Kolle, 176–93. Voss, Norway: Voss Folkemusem, 1986.

"Introduction." Jon Leirfall, *Old Times in Norway*, translated by C. A. Clausen, 7–11. Oslo: Det Norske Samlaget, 1986.

"Norwegian-American Historical Scholarship: A Survey of Its History." In *Essays on Norwegian-American Literature and History,* edited by Dorothy Burton Skårdal and Ingeborg R. Kongslien, 223–40. Oslo: NAHA-Norway, 1986.

"*Washington-Posten*: A Window on a Norwegian-American Urban Community." *Norwegian-American Studies* 31 (1986): 163–86.

"A Perspective on the Life of Norwegian America: Norwegian Enclaves in Chicago in the 1920s." *Migranten/The Migrant,* nr. 1 (1988): 24–37.

"*Gaa Paa*: A Scandinavian Voice of Protest." *Minnesota History* 52, no. 3 (Fall 1990): 86–99.

"A Pioneer Chicago Colony from Voss, Norway: Its Impact on the Overseas Migration, 1836–1860." In *A Century of European Migrations, 1830–1930,* edited by Rudolph J. Vecoli and Suzanne M. Sinke, 182–99. Champaign: University of Illinois Press, 1991.

Norwegians on the Land. Address for the Society for the Study of Local and Regional History. Historical Essays on Rural Life. Marshall, MN: Southwest State University, 1992.

"A Scandinavian Melting-Pot in Chicago." In *Swedish-American Life in Chicago: Cultural and Urban Aspects of an Immigrant People, 1850–1930,* edited by Philip J. Anderson and Dag Blanck, 60–67. Champaign: University of Illinois Press, 1992.

"The Danish Thingvalla Line in the Nordic Competition for Emigration Traffic." In *On Distant Shores: Proceedings of Marcus Lee Hansen Immigration Conference, Aalborg, Denmark, June 29–July 1, 1992,* edited by Birgit Flemming Larsen, Henning Bender, and Karen Veien, 83–98. Aalborg, Denmark: Danes Worldwide Archive, 1993.

"'For People Who Are Not in a Hurry': The Danish Thingvalla Line and the Transportation of Scandinavian Emigrants." *Journal of American Ethnic History* (Fall 1993): 48–67.

"Norwegian-American Mutuality in the Iron Decade: 'Nordlyset' of Chicago." In *Fin(s) de Siècle in Scandinavian Perspective: Studies in Honor of Harald Naess,* edited by Faith Ingwersen and Mary Kay Norseng, 179–91. Columbia, SC: Camden House, 1993.

"Swedes, Norwegians, and the Columbian Exposition of 1893." In *Swedes in America: Intercultural and Interethnic Perspectives on Contemporary Research*, edited by Ulf Beijbom, 185–94. Växjö, Sweden: Swedish Emigrant Institute, 1993.

"Innvandrernes Amerika." *Heimen* 3 (1994): 147–55.

"The Rural Bond of Norwegians in America." *The Norseman* 34, no. 2 (March 1994): 16–21.

"Harro Harring und seine Vertreibung aus Norwegen." Translated by Joachim Reppmann. *Mitteilungen der Harro-Harring-Gesellschaft* 13/14 (1994–95): 46–56.

"Emigration and Settlement Patterns as They Relate to the Migration of Norwegian Folk Art." In *Norwegian Folk Art: The Migration of a Tradition*, edited by Marion J. Nelson, 125–32. New York: Abbeville, 1995.

"Norwegian Americans." In *Gale Encyclopedia of Multicultural America*, edited by Judy Galens, Anna Sheets, and Robyn V. Young, 2:1001–15. New York: Gale Research, 1995.

"Paul Hjelm-Hansen: Norwegian 'Discoverer' of the Red River Valley of Minnesota and Settlement Promoter." In *Performances in American Literature and Culture: Essays in Honor of Professor Orm Øverland on His 60th Birthday*, edited by Vidar Pedersen and Zeljka Svrljuga, 161–78. Bergen: University of Bergen, 1995.

"Better than a Visit to the Old Country: The *Stevne* of the Sognalag in America." In *Norwegian-American Essays*, edited by Øyvind T. Gulliksen, David C. Mauk, and Dina Tolfsby, 3–29. Oslo: NAHA-Norway, 1996. Dedicated to Odd S. Lovoll.

"Et valdrisgjestebø i Amerika, Valdris Samband." *Årbok for Valdres* (1997): 194–200.

"Cleng Peerson." In *American National Biography*, 17:241–42. New York: Oxford University Press, 1999.

"Norwegian Emigration to America—A Dramatic National Experience." *The Norseman* 39, no. 4–5 (1999): 4–12.

"Den norske kirke i Amerika som kulturbærer." In *Immigrantane og norsk kyrkjeliv i Amerika. Sogndalseminaret 1988, 24. og 25. september*, 34–40. Sogndal, Norway: Sogndal kommune, 2000.

"Norway's Children, Americans All: A Contemporary Portrait of Norwegian Americans." In *Norwegians in New York, 1825–2000: Builders of City, Community and Culture*, edited by Liv Irene Myhre, 103–12. New York: The Norwegian Immigration Association, Inc., 2000.

"Canada Fever—The Odyssey of Minnesota's Bardo Norwegians." *Minnesota History* 57, no. 7 (Fall 2001): 356–67.

"The Changing Role of May 17 as a Norwegian-American 'Key Symbol.'" In *Nasjonaldagsfeiring i fleirkulturelle demokrati*, edited by Brit Marie Hovland and Olaf Aagedal, 65–78. Copenhagen: København Nordisk Ministerråd, 2001.

"The Creation of Historical Memory in a Multicultural Society." In *Norwegian-American Essays*, edited by Harry T. Cleven, Knut Djupedal, and Dina Tolfsby, 27–40. Oslo: NAHA-Norway, 2001.

"Immigration and Immigrants: Scandinavia and Finland." In *The Encyclopedia of the United States in the Nineteenth Century*, 2:86–88. New York: Charles Scribners' Sons, 2001.

"Leiv Eriksson som symbol i det norske Amerika." In *Leiv Eriksson, Helge Ingstad og Vinland. Kjelder og tradisjonar*, edited by Jan Ragnar Hagland and Steinar Supphellen, 119–33. Trondheim: Tapir, 2001.

"Nytt fra løftets land. Det private brev og emigrasjon." In *Amerikabrev. Sogndalseminaret 2000, 28. og 29. september*, 6–11. Sogndal, Norway: Kaupanger Seminaret, 2001.

"Religiøse overganger på historisk bakgrunn blant nordmenn i Amerika." In *Dissentere og emigrasjonen. Rapport fra Seminar i Tysværtunet kulturhus Aksdal, Tysvær, 22.-23. september 2000*, edited by Dag Nygård and Hans Eirik Aarek, 65–73. Stavanger, Norway: Norges Frikirkeråd, 2001.

"The Norwegian-American Old-Home Societies Viewed as a Mediating Culture Between 'Consent' and 'Descent.'" In *Hembygden och världen. Festskrift till Ulf Beijbom*, edited by Lars Olsson and Sune Åckerman, 117–33. Gothenburg: Svenska Emigrantinstitutet, 2002.

"Norwegians in America." In *Nordic Immigration to North America*, edited by Faith C. Ingwersen, 13–22. Madison: NCCP, Department of Scandinavian Studies, University of Wisconsin, 2002.

"Rasmus Sunde: Vikjer på fjorden—vikjer på prærien. Ein demografisk studie med utgangspunkt i Vik i Sogn." *Historisk Tidsskrift* 1, no. 2 (Winter 2002).

"Andrew Furuseth." *The Norseman* 44 (2004).

"In Pursuit of the Norwegian American: A Contemporary History Project." In *Scandinavians in Old and New Lands: Essays in Honor of H. Arnold Barton*, edited by Philip J. Anderson, Dag Blanck, and Byron J. Nordstrom, 265–83. Chicago: Swedish-American Historical Society, 2004.

"Norwegian Emigration to America." In *Encyclopedia of the Midwest*. Bloomington: Indiana University Press, 2004.

"The Dissolution of the Swedish-Norwegian Union and Norwegian America." *The Norseman* 45, no. 1 (2005).

"Norwegians." In *Encyclopedia of Chicago History.* Chicago: Chicago History Museum, 2005. Online resource.

"A Patriotic Celebration." *St. Olaf College Magazine,* May 2005.

"Unionsoppløsningen og Det norske Amerika." In *100 år var det alt?* edited by Øystein Rian, Harriet Rudd, and Håvard Tangen, 92–99. Oslo: Nei til EU, 2005.

"Carl Søyland: Norwegian Colossus of the Norwegian Colony in Brooklyn." *The Norseman* 46, no. 3 (2006).

"Common Historical Memory." *The Norseman* 47, no. 2 (2007).

"A Greater Norway." *The Norseman* 47, no. 1 (2007).

"One Hundred Years." *The Norseman* 47, no. 5 (2007).

"War and Peace." *The Norseman* 47, no. 3 (2007).

"The Way Forward." *The Norseman* 47, no. 4 (2007).

"A History of the Norwegian-American Press." *The Norseman* 48, no. 1 (2008).

"They're All Bound for Minnesota." *The Norseman* 48, no. 4 (2008).

"Carl G. O. Hansen and His Minneapolis." *The Norseman* 50, no. 1 (2010).

"The Norwegian-Language Press in America." *Scandinavian Review* 2 (Summer 2010): 53–61.

"Norwegian Immigration and Women." In *Norwegian American Women: Migration, Communities, and Identities,* edited by Betty A. Bergland and Lori Ann Lahlum, 51–73. St. Paul: Minnesota Historical Society Press, 2011.

"The Past Before Us: Oral History and the Norwegian-American Experience." In *Norwegian-American Essays: "Transnationalism and the Norwegian-American Experience,"* edited by Øyvind T. Gulliksen and Harry T. Cleven, 215–32. Oslo: Novus Press, 2011.

"Preserving a Cultural Heritage across Boundaries: A Comparative Perspective on Riksföreningen Sverigekontakt and Nordmanns-Forbundet." In *Norwegians and Swedes in the United States: Friends and Neighbors,* edited by Philip J. Anderson and Dag Blanck, 37–53. St. Paul: Minnesota Historical Society Press, 2011.

"Introduction." Thurine Oleson. *Wisconsin My Home.* Madison: University of Wisconsin Press, 2012.

"Norske aviser i Amerika. Deres geografiske spredning og historiske rolle som samfunnsbygger og forbindelsesledd mellom Norge og nordmenn i Amerika." In *Pionerliv i Amerika og bygdeutvikling på Sletta,* edited by Rolf Svellingen, 33–46. Bergen, Norway: Vestnorsk Utvandringssenter, 2012.

"Norwegians and Norwegian-Americans, 1940–Present." In *Immigrants in American History: Arrival, Adaptation, and Integration,* edited by Elliott Barkan, 3:1163–73. Santa Barbara, CA: ABC-CLIO, 2013.

"The Canadian Gateway." *Norwegians Worldwide,* August 2014.

"Norsk utvandring til USA etter 1945. Et samtidshistorisk perspektiv." In *Nordmenn i Amerika,* edited by Rolf Svellingen, 26–35. Sletta, Norway: Vestnorsk utvandringssenter, 2014.

"Norwegian Immigration to Canada." *Viking Magazine,* September 2016.

Acknowledgments

Writing this book indebted me to a number of people who generously gave their advice and assistance. Placing my life story in a large historical context, while requiring much additional research, also became a major theme and a rewarding approach. However, much of the book revolves around the exceptional position of my family. A peer reviewer wrote, "Throughout the book the author's big heart beats for his family in warm and close descriptions from his long life. His relation to his family and to a large gallery of people mirrors the author and gives the reader much knowledge about him."

I am most grateful to daughter Audrey Syversen and son Ronald Lovoll for their encouragement and counsel when writing my memoirs; sister Svanhild and Kåre Wergeland as well made important contributions, including photos. Son-in-law Helge Syversen was consistently helpful and encouraging, as was daughter-in-law Margit Lovoll. Grandsons Martin and Kristian and their "Grampa Rapp" in 2001 come to mind, as do granddaughter Andrea's tribute to her grandmother in 2011 and grandsons Peter and Jon for their inspiring presence at home and in 2015 when touring Norway.

Friends, family, and colleagues took part in the project. I am grateful to Kenneth Nesset, friend from childhood, for his insights on my years in Seattle. I thank Vidar Parr, owner and editor of *Synste Møre*, the paper for the locality of Bjørlykke, for his fine article when Ronald,

Margit, Peter, Jon, and I visited my birthplace in August 2015. We were warmly welcomed by the owners, cousin Magne and Ragnhild Løvoll, and their family and other relatives. While I was researching in Volda and Ålesund in October 2016, cousin Bodil and her husband John Rotevatn arranged a reunion with former students, John himself being one of them. Gunnar Botn secured a photo of the event. I greatly appreciated spending time with them.

I thank journalist Liv Jorunn Nyhagen for her articles about my research published in the local Volda newspaper *Møre*. Cousin Hilde and Wictor Kolås were also most helpful. In Ålesund, journalist Lars Inge Skrede in *Sunnmørsposten*, the main journal in the Sunnmøre district, carried an interview with me about my memoir, titled "En livsreise med to hjemland" (A Life Journey with Two Homelands). My visit to Ålesund became especially rewarding because of many people's enthusiastic assistance, among these most especially Per Tonning-Olsen, who provided transportation and was my guide; Arne Birger Tunheim, who shared information about the area; Idar Leif Valkvæ, who as museum director hosted a dinner at the Godøy Museum; Magne Godøy, who presented me with a copy of his wartime history of the Godøy island and environs; and Håkon Gill, who helped plan my visit. I thank Therese Alvik for the images of the Steinfeld family. Richard Lindin assisted me at Ålesund Museum, and director Ivar Gunnar Braaten gave me a guided tour of the Sunnmøre Museum. I extend a special thanks to Knut Slinning Bjørdal at Ålesund bibliotek (library) for literature on Sunnmøre and World War II.

Audrey and I visited Vestfoldarkivet, the Vestfold Archives, in Sandefjord, where we were most heartily welcomed. The staff made our inquiry a great success. For their help I recognize archivists Heidi Meen and Marit Slyngstad and archival consultant Lone Kirchhoff, and Øyvind Thuresson, consultant in Hvalfangstmuseet (Whaling Museum). Friend Harry Cleven accompanied me to Holocaustsenteret (the Holocaust Center), on the Bygdøy peninsula. I thank Guri Hjeltnes, the center's director; Georg Andreas Broch, special advisor; Even Trygve Hansen, advisor; and Ewa Maria Mork, in documents, who all made our visit most cordial and instructive. Research in Norway was funded by Fritt Ord.

I owe much thanks to a number of people regarding the history of the Norwegian-speaking 99th Infantry Battalion. My first contact was Bruce Bjorgum, secretary of the 99th Infantry Battalion Separate Educational Foundation; he introduced me to its president, Erik Brun. They both involved themselves most enthusiastically in my project; *The Viking Battalion*, a DVD documentary by filmmaker Steinar Hybertsen, was most enlightening. I interviewed and received much information and material from longtime acquaintances David Minge and G. Rolf Svendsen, both sons of men who served in the battalion. I also thank Morten A. Tuftedal, who in 1996, when I was working on *The Promise Fulfilled*, provided literature on the battalion. Professor Ward Kyle, a military historian, has been most helpful. Erik B. Wiborg, vice president of the 99th Battalion Separate Educational Foundation, provided images he had collected for the 2014 English translation *The 99th Battalion*.

In studying language learning and retention, including second language loss in the elderly, I had the expert assistance of especially Professor Vittorina Cecchetto, but also Professor Magda Stroinska, at McMaster University, Hamilton, Canada. I am most grateful for their friendly responses to my queries and for the scholarly literature they provided.

The St. Olaf College Library staff assisted me, as in past projects, with patience and experience. I relied much on Aimee Brown, special collections librarian, for assistance and special literature. My close relationship with the Norwegian-American Historical Association made it a special place during my work. I express deep gratitude to Amy Boxrud, director; Jeff Suave, archivist; Ann Mulfort, interim archivist; Kristell Benson, interim archivist; and Betty Bergland, boardmember. I also thank Gary DeKrey, college archivist; Dale Hovland, archive volunteer; and Cassidy Neuner, student worker. Dennis Gimmestad, current NAHA president, and Daron Olson, chair of publications, have been most supportive.

Curt Hanson, head, Elwyn B. Robinson Department of Special Collections, University of North Dakota, provided material on the laws of North Dakota passed by the 1891 legislative assembly. Jon Erik Wergeland of Halden, Norway, most generously provided images to be considered for illustrations.

A number of people I have associated with as instructor or colleague or in other ways contributed comments about their experiences and observations. I had a special partnership with Mary Hove, and I enjoyed reflecting on it with her. I have appreciated my long friendship with Professor Emeritus J. R. Christianson and his good advice through the years. I thank Terje Mikael Hasle Joranger for his friendship, encouragement, and considered advice. I am indebted to Erik Rudeng for his continuous support, as publisher and as director of Fritt Ord (Freedom of Expression).

Professor Emeritus Øystein Rian, Professor Emerita Ingeborg Kongslien, and Professor Emeritus Dagfinn Worren, University of Oslo, and Professor Michael Lansing, Augsburg University, all took a special interest in my memoirs. Aaron Hanson, *Norwegians on the Prairie* research assistant; Harry Cleven, earlier editor of *The Norseman*; Gary Erickson, constant enthusiastic supporter; and Jostein Molde, Chicago research assistant, also deserve my thanks for their encouragement and good wishes.

I thank my former students at St. Olaf College and at the University of Oslo—including Idar Ree, Chad Rossow, Joel Magrane, Michael Paulson, and Jeff Kindseth—for their kind reflections.

It was great to have Shannon Pennefeather as the responsible editor and to benefit from her expertise and friendship; I thank her most sincerely. I also express my appreciation to Josh Leventhal, director of Minnesota Historical Society Press, for his encouragement and support.

Index